Quent

BISON
BOOKS

THE

LITTLE WAR

OF

University of Nebraska Press
Lincoln and London

CHARLES JOHNSON POST

WITH ILLUSTRATIONS BY THE AUTHOR

INTRODUCTION TO THE BISON BOOKS EDITION BY

Graham A. Cosmas and Marylou K. Gjernes

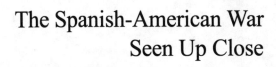

PRIVATE

POST

The Spanish-American War
Seen Up Close

Manufactured in the United States of America

⊗

First Bison Books printing: 1999
Most recent printing indicated by the last digit below:
10   9   8   -7   6   5   4   3   2   1

Library of Congress Cataloging-in-Publication Data
Post, Charles Johnson, 1873–1956.
The little war of Private Post: the Spanish-American War seen up
close / Charles Johnson Post; with illustrations by the author;
introduction to the Bison Books edition by Graham A. Cosmas and
Marylou K. Gjernes.
p.   cm.
Originally published: Boston: Little, Brown, 1960.
ISBN 0-8032-8757-7 (pbk.: alk. paper)
1. Post, Charles Johnson, 1873–1956.   2. Santiago Campaign,
1898—Personal narratives.   3. Spanish-American War, 1898—
Personal narratives.   4. United States. Army. New York Infantry
Regiment, 71st (Militia), (1852–   )   5. Santiago Campaign,
1898—Pictorial works.   6. Spanish-American War, 1898—Pictorial
works.   7. Soldiers as artists—United States—Biography.   I. Title.
E717.1.P6   1999
973.8'93—dc21
99-10211   CIP

Reprinted from the original 1960 edition by Little, Brown and
Company, Boston.

INTRODUCTION TO THE BISON BOOKS EDITION

Graham A. Cosmas and Marylou K. Gjernes

The Spanish-American War of 1898 has received many nicknames, including "the splendid little war" and "the gentlemen's war." Perhaps it was a splendid little war to the correspondents who covered it from converted yachts and the commanders who directed it from hilltop observation posts. Charles Johnson Post, a private in the Seventy-first New York U.S. Volunteers who participated in the war's principal campaign, the attack on Santiago de Cuba, tells a very different story about that "splendid little war."

Post was born in New York City in 1873. He worked as a cartoonist in Philadelphia and New York and was with the *Journal*, a paper owned by William Randolph Hearst, when the USS *Maine* blew up. When the United States declared war on Spain, he enlisted eagerly in the Seventy-first New York and set out for adventure. Fortunately he took his sketchbooks and imagination along, and they never left him. After his return from Cuba, even years later, after he retired from government service, he recorded in images and in words what he had experienced. The resulting unique collection of approximately eighty pieces of combat art tells the story of the Santiago campaign from the viewpoint of a rifleman, an ordinary soldier. Sixteen of his paintings served as illustrations for *The Little War of Private Post* when it was originally published in 1960.

Post's regiment, the Seventy-first New York, was typical of the state units that constituted the vast majority of the three hundred thousand troops the United States mobilized for the war with Spain. An established New York National Guard regiment, it was mustered into U.S. service under President McKinley's first call for troops of April 23, 1898, to serve for two years or the duration of hostilities, whichever was shorter. With a core of veteran national guardsmen, the Seventy-first expanded to its war strength of about one thousand officers and men by enlisting civilian recruits, among them Charles Johnson Post. The regiment formally entered U.S. service on May 10, 1898, at Camp Black, Hempstead, Long Island. Unlike most of the volunteer regiments, which spent the war in camps in the United States, the Seventy-first saw combat in the Santiago campaign. It left Santiago for the United States on August 8, arrived at Montauk Point, New York, on August 18, and was mustered out of U.S. service on November 15. According to official records, the regiment's battle deaths during its tour of duty totaled fifteen. Seventy-seven more men died of disease, three perished in accidents, and one committed suicide. Sixty-seven of Post's comrades were wounded in action.

The Santiago campaign was a hastily improvised operation launched within a month of the beginning of mobilization; hence the confusion, shortages, and hardships so vividly described by Post. Its purpose was to assist the navy in destroying Admiral Cervera's Spanish squadron, which had taken refuge in the harbor of Santiago de Cuba. The Fifth Corps, which carried out the attack, consisted of most of the peacetime regular army reinforced with three volunteer regiments: the Seventy-first New York, the Second Massachusetts, and the First U.S. Volunteer Cavalry (the "Rough Riders").

Commanded by Major General William R. Shafter, an elderly, corpulent veteran of the Civil and Indian Wars, the Fifth Corps landed at Daiquiri and Siboney, east of Santiago, on June 22. Short of landing craft and wagons and hampered by poor roads, the corps campaigned on a logistical shoestring, the troops living on canned beef (much of it of poor quality), beans, hardtack, and coffee. In spite of supply difficulties, Shafter pressed forward. After a preliminary skirmish at Las Guasimas on June 24, his command stormed the outer defenses of Santiago at San Juan Hill and El Caney on July 1. This costly but successful action, the war's only major land battle, placed the Fifth Corps in position to besiege Santiago. In response, on July 3 Cervera's squadron made a

vain dash for freedom, only to be destroyed by the American fleet
in a three-hour running battle. After a two-week siege the Spanish garrison of Santiago, sick and starving, surrendered on July
17. The capitulation included several other Spanish posts in eastern Cuba that depended on Santiago for supply and reinforce-
ments.

The Spanish surrender came none too soon. Disease, princi-
pally malaria and various forms of dysentery, was spreading
through the ranks of the Fifth Corps. Officials at Santiago and in
Washington DC feared an outbreak of the deadly yellow fever, although in fact few soldiers of the Fifth Corps appear to have contracted that disease. (Diagnosis in that era was less than precise;
Post's doctors concluded that he had "Compound Enteric Typhoid
Malaria," which seemed to account for most of his symptoms.)
Soon the conquerors of Santiago were reduced to the shambling,
emaciated convalescents protrayed in Post's paintings. Initially
afraid to return the troops to the United States lest they spread
yellow fever on the mainland, the War Department, belatedly
warned of the corps's plight, in August hastily evacuated the force
to an improvised quarantine camp at Montauk Point. There the
men of the Fifth Corps gradually recovered a semblance of health.
The volunteer regiments were discharged and the regulars sent to
their permanent posts.

Private Post recorded his view of these events with pen and
paintbrush and was eloquent with both. His memoir is accurate
insofar as it deals with what Post personally saw and experienced.
On the other hand, his judgments and speculations on the strategy of the campaign, in chapter 19 for instance, should be treated
with caution, as they reflect prejudices and rumors of the time.
Post gives an honest account of his regiment's less than stellar
performance in the attack on San Juan Hill. He correctly describes
how the Seventy-first New York fell into confusion during its advance along a narrow jungle trail under fire and finally marched
up the hill only after regular units had secured the crest and blockhouse. His vignettes of battle, some horrific, others humorous or
bizarre, have a ring of truth, as do his unheroic but generally

affectionate characterizations of his fellow soldiers. Post gives mixed reviews to his officers. He admires some but denounces others, including the regimental chaplain, as self-seeking time-servers.

Post portrays himself as a champion scrounger. Whether trading portrait sketches for meals with the engineers on the transport *Vigilancia*, camping in a supply warehouse on the wharf at Santiago, or stealing a bath in the officers' tub on a ship bound for Montauk Point, Post appears to have had an unerring eye for whatever meager comforts were available and the cleverness to secure them for himself and his mates.

Comforts were few at best, however. Some of Post's most eloquent and angry writing tells of his own and the Fifth Corps's slow debilitation by hunger and disease and describes the callous treatment the troops received on the homebound ships and in the camp at Montauk Point. Passage after passage evokes images of sick, filthy, emaciated men struggling to retain a semblance of dignity and soldierly bearing when scarcely able to stand, let alone walk. Some suffered stoically and died quietly in their tents. Eventually discovered, they were buried without volleys and bugle calls to avoid demoralizing the survivors. In the comfortless convalescent camp at Montauk Point, "the grass between the tented streets was flecked with blood and dysentery. Few could make the latrine at the far end of the camp. Tents were latrines. . . . We measured time in food; in the time between chills; and when the fever left us, and we were partly brisk and living again, we measured it in dysentery, and in latrines."

Post's recollections of the campaign with sketchpad and paintbrush are if anything more eloquent than his words. As a group, his drawings and paintings give a general chronology of the Santiago campaign, beginning with the preparatory camp scenes in Florida and ending with the sick and wounded returning home to New York on the vessel *Grand Duchesse*. It is interesting to note the differences in the paintings. Those depicting campaign preparations are humorous, have lots of activity, and show lively soldiers in neat, clean uniforms. The soldiers appear to be as excited as if they were going to a picnic. The midcampaign pictures are of more sober men filled with confidence and determination. They realize they are going into battle and they could be hurt or killed. The last paintings depict sick, tired men who have seen hell in fear, panic, and death, dysentery and yellow fever. They no longer want the excitement and glory of battle. Now they want only a soft bed, a hot bath, and a good meal. They want to go home.

The selection of Post's paintings in *The Little War of Private Post* is drawn from all periods of the campaign. It begins with scenes of the Seventy-first New York arriving at Tampa and of the "sporting sandbar" near the docks, where soldiers could obtain amusement and refreshment, both wholesome and otherwise. Other illustrations cover the landing and the action in Cuba. The picture titled *Bloody Ford* shows the Seventy-first New York at San Juan Hill as it emerged from a trail that was in the direct line of Spanish fire. Here the regiment fell into mass confusion, with men milling in the crowded pathway and wounded falling or trying to roll themselves into the brush. The men in the jungle could not even see the enemy to fire back. The painting shows the reformed regiment marching up the hill toward the blockhouse in a column of fours, following up the earlier successful attack of the regulars. This may have been the last time U.S. troops went into battle in close-order drill formation.

Another San Juan Hill painting shows an improvised field hospital down the slope from the captured blockhouse. Of this watercolor, Post said, "the wounded were laid out under a tree until their turn for care. Surgeons worked all night and [the dead] under the trees were sorted out in the morning." Hospital corpsmen are doing what they can for the wounded, but four men and a trunk full of first-aid equipment cannot do much. Most of the group is watching the treatment in anticipation, but the two sitting nearest the tree and facing the viewer are not impressed or excited by the efforts. They stare into space, perhaps wishing they were still at the front, perhaps wishing they were anywhere else. It is interesting that one man is black, the other white. African

American soldiers of the Twenty-fourth U.S. Infantry and the Ninth and Tenth U.S. Cavalry took a prominent part in the assault on San Juan Hill. In combat, pain, fear, sickness, and bullets do not see any color difference.

Some of Post's paintings may not reflect his eyewitness experience. An example is the picture of Theodore Roosevelt's Rough Riders joining the assault. From the Seventy-first's position Post could not have seen Roosevelt's men advance. The artist must have drawn this scene on the basis of what he was told when his regiment was in the trenches near the Rough Riders or from accounts he read later.

At the beginning of Post's series of paintings, his scenes are brightly colored and lively, with a great deal of action both in the scene and in the background, which is quite pronounced. As the work progresses through the chronology of his experience in Cuba with the Seventy-first, the focus of the scenes gradually shifts inward until, in the last pieces, the trip home has no background. This can be seen in the book in the pictures of Captain Rafferty's detail and the quarantine camp at Montauk Point. The men, Post included, were sick, feverish, hungry, and dying. The world they knew was the internal world of pain. They could tell time only by the ebb and flow of fever. Time, a link to the outside world, is meaningless unless it can bring hope of relief from misery.

After a period in the quarantine camp at Montauk Point and three months in a New York City hospital, Post was able to resume his life as a civilian, but he never lost his taste for adventure. He was at various times an explorer, a labor counsel, an inventor, a soldier, and a political cartoonist. In 1946 he retired from the Department of Labor, where he had served as commissioner of conciliation, and turned to painting and writing about his life's experiences. He died in 1956 at the age of eighty-three.

The Little War of Private Post is of lasting significance as a soldier's-eye view of the Santiago campaign, an eloquent evocation of the valor and suffering of those who actually fought the "splendid little war." In addition, it recalls to the public Post's significant achievements in what is today called combat art. His work is in a genre of military paintings that was begun almost the same moment men first went to war. In U.S. history, Post is in the thematic tradition of John Trumbull of the Revolutionary War, Winslow Homer of the Civil War, Kerr Eby of World War I, and Aaron Bohrod of World War II. These and many other men and women who are part of military activities, whether in war or peace, find it essential to record in ink, watercolor, or oil the emotions of fear, pride, excitement, confusion, or disillusionment they see around them. In doing so they make a statement about people and about war that cannot be captured in a photograph. The world is better for their having made the statement.

Contents

Illustrations

Introduction

ANY book about the Spanish–American War of 1898 needs a word of introduction. For this particular subject is regarded as among the little wars that are the mere trivia of history.

Yet, for those who are in war and battles and on the fighting line, there is no triviality in shaking dice with death. It makes no difference whether a man gets his along with twenty thousand others, or falls while on outpost duty all by himself. He is a hundred per cent casualty to himself. For him there is no lesser percentage. What more could there be to give?

So this will explain what this book is not: it is not a treatise in the comparative anatomy of history or a cosmic chronology of grandiose events. It is, to classify it at all, a mild chronicle of many little men who were painting on a big canvas, and of their little epic routines of life, with a common death at their elbow. It is only the little, but keen, tribulations that made the epic routine of an old-fashioned war.

This, then, is not to be a book of dates and departures and hours of arrivals or tables of statistics. It is simply of human experiences, my own and others, and if a dedication be in order, I dedicate it here:

To the men of the Fifth Army Corps . . .

THE LITTLE WAR

of PRIVATE POST

1

The Maine *is sunk. The United States declares war on Spain. Patriotism and romance — Hearst stirs the blood. I enlist. Free drinks and red flannel bellybands.*

THE *Maine* was a tangled wreck in the harbor of Havana. We were at war with Spain. And red flannel was at a premium.

Everywhere nice young girls were sewing red flannel bellybands. Two young maidens were sewing them for me. Naturally, in those days of decorum and delicacy, they were modest young ladies, and the size of my midsection was not to be approached by direct questioning. Thus it was that a mellow married aunt produced a tape measure and acquired the requisite engineering data. Shortly afterward, two Christmas-like packages were presented to me, the modest donors being carefully chaperoned by my aunt. Each package held a red flannel bellyband with three black tapes at each end with which to lash it to my person. Thereupon, I was to be secure from all forms of pestilence and intestinal fevers.

I had enlisted. I had been stripped naked and passed down a line of well-dressed medical inquisitors to join a group of naked enlistees who were jumping up and down as if practicing to stamp the Spaniards to death. This was a scientific test to see if our hearts were in the right place.

I passed the jumping test. I passed the coughing test, which proved I was not ruptured. And I passed the eyesight test (since I wore glasses) when I explained that I was a bit better than a good pool shark and had once run thirty-five balls. Thus I became a soldier, with bed, board, and all "found," as the indenture papers have it. The wage was thirteen dollars per month, which, later, owing to the hazards of battle and front-line campaigning, was increased by the addition of $1.30 combat pay per month. On most of the other items the Army fell down, but it never reduced my pay or docked me for being, at times, somewhat undernourished in the trenches.

Enlisting then was not like enlisting today. When you enlisted then, you first shopped for a regiment. Anyone with money or credit to rent a vacant store could recruit for his regiment, and he would be colonel. There was vast enthusiasm. In fact, one had only to go into any of the three or four saloons at each street intersection and start a conversation with almost any casual stranger and, first thing you knew, the bartender would invite you to have one on the house and recommend a regiment for you to join or transfer to. Mr. William Randolph Hearst had just bought the New York *Journal* and was mixing war, patriotism, and romance with Eva Cisneros — a Spanish captive in Havana, reported by Hearst to be of superlative and languishing beauty. This reporting was fragrant with circulation results, while we commoner folk began to boil and seethe with ardor to kill a Spaniard.

So it was that vacant stores on every avenue suddenly blossomed into recruiting stations, with pictures of the *Maine* before and after sinking, and with pullers-in at their doors straight from the *Social Register* or the nearest ward leader. Each store was intent upon recruiting a regiment. Officers were needed. And before each store was a line of expectant officers. This was a system that dated back to the Civil War — probably back to the barons of the Magna Charta. You wanted to be an officer — and who did not? You brought in enough followers to make a platoon, and you became its lieutenant. Enough for a company, and you became a captain. And who made you an officer? Why, the man who paid the rent for the store and who was going to be the colonel of the regiment.

Substations opened up for recruiting — mere desks on the sidewalk. The Old Guard, those portly gentlemen with a bearskin barrel for a hat, opened a tent in Union Square with a magnificent soldier from their own company as a sample. The venerable paunch of this gentleman set off well the creamy doeskin of his gold-buttoned mess jacket. Above the jacket there rose and floated, in even greater glory, the most military mustache that New York had ever known; it curled outward and downward like the inverted horns of a Texas steer. It was worth going miles to see, whether one enlisted or not.

I counted up my military experience and military lore. Of the former I had none. Of the latter, I had read *The Boys of '61* and had once been taught the manual of arms as a small boy, but had forgotten it. Clearly, Nature had designed me for mere cannon fodder, so I enlisted, taking the step that qualified me for a drink on the house almost anywhere between Eighth Street and Twenty-third Street, between the Hudson and the East rivers. Also, it qualified me for a red flannel bellyband from any patriotic young female, and thus the two very lovely young ladies had stepped forward.

Bellybands, most preferably of red flannel — red being regarded as a highly medicinal color — were the intended protection against all the tropical ills: blackwater fever, yellow jack, black jack, Chagres fever, and a dozen other names of increasing horrendousness.

Much interest also attached to the mechanisms of the abdomen, and it was thought that a bellyband which would keep all heat in, perhaps even from the dangerous airs of the nighttime, would help our brave soldier boys resist the Spanish miasmas of Cuba.

So the womenfolk fell to with their needles. Mr. Jaeger, the leading maker of hygienic clothing in those days, invented a sort of knitted barrel into which one could crawl. But this, while it may have had a utilitarian value, was utterly devoid of romance.

I shall always recall with pride that my own red flannel bellybands were not.

2

Camp Black. Drill, we learn the bugles, drill, police the area, drill. We learn to curse hardtack and enjoy whisky and good fellowship.

I WAS now a soldier. That is, so far as the general public was concerned. Not that I yet had the thirteen dollars, or any part thereof. That was six weeks yet in the offing.

True, I had a uniform — cerulean-blue pants with a broad, deep blue stripe down the sides, and they fitted reasonably well. But my blouse! I had always thought that a "blouse" was specifically an article of feminine apparel, a sort of loose shirtwaist with a snappy, come-hither effect. But in that man's army, a blouse was anything worn outside a shirt and inside an overcoat, and instantly provocative of a sergeant's acute anguish if it wasn't buttoned. Also, it was supposed to fit.

They were short on blouses when mine was issued; that is, short of normal blouses for normal men. So my blouse was left over from some outsized predecessor, a mere fragment of whose clothing would have outfitted me inside and out, with a Sunday suit left over. The turned-back sleeves reached my elbows; the blouse folded around me so that its buttons were at all times under my arms, and it reached to my knees like a frock coat. But my choice was this, or not marching at all in the parade that would start us into the real war, at Camp Black out on Hempstead Plains, Long Island. So I took the blouse, crept into it, and marched, undoubtedly passing as some sort of regimental mascot.

At Camp Black we raw recruits were separated, the sheep from the goats. The goats were those who had not yet had any part of a uniform issued to them. They drilled as an awkward squad in their wrinkled, slept-in civilian jackets, trousers, and derby hats.

The tents were already up when we arrived; one bale of straw to a tent, and bedding for the four men to that tent. It was April and the ground was wet and soggy with spring. I had roughed it a bit in the open and knew enough to put my poncho rubber-side-down next to the sod. Some men didn't. But with the blanket over the straw, it made a fine bed, soft and warm.

The regiments kept rolling in. As far as the eye could see, there were the long rows of white tents. All day the bugles kept calling or blowing the commands at drill. "Fours right — march!" The bugle ascended in scale, and with the word "march" came the staccato note that gave us the instant of action. "Fours left — march!" The same notes in retrograde, a pause, and the note of final command. "Right front into line!" "On right into line!" "Right by twos!" "Fours right about!" "Right by file!" All the commands that had not varied from the time of the Civil War.

We learned the bugles. Then came battalion drill, with four companies together. More bugles to learn. And getting up in the morning was a pleasure — at least to me. It would be somewhere around five o'clock. Slowly, one became conscious of a throbbing, rhythmic cadence of vibrating drums — forty of them, out on the parade ground beating out the top-o'-the-morning and almost drowning the shrill yelps of the fifers. For ten minutes they serenaded the camp; then the bugles started reveille. With the last note of reveille, we were dressed and out in the company line-up for roll call. Now, much later, I am willing to join in damning reveille just as a matter of the old school tie, but actually I think back with joyous thrill to the time I crawled out from under the blankets to the serenade of forty drummers, twelve buglers, and twelve fifers.

Bill Garthwaite was a first sergeant when we went into Camp Black. Then he was made first lieutenant. Jim McDermott went up to the first sergeantcy, and no finer, fairer first sergeant ever wore the chevrons-and-lozenge.

After roll call came the policing of the company street. This meant, literally, sweeping the street. Its tramped sod must be cleared of every careless cigarette butt, of every dried twig, of every shred of wanton paper too small for any eye but that of the bossing color-sergeant to see. Next day we scoured the plains of Hempstead for bunches of dried twigs to make into brooms so that we could sweep and shine our tented avenues.

At the end opposite the captain's tent was the cook shack. The cooking apparatus was what was officially designated as a "Buzzacot Oven." This was a series of huge pots and pans (including a wash boiler) nesting one within the other, all enfolded within two sections of an iron grill. The Buzzacot could cook for a hundred men with ease, and burned fuel like a blast furnace. In those days, when war was not waged by machinery, and when soldiers went into comfortable winter quarters for the Thanksgiving and Christmas seasons, no more effective cooking device could have been invented.

I learned to operate one later. In operating it, mere cooking was one of the minor elements to be mastered. You had to nurse the grill like a premature infant. The grid was the type made famous by St. Lawrence. You watched the wind, you banked one side or tore it down a bit. You made big, fat embers and then put them on the lid of one of the huge pans you were using as an oven, to get the heat down on the upper side of your roast or beans. You fanned it with your hat, or you coaxed it and cussed it in a thousand ways. And sometimes you succeeded rather well. But for an army in the field before Q, X, or K rations were invented, for soldiers who were not merely hitchhikers on baggage wagons or tanks, I want to say that the Buzzacot was a superb though eccentric instrument.

Before we went into camp, our company had hired a cook. Of course, he was enlisted like the rest of us. But he was not only a cook, he was a *chef* — a regular hotel chef! No wonder our captain, J. Hollis Wells, had gone up to become major of our battalion, or that Sergeant Garthwaite had become Lieutenant Garthwaite! Of course, not all things could be expected to happen at once, right off the bat, so when we got ham and eggs, they seemed just like ham and eggs. And when the stew was ladled out into our mess pans, it did not seem to vary much from any other rather indifferently boiled meat and potatoes. Give him time, Rome wasn't built in a day. Our confidence persisted, and our hopes. Then, suddenly, the hotel chef was detailed to the awkward squad. We had lost our chef and gained only another soldier. The quartermaster sergeant said nothing but cooked in person. Sometimes it was not good and sometimes it was worse. Various members of our company were tried out as cooks, particularly if they criticized too much. As for me, the cuisine of that cook shack never had a more open admirer, verbally. As a result, I never peeled a potato. There is much to be said for tactful meekness.

Later on, I heard about *l'affaire chef* in detail. It had been this way.

Our hotel chef was named John Chaubin. Instantly, he was given the nickname of Chumbum. He was built like a piano mover and had direct, beady black eyes, and an indefinable accent that might have been nurtured anywhere from Poland to Paris. On the first day of his chefship in camp, he watched the disassembling of the Buzzacot with stoic calm.

He looked at the wash boiler. "Wat for, dat?" he asked.

"For coffee," said Sergeant Werdenschlag, the quartermaster sergeant. "You make coffee in wash boiler, savvy?"

"Wash boiler! Lak hell!" said Chef Chumbum. "Okay. Then you get wash boiler coffee!"

And, as it turned out, it was just as Chef Chumbum said. The coffee was terrible. It was made on a sort of co-operative system of guesswork. The wash boiler was first loaded up with water to a height estimated by the K.P. water-tender. There were no water pipes in the camp; a sprinkler cart from some neighboring municipality regularly carted the water to the regiment, and each company bailed out of the tank what water they could stow in the Buzzacot pots and pans not then in use. Sometimes the coffee was a palish amber, and sometimes it was a full-blooded deep brown. But, as Chumbum suggested in his scorn, it always tasted "lak hell."

We began to realize that something was not quite as it should be. There was a showdown. The burden of attack, or defense, fell on the Buzzacot. Who ever heard of a goddam stove that was all fragmentation and had to be used over an open fire!

"I am a cook — a chef — goddam!" said Chumbum.

There had been another error in compounding the coffee. Somebody had guessed wrong on how many of the waxed paper sacks of Arbuckle's Coffee should have gone into the wash boiler. Or the coffee ran out before the last man on the company roster had his. Then there were other lapses. This was called to Chumbum's attention.

"Wat like hell you t'ink I am, heh!" he shouted. "I am bes' goddam cook — chef — you know. You mak' salad I show you. I am bes' goddam salad chef you never see!"

Perhaps he was. At any rate, cooking to him meant making a salad. He was, in fine, a specialist and had a specialist's pride. This pride had been outraged ever since he had set eyes upon the Buzzacot, ever since he had had to deal with the coarser groceries and the wash boiler. In his world, coffee had been made by scullions and not by the artists of saladry. He had borne with us patiently, but he could take it no longer. So he became resigned, and relapsed into being a plain doughboy like the rest of us. He was a good soldier. Later, down on Misery Hill outside of Santiago, he and Jack O'Brien bunked together in their dog tent, nerveless and cheerful, until one day Jack went down with the fever and the day after was dead. Chumbum's shouting robustness and conglomerate idiom, accented with Brooklynese, lost its vivid cadences.

With Chumbum in the ranks, there was no noticeable change in the mess. The brisk April air, the drills that were even brisker, and the jobs of jacking garbage or unloading freight cars full of blankets, clothing, food, and rifles, gave us an appetite that made all things edible. We were getting initiated into hardtack — that staple curse of all armies from Caesar's on down — by gentle degrees; for the Army is artful. Hardtack was smashed up into chips and mingled with the stew, or the boiled tomatoes, or anything that was liquid. Thus softened in hash or stew as a sort of culinary grout, it could pass unnoticed. Later, when we had hardtack, we learned to curse it. Hardtack belongs in the ceramic group and is the best substitute for a durable bathroom tile yet discovered.

Sowbelly we did not get at Camp Black. It was reserved for journeymen soldiers, not for the apprentice class. Sowbelly is exactly what its name implies, the belly of a very adult lady pig, faucets and all. It comes about two to three inches in thickness, and the plastron of sowbelly is the full size intact of its original owner. On one side is the meat; on the other, the leather. And no one but an old Army sergeant or a leather fancier can tell one from the other. However, it makes but little difference, since one side is quite as nourishing as the other and both are equally tasty.

Between three layers of leather is fat, pure, callous fat with a potential, under heat, of liquid lard. When we jacked sowbelly in the tropic sun down between Siboney and San Juan, we reached our battalion and company dripping from wool shirt to canvas leggings with melted lard. Later in the campaign, when hunger bested us, it was a nicely balanced question whether to fry our shirt or our sowbelly. Still, I remember that on Misery Hill there was a time when we did not have either hardtack or sowbelly, and we sought the abandoned haversacks of the dead for both.

"Sowbelly," incidentally, is the epithet used by the common soldier. The official Army term is "bacon."

At Camp Black we had canned peaches, canned pears, potatoes mashed, hashed, or browned. We had coffee — roasted, and not raw as it was issued to us later in the trenches of Cuba. We even had roast beef from the cavernous pans of the Buzzacot. And once we had ice cream. Cake, too, fresh from the bakers, and white bread, two slices and seconds, every day.

The water was finally laid in, one tap at the foot of each company street. No longer did we have to dole from our daily canteenful. Any man could have a plentiful supply. The shortage of water had been a problem, for the need was great. Our company had two plumbers, and they were detailed to help lay the pipes and taps for headquarters and the twelve company streets. They worked one day and most of the night; the next morning we had water. Major Wells had promised them pay for their work over and above the Army salary. He gave it to them — $2.50 each, from his privy purse. This was at roll call the following morning, as they were ordered two paces to the front and center.

They looked at the money.

"Some mistake, Major," said one.

"Yeah," said the other, contemptuously. "Two dollars and a half! This ain't the scale, Major. We're plumbers. The union . . ."

The major interrupted. I observed for the first time what an angry Army man could look like.

"Wrong!" remarked the major, and there was fire in his voice. "You're not plumbers, you are soldiers. I've given you a present because I'm as big a numskull as you are. Next time you'll do a job as soldiers! *Any job!*"

Of course, they never forgave him.

We could now have water as a chaser after a genteel slug of whisky taken straight from the neck of the bottle, which was always politely wiped with the back of the hand before it was passed along. Every man had at least a brown-bottle pint at all times, which could be replenished by the newsboy bootleggers, or those of a higher category who dealt only in quarts and cases. Not to have a bottle of whisky was simply open confession of abject poverty or poor bringing up. Thus we established friends and acquaintances in companies other than our own, and it was mere manners anywhere to bring along a bottle, for you always came back with more inside than you had brought outside.

Company C had the finest tent in camp—the finest that I knew, anyhow. The back wall of this tent was piled high with case goods, each case solid with rye. It was a club, in its way, and every night it held open house. There was Bob Roby, Jr., a singer from vaude-

ville, who sang the verses while we joined in the chorus
of every popular song of the day.

There was also Burgess Cluff, who was a most
amazing taleteller, a songless minstrel of superb dia-
logue. His stories, true, false, or bawdy, were a de-
light. Sometimes he got drunk, but it made no difference in his picaresque talks. And outside the tent, in the
darkness, groups of men listened to the tales through
the tent walls and joined in the singing. The songs?
Well, you may know some of them today, but we all
knew every word of all of them, then; they were
part of our social education — "Comrades," "Little
Annie Rooney," "Sweet Marie," "Hot Time in the
Old Town," "Goodby Nellie Gray," "There Were
Three Flies in Our Town," "The Old Gray Mare"
. . . and a dozen others, some bawdy, some tender
with easy sentiment, and some rather rugged. It was
the day when quasi-Negro songs were popular, like "I
Don't Like No Cheap Man," "Bill Bailey," "She's
Not Colored, She Was Bawn That Way."

The evening generally wound up with "Tenting Tonight," and the little group outside would melt away
and, with one farewell passing of the bottle, we would
all turn in. Tattoo had long since blown. So, often, had
taps. But that little No. 2 tent of C Company led a
charmed life. Curiously, there were but few drunks at
the end of each evening. A little jingled up, maybe, a
little more sentimental and a little more thrilled with
Army life. It was a wonderful place to spend an evening.

3

Comrades-in-arms — a cross section of America. I acquire a nickname. We board the steamship Seneca, *bound for Cuba and glory. We disembark at Hoboken.*

SLOWLY, at Camp Black, we began to know one another. There were three artists in my company, but I was the only one who had ever held an artist's job and been paid, and I was therefore senior in the company's art department. There were, also, two young lawyers; a theatrical press agent, John Shaw, who later died on Misery Hill; and a theatrical manager, Gus Pitou, whose father was a famous play producer. We had a bartender, Lem Eiseman — badly wounded at the San Juan blockhouse on July 1st — whose father owned a saloon just above Thirty-fourth Street and Sixth Avenue. Lem's father had promised us a prize of $500 cash for the first man to capture a Spanish flag, and a half-partnership in his saloon if the capturer should be Lem. We had a printer, Amos Barnett, who later spent his summers in the Adirondacks and his winters in Florida. There was Lipman Stanfer, who made and rented fancy costumes for Eighth Avenue balls, and dress suits for orthodox weddings. Earle Hall was an undertaker, a mild, blond man with steel nerves who, shot through the stomach from rib to rib, hobbled back with Jesse Pohalski to the field hospital where he was laid out to die in the shade of a tree, where he cursed the doctors and whispered that he would not die. And he didn't.

But this was still ahead of us.

There were the Booth twins from Biloxi, Mississippi —identical except for careers. Jim, a druggist, held a pew in the Calvary Baptist Church and was given to a modest piety which he never flaunted. Ed Booth was not given to churchly ways. He unhesitatingly announced that he was a hobo printer — a blanket-stiff — who wanted to travel. He was also a gambler, poker his specialty. Ed became a corporal, and a good one.

The Post Office was represented by Barney Goldberg. The American Federation of Labor had two delegates from the plumbers' union — the fellows who laid in the water pipes — who never forgot their union scale and felt they were scabbing as they took the government pay of $13 a month and found. They faced non-union hours — since we all had to work at night on guard duty. And, worse, our tents did not have the board floors which were required by what they evidently regarded as union-shop rules. They went on strike near San Juan Hill.

There was Ed Kroupa, a quiet, self-contained boy

The 71st Infantry arriving in Florida — Ybor City.

The sporting sandbar at Port Tampa.

Horses and mules being pushed overboard for the long swim to Siboney.

The *Vigilancia* unloading troops.

— friendly and shy — who died as quietly as he had lived, picked out of his tent cold and stiff one morning on Misery Hill. And my corporal, Henry Scheid, round-faced and well drilled in his book. Henry was shot through the middle with a Mauser bullet, but managed to get back to the field hospital, whimpering in pain. Our chaplain saw he was dying and told him so clearly. Henry died calm and without uncertainty.

We were a cross section of America. We came from every stratum. There were men who loved the rough side of soldiering and men to whom daintiness of living was a habit that made soldiering difficult. There were short men, tall men, stout ones, or men just passing the standard soldier height of five feet six inches. We liked each other or not, but always we were a company unit. A solidarity grew among us that seemed to come from the sharing of a common enterprise. The cementing of this solidarity was to come later, in battle. After that the men gauged each other in terms of what they knew of each other that July 1st.

Everyone had a nickname. I was Four-eyes, or Doc — the latter a common name for anyone wearing glasses. And there were two men, brothers, good soldiers but quiet, who were promptly nicknamed Dope No. 1 and Dope No. 2. They accepted this with a grin. But after the affair at San Juan one of them mildly explained that he and his brother really did not like to be known as Dope No. 1 and 2; they had even been called on roll call by these. We knew them on the Hill and the nickname was dropped.

Our company also had several other sets of brothers — the Booth Twins, of course, one of whom was ordered to shave and the other to grow whiskers so First Sergeant Jim McDermott could tell them apart — and the Knobloch brothers — one got his by an overhead shell burst in the jungle that shattered his shoulder blade — and the Reigher brothers, Joe and Louis, who came from a delightful little Rhine wine restaurant on Sixth Avenue where you could get the real May wine each spring, and Liebfraumilch — if you had the price — to go with roast goose at Christmas and New Year. There were the Seligman brothers, Henry and Joseph; and the Brown brothers, Charles and Harry.

The sergeants and corporals were as sergeants and corporals always are. They knew their book. Those were the days of close order, and we drilled in it much as in the days of Waterloo or Gettysburg, when troops formed for battle at long-range cannon shot, and in full view each of the other, unless one side was entrenched. The only substantial innovation was the "advance by rushes" when each squad alternately advanced while the other covered them with volleys.

Jim McDermott was a fine first sergeant, kindly, fair, and considerate in all his details. Dave Werdenschlag was a good quartermaster sergeant and we appreciated his butchering. John Moore, first duty sergeant and a carpenter in civilian life, had left his wife and one child — with another baby on the way. Sergeant John Meyer was a ferryman on the Long Island

Rail Road, a jovial man who picked up a stray yellow
mongrel somewhere in Tampa and smuggled it aboard
the transport. It followed him devotedly, even up San
Juan Hill and over when we covered Best's battery.
John often used to tell how it galloped along with him
over the Hill, snapping at the Mauser bullets as they
zinged past. "Goddamit, he thought they were bugs!"
John would explain. The little dog died peacefully,
years after, in John's Long Island home.

Slowly, we got to know our captain, Malcolm A. Rafferty, and no company was ever luckier. He was later
recommended for brevet rank and promotion at the
Hill, though he never received it. Captain Rafferty was
an Irishman, born in England. He had served in both
the cavalry and infantry; he had been in the Sudan and
in a campaign up in the Punjab in India. And he knew
his business. He left the cavalry, he explained to us one
night as we sat like a little group of prairie dogs peering over our trenches at distant Santiago, because of an
incident. He chuckled.

"The sabers were dull," he explained, "and, as a
weapon, that seemed to me rather stupid. So I sharp-
ened mine. The next drill we had saber exercise, right
moulinet and left moulinet — a sort of windmill swing
of the saber with the wrist as an axle. It gives strength
to the wrist and speed, and all sorts of things that
come in handy. It was a right moulinet and I cut off my
horse's ear. It was a favorite horse of my uncle. So I
became an infantryman."

It was Captain Rafferty who, in broad daylight,

broke into a string of freight cars on the Hempstead siding containing our regimental food and issue, when Army red tape had got gummed up. He became, in Army law, no better than a common burglar and bandit, looter of the sacred supplies and quintuplicate vouchers. Our Colonel Greene, later Brigadier General Francis Vinton Greene, a West Pointer, laughed and thereafter kept an eye on Rafferty —a very, very favorable eye! Thus we continued to eat, and official Washington gritted its teeth in formal, quintuplicate frustration.

We were sworn into the U. S. Army out on the gusty plains of Hempstead. The Articles of War were read to us by a microscopic, uniformed figure in the distance. We missed a good laugh by not being able to hear them. Later, in Lakeland, Florida, the Articles were again officially read to us, on a calm evening while a sergeant held a lantern so Major Wells could see them. They listed a vast number of infractions, with suitable punishments ranging from a bread-and-water diet to loss of pay, hanging, or such other discipline as the court might direct. Among these infractions was the use of profanity in any form, regardless of circumstances. And in this general category there were social subdivisions; an officer caught swearing was to be fined out of his pay to the amount of one shilling, a non-commissioned officer sixpence, and a mere soldier threepence! Whether the grades of the fines were laid on in accordance with the measure of proficiency of the grades of the Army, was always a moot point. I felt then, and still do, that the common soldier was entitled to a higher degree of punitive praise than a mere threepence!

After the first reading of the Articles of War, and the swearing into federal service, there was a review by Governor Black of New York, in whose honor the camp had been named. Then, back in the company street the bugles blew, the tents were struck, the Buzzacot was assembled in its nestings and clasped in the great grids. Two baggage wagons were assigned to each company for campaign or combat, and we marched down to the Hempstead siding and boarded the train for Long Island City.

We were the first regiment of volunteers to start for the front. The newspapers shrieked with headlines. Already we were heroes. "Brave Boys in Blue" — for we had the same uniforms made famous by the Civil War.

The plains of Hempstead swarmed with spectators and friends and relatives. And it seemed as if every friend had brought all the whisky he could carry. I doubt if there remained a canteenful of water in the entire regiment. It was dumped for whisky. Every rolled blanket atop the Merriam pack (the knapsack of those days) had a quart rolled inside. In fact, the Merriam pack seemed to have been admirably designed for just such an emergency. Its center was a canvas box about the size of the Civil War knapsack, which would hold just a quart bottle comfortably with some space left for socks, shaving materials, and a deck of cards or so. The blanket was formed into a long roll across the top of the pack and down each side. This blanket could accommodate three bottles, one atop and one each to port and starboard, and the pack straps held it securely so that every bottle was safe and well padded. Beneath the Merriam pack were two more straps. These were for one's rolled overcoat, which could accommodate another bottle or, better yet, a moderate-sized demijohn. I know, because a friend of mine brought a demijohn to me with the compliments of the gang at Johnny Boschen's saloon on West Tenth Street. Not all were rigged out as thoroughly as I have outlined here; there were impatient souls who lightened their cargo by stowing it in the hold instead of on deck. These were helped aboard the train by friendly hands while officers looked the other way or found it the moment to cuss out a wagon driver.

Incidentally, the Merriam pack had two hickory sticks at each side fastened to the two upper corners of the pack. The other end fitted into the end pockets of a half-belt, which rested below one's kidneys. The Army believed that this took the load off a soldier's shoulders. We carried the Merriam packs on our kidneys, and the leverage of the sticks pulled our shoulders back so that we were perpetually being pulled back downhill with the swing of leverage in each stride. At Tampa, by official order, we abandoned the packs and went back to the old horse-collar blanket roll of the Civil War, invented by the men who had to wear them.

The hacks of Hempstead did a roaring business.

They pulled up along the siding and trundled the civilian folks off to the Long Island Rail Road station, where the good people embarked for Long Island City to prepare another reception in the railroad yards for which our troop train was bound.

Yet it was not all jollity and whisky. Here and there a woman sobbed and her husband led her away, his arms around her. They were plain, worn, homespun people; the people who furnish the cannon fodder and give three cheers that any Yank can lick his weight in Chink wildcats or limejuicers. Here and there a soldier was sick with too much whisky; or, drunk as Billy-be-damn, began to shout some bawdy song or the obscene words to a bugle march — and was promptly fought into mumbling lethargy by his car mates. Here and there in the troop cars, some young chap would cautiously do his beads or read a prayer book that had just been thrust upon him by some missionary peddler or fond mother.

It was a wonder that there was a button left on a uniform. Girls, and there were girls everywhere, looked longingly at the brass buttons on our blouses and some, more thoughtful, would trade a safety pin for a button. Also, if it could be arranged with reasonable privacy, a campaign-hat insignia with its crossed rifles could bring a kiss. It was a gay time. War — war itself, was on. War had begun.

At Long Island City a guard was posted around the train and at the railroad gates. One couple had come from upstate to see their boy off; they had a basket of

home-cooked food. Kindly Captain Rafferty explained
that their boy was on detail back in camp and would
join the company later. But Captain Rafferty knew —
we all knew — that their boy was drunk, fighting
drunk; it took five men to hold him. The little mother
wept; the father comforted her clumsily. War has its
duties, he said, and handed over the basket to give the
boy. Back in the car, their boy had pulled a knife. Later,
and for an entirely different matter, he was sent up the
river, and then to Dannemora, for homicide.

There were two men, with their Merriam packs and
haversacks, to a seat. Every car was crowded. We
slept as best we could. At midnight the bugles blew
again and we stumbled over the railroad tracks to the
ferryboat. At dawn we cast off and churned down the
East River, our cabins, runways, and decks jammed
with companies standing in formation. The early morning tugs whistled in salute as we passed. Here and
there a steamship blew a blast, and on the upper deck
of our ferryboat the drum corps played "The Girl I
Left Behind Me" and "When Johnny Comes Marching
Home." We could see people on the docks waving
flags and cheering as we passed. Under the Brooklyn
Bridge we churned, then on south through Buttermilk
Channel.

We swung west and scraped up alongside our transport. It was the *Seneca,* a little coastwise steamship,
shabby and inadequate. Bunks had been hastily built
from the bottom of her hold to the main deck, four to
a tier that reached to the deck above. Each bunk was

built to the exact size of a man flat on his back — like a coffin. Between the tiers of bunks, we had to walk sideways. When two doughboys met, one had to crawl into a bunk to let the other pass. With my pack, overcoat, blanket, haversack, and canteen in my bunk, there was no room for me. I slept aft of the single smokestack on the upper deck, warm, snug, and comfortable. I had hoboed down the Hudson River once, deck-passage, and learned that trick.

There was no ventilation for the lower holds and their bunks, except for the open side ports about three feet above the waterline. In a bit of weather these would have to be closed — a pleasant prospect for the soldiers assigned to those holds, as we all were.

Everything was by Army contract. The bunks were too small because lumber could be scamped and the shipowners thereby make greater profits. The ship's galley had been guaranteed for our use, but the crew had first claim on it and not until they had been fed could our rations be cooked. The ship had contracted to provide coffee for the regiment when it came aboard. It did. Our regimental surgeon, Major Bell, looked at it, smelled it, tasted it. Then he ordered it all thrown overboard.

The Army had chartered ships, and boats such as the worthless and inadequate *Seneca* were foisted upon it. Sheets, linen, tableware, all were removed — even from the quarters reserved for officers. The *Seneca* had a galley and was prepared to cook for a crew and perhaps a hundred or so passengers. Yet, overnight, as soon as the last nail had been driven, a regiment of over 1,000 men was stowed aboard. The galley could not begin to feed us. It held one large kettle, about half the size of an ordinary barrel. And that kettle worked from dawn until ten at night. We were fed in relays, around the clock, on half-cooked rations.

So, within reach of a city in which not a man aboard would have been allowed to pay for a meal from the Battery to Harlem, 1,000 men were fed wretchedly. They gave us oatmeal for breakfast, cooked in three batches, one for each battalion. There was no milk, and only the water of our canteens — or whisky, if anyone had saved that more precious fluid. We also had hardtack, hard as a ship broker's conscience. The coffee, never more than ash blond, was only somewhat warm at the time of its issue. We followed Major Bell's example and threw it over the rail.

Noon, of course, called for a heartier meal, and sowbelly came on the menu. Sowbelly, cut in chunks, was tossed into the kettle and, in a manner of speaking, stewed. Warm, soft, and greasy, the chunks were bailed out of the kettles and dumped into our tin mess kits. Half raw, or to be more exact, about three-quarters raw, they were wholly inedible. As the men in the mess line of each battalion reached the galley door and was handed his cube of morbid pig, he would walk to the rail and toss it overboard. We all chucked it. But it was government property and, by regimental order from the colonel, such waste was prohibited. Nothing, of course, was said as to other means of its disposal.

So the latrines became choked, and the scuppers —
which, of course, are not overboard though they help
toward that direction — became cluttered with a sickening slush of parboiled Army "bacon."

Then the galley tried baked beans. Beans need to be
soaked and softened before cooking — at least Army
beans must be so treated. But it was as if the beans had
been dumped, unsoaked, into the kettle of sowbelly-
lard and issued while still hot. Overside they went —
nothing having been said about not throwing *beans*
away. All day long we nibbled hardtack — for it defies
any method but that of gnawing and nibbling. We were
mad. Chumbum, with his huge arms and thick neck,
and others, made indecent remarks as the ship's officers passed. But the ship's officers did not respond. We
lesser fry would have helped any of them to follow the
sowbelly and beans overside.

The officers of the regiment sympathized with the
men; they fared scarcely any better themselves. The
owners of the *Seneca* were out for whatever chips they
could rake in, come-hell-or-high-water. The *Seneca*
was the most shameless swindle ever finagled into a
government contract. I doubt whether there has ever
been bred a more rapacious set of scoundrels than
those responsible for the arrangements of our troop
transports.

A casual friendship with the sailors in the fo'c's'le
of the *Seneca* occasionally got us the leavings of their
food. Some sailors even called for seconds in order to
have more leavings for a soldier friend. We traded

whisky, of which we had plenty, for these leavings from the crew's mess. And yet, only two miles away to the north, there was New York and food! And credit or "on the house" for any man in uniform!

Excursion boats loaded to the gunwales and with their off paddle wheels scarcely beating the water, circled us in steady trips with the bunting flying and the passengers waving and cheering. All day long they drifted past, staring with patriotic eyes as they cheered the puny, coastwise tin can turned into a troopship jammed with a thousand hungry soldiers. Newspapers chartered tugs that megaphoned us from their decks as they circled around; but no reporters were allowed on board as we swung idly at anchor in upper New York Bay. We were incommunicado.

One man deserted. Technically, it was simply an AWOL. He hid on the tug that had been unloading supplies through a lower port. He was caught in New York the second day and returned, but in the meantime life was brightened by lively discussions as to whether he would be hanged or shot. When he was brought back it was to the hoots and jeers of the ship.

We had two days on that wretched *Seneca*. It seemed like weeks. Then came orders to disembark at Hoboken, there to entrain for Florida. We learned that this was because the fleet of the Spanish Navy, under Admiral Cervera, was abroad somewhere on the high seas, location unknown, and the inland railroad would be safer. Florida was a better jumping-off place for Cuba than New York City.

It was a sound decision. But I am inclined to believe that somewhere within the War Department they had discovered the damn fool who had chartered the *Seneca* and realized that a departmental mechanism which could calmly charter a flimsy coastwise steamer to feed and carry over a thousand men to an enemy country, needed some official pause. It is also more than possible that our Colonel Francis Vinton Greene, who besides being a West Point graduate was also president of the Barber Asphalt Company and knew his way about Washington, had sent various persons in Washington some pungent telegrams. Perhaps it was one of the fragrant operations of Abner McKinley, brother to President McKinley, in ship brokerage; for he was an eager little man.

Hoboken was just another railroad yard, as Long Island City had been. Nearby church groups hustled up lemonade, cakes, and sandwiches. And there were girls to hand them out. Once again it was good to be a soldier.

At midnight the train pulled out. The lovely girls had long since faded back to their homes with their empty lemonade pitchers, and the formal sentries at the railroad gates had been called in. We waked the men who were sleeping and gave a final cheer. The vibrant thrill of motion, the click of the wheels as we pulled over the siding switches, and the very night seemed to have an epic quality.

We were off to War!

4

Our "march" to the sea by railroad. The Yankees and Richmond again. We get a mascot. Naked in the State of Georgia, or Southern Hospitality.

WHEN we awoke at dawn we were in Washington, on a siding in a railroad yard.

The dome of the Capitol glowed softly in the lovely coolness of the early morning light. It was May, the first fortnight of May, and the most alluring time of the year.

I had been in Washington before. I had walked down Pennsylvania Avenue from the Capitol ground to the Treasury Building at the other end. I had counted the saloons on one whimsical trip — there were fifty-seven of them. The rest of the street was dingy shops, dingy lodging houses, and alleys that opened into moldy slums. It was the shabbiest avenue that was ever part of a nation's ranking city.

But Pennsylvania Avenue was broad and was made thus, with prescience, a century ago, for the parades to come and the great rituals in our country's progress. I could imagine it as it was in the days of Sherman and Grant and Lincoln, and see that last parade of the "Boys in Blue" with the Civil War that had closed but thirty years before. I could see the ranks, tanned and grizzled, of veterans of great battles and rugged campaigns that had made history, men who had faced death and survived. I envied those veterans their memories, and their Great Parade.

And now I, too, was one of the "Boys in Blue."

Perhaps this very day we too would march down Pennsylvania Avenue and across the Potomac by the Long Bridge, as McClellan had done!

However, matters turned out differently.

Guards were posted at each car door, and no one was allowed off the train. Our breakfast came: a can of corned beef to each man as his day's rations, six hardtack, and swell up on water. Also, there was coffee, real coffee, cooked in one of the eating shacks that clustered outside the railroad yard and brought in our company's Buzzacot wash boiler.

Our car was an ordinary, old-fashioned coach, with faded, red plush seats, saturated with cinders and coal gas. There was one seat to each man. Two men would turn one seat back around so that the seats faced each other, and this became the bed, for two, at night. Between the seats on the floor, our Merriam pack with its overcoat roll bridged the gap, and the two blankets made a passable mattress. At one end of the car was a water cooler, which, we were instructed, was solely for drinking and not for shaving or washing. We could wash when we got to Florida, four days later!

The hours passed. The day passed. The train sat in the railroad yard. Each meal brought the wash boiler of coffee and an added distaste for canned corned beef and hardtack. There was only a trickle of lemonade, sandwich, and cake peddlers. However, the nearby eating shacks sold sandwiches — big, thick, railroad sandwiches — with cake, pie, and coffee with milk and sugar. They did a thriving business.

Night came and we bedded down in our plush seats. And sometime that night we pulled out. Later, we learned that the President, the War Department, the Navy Department, and everybody else had been in conference — and in a funk — over our train and its regimental contents!

It seemed that there were two ways to get to Florida by rail. One of them would take us through Richmond, Virginia; the other would go around it.

Which route? We were a Northern regiment. We were "Boys in Blue"! It was only 1898, remember, and the question was profound. Would we be fired upon or would we not?

Of course, no adequate reply could be expected from Richmond itself. Yet Richmond knew we were coming; that Northern troops were coming. And Richmond would be prepared, in some way, to receive us. If we went through Richmond on our way to Cuba, would we, or would we not, turn Virginia into the Republican column? That was the question. Some said yes; some said no. All day the secret debate had waged while we dieted on the prescribed Army ration and lolled amid the fumes and soft-coal burners of the railroad yard.

Finally a decision was reached. It was a compromise, possibly arranged by President McKinley himself. General Joseph Wheeler (late in command of cavalry of the Confederate States of America), private citizen and pure Southern, was made a major general of United States Volunteers, and our troop train was directed to pass through Virginia, but not through Richmond.

So we pulled out of Washington, and in the clear light of the next dawn we saw Richmond in the distance, five or six miles away. Flecks of the gold of dawn marked its steeples and spires. Between were miles of foliage, little Negro shacks, whitewashed villas, and scrawny fields. Negro children stood here and there by the tracks, sometimes waving in an abashed fashion, sometimes not. Some adult Negroes watched us stolidly; some others gave what might be called a perfunctory whoop. We credited the latter with being the braver souls of their community.

That was what we saw of Richmond. Later the details drifted in. Richmond *had* been expecting the "Boys in Blue." All that night, from the time they knew we had pulled out of Washington, they were piling up mountains of sandwiches, frying chickens by the flock, squeezing lemons, stirring sugar — all this following an afternoon of frenzied baking of hams, sweet-potato pies and cakes, and ironing frocks and frills for the reception committees. Messengers from the railway station kept the committees supplied with rumors. We had left Washington, we had passed through Alexandria — we went onto a siding to let a freight go by — we were back again on the main line!

Down at the Richmond railway station the committees began gathering. Negroes toted baskets of food covered with white napkins. There were tables of reserve supplies. There was a choir. There was a delegation from the Richmond Greys. There was a band. All around the station the crowds had formed. There was, I may add, a delegation from the Confederate Veterans! This was the reception we were to get in Richmond. They had waited from the dawn. They waited longer.

Then the news came to them. The Boys in Blue would pass them by in silence some six miles off, beyond even the toot of an engine whistle, a Yankee cheer, or a cordial Rebel yell!

Thus Richmond was to us only a moment's glimpse of some slender spires above intervening miles of dusty trees.

We were Northerners all, and Virginia was new to us in that dawn. We had never seen anything like it. We looked in amazement at the villages: a crossroads store on one side of the tracks next to the railroad, a water tank, and, across the way, the store owner's house. Beyond that, dusty trees, a wandering dirt road, an endless landscape. And each of these whistle stops had a name. One of them with three houses was the county seat!

There was time to learn these things. Each village had its sonorous name, its cordial storekeeper, some cordial villagers, straggling lines of silent Negroes, and a superb collection of razorback "hawgs" that strolled in and out with an easy indifference that was irresistible. This was sowbelly at its source.

It dawned upon us that we did not have a company mascot. A kindly storekeeper presented one soldier with a dog. But dogs were common. It was when another genial storekeeper presented our company with a cute little razorback piglet that we got our mascot. And the little pig would eat hardtack! He was clearly a natural for Army life. He was not merely unique to behold, but useful. He kept the Army rations from being wasted and gave forth gentle grunts of pleasure while he was doing us this favor.

From Virginia we passed into North Carolina. Again the same crossroads store and water tank. As in Virginia, there was always a group to welcome us. Those people knew, as well as a conductor, when any train would pass through — which, in general, meant sometime within an hour past its scheduled time of arrival.

We were running "wild," in railroad parlance; that is, we had a special conductor and ran as best we could while another train was not using the right of way. So these little crossroad stops on a siding were always a welcome break from our cinder-infested plush seats.

We began to acquire more sowbelly on the hoof as mascots. They did not look either valuable or edible, and we could not imagine that anyone else could think they were, either. Our car had four by this time, all small and quite portable, under the seats.

Then we entered South Carolina. Here the battalion acquired a few more mascots. These were a trifle larger, it seemed, and some were too fleet and got away. We had rather reached the stage where it wasn't so much the pig for a mascot as it was the principle of the thing. We had become collectors of neglected pork, the principle appearing to be to acquire a razorback mascot for each man in a company, whether he wanted it or not.

We passed into Georgia. Sunrise came and went and was measured in terms of canned corned beef and hardtack, which came from the baggage car ahead each day, via Quartermaster Sergeant Werdenschlag. For three days and nights we had not washed or shaved. We were grimy with coal soot from the engine and gritty from hair to socks with its cinders.

Then, one dawn, we pulled into a railroad siding. There was the unpainted, weatherbeaten crossroads store with its hound dogs dozing in the dust, the razorbacks, and a lone, rambling Negro. Two or three houses were visible before the pinelands and patches began. One was a big house with blinds. And in its yard was a pump. Around all was a picket fence waiting for its annual coat of whitewash. Beyond that picket fence were hogsheads sawed in half — huge half-barrels scattered about the high grass of the lawn. It would have been impolite to open a gate unasked, and walk in. So, politely and considerately, a dozen of us climbed over the picket fence. The pump, thank God, pumped, and we smote it hip and thigh until water gushed forth. We trained the pump onto the trough and the trough into the nearest barrel tubs. Two dozen men, naked as the day they were born, sloshed around that yard both in and out of the sawed-off barrels. As many more were in the intermediate and hasty stages that precede complete nudity. The sentries posted at each car door were helpless. Men poured past them or saved time by dropping out of the windows, stripping as they dropped. There was no shouting, no disorder. Three hundred men were hell-bent on nakedness and having a bath. There were not three hundred tubs, and we knew that we would soon be stopped.

From the house there came not a sound. Not a curtain moved nor window raised. There was no whisper from it; it was silent as the tomb. But the store was now wide awake and its stoop was lined with natives, black and white — all men. Which, in those decorous times when legs were limbs, was as it should be.

But suddenly, from the officers' Pullman — the last car of the train — there surged forth our Major J. Hollis Wells, roaring. An adjutant, a battalion sergeant major, a pair of captains, and, on the lower steps of the car, Colonel Greene himself, were gesticulating. From the yard of the house we could not hear the colonel. But we could hear Major Wells.

"Get out of there!" he was yelling, as he ran toward us. "Get out of there, you goddamned . . . !" I was at the pump and could not quite hear the rest of it; the pump made too much clatter.

Out of the corner of my eye, I noted a tall gentleman approaching the major. He had on a butternut homespun of civilian cut, mail order.

"Colonel," he said, correctly saluting the major. "Ah'm —"

"Major, sir, Major J. Hollis Wells," said our major.

"Ah'm delighted to make yo' acquaintance . . ."

"Pardon me, sir," said the major. "Just as soon as I get these goddam blasted naked sons of Belial out of here . . ."

"Suh, Major, I beg yo' pardon, that's what I wished to speak to you about, suh. Ah'm —"

"I apologize, sir, for this outrage," interrupted the major. "I present the sincere apologies of our colonel to you for this outrage in this town."

"Major, make no apology, suh, this is my prop'ty and I . . ."

"Sir, the colonel, Colonel Greene, in command, desires me to present you his utmost regret." The major paused.

Washington had given firm instructions that the South must be protected from the Northern rascals, and this outrage was occurring in Georgia through which Sherman had marched. Now what would the folks back home say to a whole Georgia town being overrun by an army of naked Northerners!

"If you'll pa'don me, Major, I wish to say that I have asked all the women folk to stay on the far side of the house, suh, and in fact it was their suggestion, and if you'll invite yo' entire regiment to have a bath, suh, me and my fam'ly will be most honored, suh."

The major looked at him.

"I wish to say fu'ther, suh, that these gentlemen" — he indicated the naked horde in his yard — "these gentlemen are here at my invitation and are in no sense trespassin'. I can only regret, suh, that mo' barrels were not sawed up."

That was a Southerner for you — and I still am willing to bet that he spoke for the whole South. I figured he was a colonel himself, once, with his saluting the major and giving him a step-up in rank.

When we pulled out of that siding, I can also bet that the cheer we gave him could be heard in Charleston. At any rate, it drowned out the whistle of the locomotive. The house owner did not salute as our train pulled out slowly. Instead he waved his hand high. I decided that he was at least a general, Confederate States of America. Generals do not have to salute. They can wave.

5

The Waycross Coffee Riot. Alligator fishing — Lakeland, Florida. I become a mule skinner. Camp athletics: poker, craps and whip duels.

GEORGIA was a state of more railroad sidings, more long stretches of pine and hills and water tanks and crossroad stores. More razorback hogs, and we added to their number by releasing our piglet mascots.

We had had no coffee since we left Washington. There was not an eating shack big enough to provide coffee for 350 men between Washington and Waycross, Georgia. Waycross was a railroad center, with a restaurant in its station that could provide coffee. Major Wells passed the news as he went through the train. Wires had been sent on ahead and coffee contracted for, enough for the entire regiment. Of course, this was morning and we would not arrive in Waycross until after dark. No matter. The coffee would be there, we could smell its aroma at every siding.

It was dark when we pulled into the main station.

There were the committees with sandwiches, cake, and lemonade. The coffee was in the station waiting room for "Whites Only" and we made for it. Huge urns of regulation restaurant-type were full of coffee. On the minute the room was jammed. Coffee, five cents a cup. The crowd was six deep. It went to a dime. It got to a quarter. A quarter, hell! The doorways were jammed. Coffee, a quarter! Anger began to show. The station waiting room was a milling mass of soldiers. The two men and women behind the counter were flustered, then frightened. They began swearing at the soldiers. Their faces showed panic; soldiers were grabbing the coffee and refusing profanely to pay the quarter.

"A quarter for coffee! *A quarter for coffee!*" The words were passing back angrily through the soldiers struggling at the doors to get in. The anger was spreading fast. It would have taken nothing to start a riot — nothing but the first smash of glass or crash of wood. We would have wrecked the place. No longer were we a battalion of good-natured, bantering young men. We were a mob in the stage just before the first splintering of wood or tinkle of a broken pane can pull the trigger of riot.

Out and down the line of cars passed the cry, *"A quarter a cup!"*

Major Wells came thrusting his way through the station.

"Stop selling that coffee!" he shouted. He shoved and fought to the counter.

"Get back to your cars!" he ordered. "You'll get coffee — every one of you!" He turned to the man in charge. "You're selling these men the coffee that the government has already paid for. Sell another cup and I'll put you under arrest, goddam you!"

The station waiting room was cleared and our guards put on its doors.

"Go on, boys, back to the train," shouted Major Wells. "They sold you your own coffee, so they'll have to make it good. You'll get it!"

We did. It came to the train in our Buzzacot wash boiler, and we dipped it out with our pint cups. Back in the station, the major had words with the sullen white trash who had gypped us. The words were all by the major. A guard stood by and no one was permitted to buy anything. Adjutant Fisher backed up the sentry.

The coffee was *good*. No pleasanter night ever followed a day than when we pulled out of Waycross with our bellies coffee-lined.

We dawdled along through Florida. Its swamps and the trees with their festoons of gray moss were novelties. The scarcity of villages was even more accented here by long stretches of swamp and low pine barrens.

Lakeland, in the far south, was our destination, and it was but little more than the crossroad-and-tank villages we had sided by so many times. It had a station, with doors for white and colored, and a couple of freight warehouses. From it stretched a street, with an occasional house showing its front outline against the fringe of oleanders and pines. Other troops had arrived before us and there were a few officers and some soldier details around the warehouses. A scattering of townspeople were on hand, somewhat blasé. By this time, they had become acclimated to soldiers.

Nonetheless people waved from the plank sidewalks or gathered at the edge of the trodden, grass-lined paths.

An officer from the Regular Army, by the side of our colonel, led us to the camp ground. It was just at the edge of the town in a grove of slim, gaunt pine trees that flecked the ground with a lovely spotted shade all day long. Into the grove, we formed columns of companies and each company then had its company street before it. Beyond, not thirty feet away, was a little lake. Even before details could be formed to bring the tentage up from the freight station, a soldier was fishing in the lake. He got a bite in a minute, and jerked his new-cut pole upward. A baby alligator dangled at the end and — believe it or not — he did not know what it was. Further attempts proved that you could catch nothing in that lake but little baby alligators and an occasional turtle.

I was put on baggage detail. My job was to go with a regular army teamster, along with a half-dozen more of us, and jack tents out of the baggage car and into the Army wagon. The Army wagon was what all Army wagons have been ever since the Revolution. It was not driven from a seat, with reins. It was hauled by a jerk-line team of mules: three teams of mules and no reins. The driver rode the wheel mule, that is, the one just ahead of the wagon. A single rein led through the cheek-strap of the mule he was riding, along to a simi-lar loop on the bridle of the mule ahead, and then on up to the bit of the nigh lead mule. This was the sole appa-ratus for pilotage.

To start the engines, you yelled at the mules, gener-ally in technical profanity. Then, if you wished to go to port, you hauled in hard on the jerk-line. I have since then been utterly amazed at the intuitive and intellec-tual processes of the mule. No mule turns but the lead mule; while all the rest, in their docile procession, fol-low him — or it — up to and around his exact turning point. Then, if you wish to go to starboard, you rattle and slap that same jerk-line. This, to the mule, means to go to the right. And the lead off-mule, sensing the push by his near-side partner, plugs off to the right, too, and again the procession pivots after him. It is an intriguing process. The master pilot of my baggage wagon was a Negro teamster of the quartermaster serv-ice. He had an open mind, and I became a temporary apprentice teamster. He walked alongside and was helpful, for driving a jerk-line through the intricate ir-regularities of a straggling pine grove is no cinch.

That first evening in camp, we had a hot stew of fresh meat, bargained for at the Lakeland meat center. We had fresh bread, and stewed tomatoes with crum-bled hardtack. It was good!

The sand made lovely beds, each shaped to the sleep-er's figure before morning. There were six of us to a tent instead of four. Daytimes, the tent's side walls were rolled up after breakfast, so that each night the air in the tent was fresh, clean, and fragrant with the incense of the pine grove.

We were beginning to get more intimately acquainted. Jimmy Lowe, my bunkie, I knew well, naturally. He had lived a block away from where I had my studio in the old West Tenth Street studio building. We had been at the Art Students' League together; and we had been together on a 400-mile hobo trip and gone broke on it before we got home. His grandfather — who looked like John Brown of Osawatomie — had invented a method of casting the gooseneck trap for sinks in one piece instead of soldering it together; he was retired and Jimmy did not have to work.

Ed and Jim Booth, the twins, were in our tent. As I mentioned earlier, poker was Ed's lay. Stud, preferably, for he regarded draw poker merely as a preliminary apprenticeship.

"You see," Ed would patiently explain to me after he had picked a worthy opponent and I watched as an apprentice, "you want to play careless-like in the beginning. Then bluff — hell, the only use of bluffing is to get caught. No matter what the books say, you don't win hands on bluffing. Play like you was a damfool for the beginning, maybe an hour or so. Show 'em how you play — show 'em your hand when you don't have to. Let 'em get set as to how they know what kind of poker you play. Then, later, play like hell! And close."

Twin Jim listened, too. With a warm admiration, for they were, as a matter of fact, very close.

"Don't you ever play, Jim?" I asked. "Sinful?"

"No," said Jim easily, "never interested me. It's just luck. Things turn up or they don't turn up and there's nothing you can do about it. I like things more where you have to do something to shape them."

"The hell they don't," said Ed. "And another thing . . ." He was speaking to me. "Don't forget that the money and play is all in *before* the draw, if you're in draw poker. Now stud, that's different. You've got to play 'em before the draw and after, too. Draw's just a showdown, mostly." He regarded draw as kid stuff.

Few played stud. We were from the East, and stud was more of a Western type of poker. Except draw poker, there were few card games in our regiment. Matching pennies, or nickels, occasionally, but there wasn't much interest in gambling until we learned to play craps — a game none of us knew before coming to Lakeland. We watched our Negro teamsters with interest that first Sunday, bending in close groups over a poncho or blanket in the shade of a wagon and hoarsely cajoling the dice. The teamsters had still another game. Each teamster had a blacksnake whip with a last long enough to reach the lead mules of his six-mule team. They wore leather boots, and two would start a game. Carefully circling around each other, blacksnake in hand, suddenly one would lash out. The other would leap in the air, doubling his legs under him to avoid the lash. They only aimed at the legs below the knee; for one of those lashes could lay the skin open to the bone if it landed on the flesh. It could sting even through a boot, and the blue jeans would be no protection at all.

It was a game, and they bent themselves to it earnestly. There was no anger, but pure skill. Like two gamecocks, they would circle amid the joyous shouts of the other teamsters. One could hear the whip's crack from the far end of the camp. When the crack of a lash *did* land, it was a joy for the spectators and no time out to rub a leg for the players.

Out farther from Lakeland was the cavalry camp. It was the days of the frontier Indian fighting, and the cavalry was the original of Frederick Remington's best pictures. Lean, slit-eyed, hard-bitten men, who played Mexican monte, or poker. Cards were no mere pastime here; they played for blood — and with blood, sometimes. Once I saw a trooper reach for his knife, and a half-dozen kibitzers swarmed over him till he calmed down. They played in silence; with all the rigors of the game, eyes half shut, cards close, and every sinew tense.

But it was the teamsters, and the Ninth and Tenth Cavalry, the only Negro cavalry regiments, that taught us Northerners craps. Before the war with Spain, craps was not prevalent as a white man's game. But it did not take us long to catch on. Before we embarked from Tampa, even the soda-water counters and ice-cream stands just beyond camp had a layout chalked on a poncho, with a soldier running the crap bank.

Ed Booth still preferred poker. I still remember his final word of advice, as we sat under that pine in the lazy Florida afternoon.

"Don't let 'em buy chips. Make 'em play what they have in front of them. Poker isn't just cards, it's human nature. And it isn't the high hands in poker, anyhow, that makes a winner. It's playing the hands you get and playing them right!"

Excellent advice.

My company landing at Siboney.

William Randolph Hearst on horseback reviewing troops.

Our commander, General Shafter, in his buckboard.

Bloody Ford below San Juan Hill, where we lost over four hundred men.

6

*The Sheriff and the Provost Guard. Local option (dry)
and how to get a bourbon milk shake. Drill!*

WE HAD drill every morning until noon, after
which the day was our own. Also, after a turn
at guard duty for twenty-four hours, or a particularly
onerous detail, we were entitled to a pass. Yet one took
a pass mostly as a matter of duty, for pleasure was limited in that little sandy village of Lakeland. There were
no saloons there, for Lakeland was in a local option
county of Florida, and had voted itself bone dry. Not a
drop could be bought anywhere for love or money unless, of course, you knew the ropes. The ropes, I may
say, did not exist until the arrival of our soldiery in
blue. Before that, I believe one could get a drink in a
friend's house, and a friend could get one in yours. But
there was no buying or selling of the demon rum in any
public place. Public sentiment rigorously enforced this
law, for Lakeland was dry on principle — the principle
of "Plenty of bourbon for the white man, but no gin for
the nigger!"

One day some of us were on supply detail at the Lakeland freight depot. Between wagon loads, we would sit on the platform and talk to the townsfolk. The sheriff and a couple of his deputies were there, and they were full of questions about New York. We Northerners were as much curiosities to Lakeland as Lakeland was to us. It was all friendly, both ways.

"You-all don't have many niggras up No'th like us down here?" remarked the sheriff.

Well, no, not exactly. But there were quite a few.

There was a short silence. The sheriff had something on his mind.

"Well," he finally said slowly, "d'ya ever have niggra cops rounding you up an' throwin' you in the jug — like here?"

I saw what he was driving at. The Army did not have "niggra cops," but some throbbing sociologist in the Army had designated the Tenth Cavalry, which was Negro, as a Provost Guard for Lakeland. Maybe it was because it was the first regiment to arrive there, or maybe it was just a totally unnecessary bit of damfoolishness. At any rate, the Tenth Cavalry was Provost Guard, and it did arrest both white and black soldiers, or demand that they produce their passes for inspection. This in a town where black men stepped off the sidewalk, touched their hats, and said, "Howdy, suh," when a white passed by.

Now a Provost Guard may be one man, or it may be a brigade or more. Their function is that of a military police, to prevent disorder, to preserve the peace, and

to protect citizens from marauding soldiers in captured cities, or vice versa. And here the Provost Guard
had been appointed from a Negro cavalry regiment!

Any day, you could see some Negro trooper riding
through the town and calling upon a soldier to come
out into the road and show his pass, or demand his
right to be out of camp. Still mounted, the Negro
trooper would examine the pass from his saddle, listen to any excuse impassively — the same as a white
trooper would. And then, perhaps, he would wave the
culprit ahead of the horse to join the little group of soldiers already under arrest and shortly to be delivered
to their regimental guard tent.

"Well," said the sheriff, after a long and thoughtful
pause, "it's sort of disturbin' to the folks around here
to see niggras arrestin' you white folk."

I explained that such was all right. Army was Army,
black or white. It was the uniform, not the wearer. It
was just Provost Guard, wholly impersonal.

The sheriff paused again. "Well, just as you say —
perhaps," he said, "you're in the Army and maybe it
don't make no difference in the Army. But it shore
gravels us folks around here. It ain't natural."

Another pause. It seemed tactful for my part to remain somewhat silent.

"Yes," he went on, "it shore don't seem right for a
niggra on a horse to be herdin' up white folks, even if
they is in the Army. Any you fellows ever punch the
black bastard?" he continued.

I assured him that Army discipline was such that we

were forbidden to punch bastards either black or white.

But the sheriff had made up his mind to something. Clearly, for some reason that seemed sound to him, I could be trusted.

"Well, young fellow," he said earnestly, "I want to tell you something. You might pass it along, too. Effenhow any you boys gets into trouble with one of these black bastards on a horse, an' so be it as you'd like any help, I'm tellin' you jest you holler for it an' you'll be gettin' a-plenty quicker'n scat. Us folk is with you boys every time."

I looked at the nickel star that made him sheriff.

"Where'll you be, Sheriff — if anything happens?"

"Me — who, me?" He laughed cordially and slapped me on the shoulder. "Why me, son, they'll be havin' one hell of a time locatin' me then or thenabouts. Or any of my deppities, either!"

The jerk-line pulled up alongside the platform and we began jacking the supply cases out of the freight car. We came across some cases of canned beef and read the name of the consignee; it was us, all right, our U.S. Army. But on the other side of the case the name of a previous consignee could still be seen, burned into the wood: "Yokohama, Japan." It had been intended for the Japanese soldiers in the China-Japan War of four years before — 1894. Its contents were indicated as "Roast Beef." We got it later, in the trenches; same cases, same cans — but no can label. When filled, those cans had simply been dipped in red barn paint. The contents were ground-up cow, bone, gristle, cartilage, and gullet, with stringy fibers scattered through a semi-liquid mess. Clara Barton knew about it in Santiago. She told Captain Rafferty in indignant words what she thought of the Chicago meat packers.

"It is what was left over after making beef extract," she said, "or worse. You could starve to death eating it!"

Later, Upton Sinclair wrote *The Jungle,* exposing the Chicago meat packers. And many good and worthy people thought that he had libeled some noble souls of the stockyards. Incidentally, the Chinese lost the war with Japan. I think it was because the Japanese let them capture those canned rations.

As we pulled out of the station with the last wagonload of the day, I saw the sheriff. He waved cordially.

"Don't forget what I told you, son," he called. "You'll be gettin' it when you need it and mighty damn quick."

The next day Jimmy Lowe and I had a pass. I had some money from poker and Jimmy had some by the most recent mail. What we wanted was a drink, not as alcoholics but as a sporting proposition to test the dryness of the county. We had been given directions by those on whom we could rely: "Go down the main street — you can't miss it. Look for one of those stores where they sell ice cream and candy — lace curtains in the windows — maybe a nice old lady fanning on the porch above. Never mind, go in. Ask for what you want and you'll get it. Anybody in uniform can get a drink, and no one else."

Jimmy and I set out gaily. We went up the porch of an ice-cream parlor, and were confronted with two store windows with white lace curtains. Inside were a few couples, no soldiers. And they were having ice cream; townfolk, obviously. We went up to the counter, behind which were a row of home-freezing ice-cream cylinders. Above them and, in fact, all over the room were cardboard signs, neatly lettered: "Try Our General Robert E. Lee Milk Shake," "General Miles Grape Juice," "A General Grant Ice Cream Soda," or "A General Beauregard Favorite — Mint Ice Cream." It was a perfect display of North-and-South fraternal patriotism. Northern and Southern generals mingled in fairly equal proportions. A small sign in the center of the wall, back of the counter, briefly stated in small letters: "No Alcoholic Liquor Sold Here." We smiled. We knew better.

"A rye highball," we said, not loudly.

"No, sir, gentlemen, sorry gentlemen, nothing like that sold here." It was not soft-pedaled in tone, either, though polite.

We winked politely.

"We're of the Army," we explained. "A highball, rye — or bourbon if you don't have rye." We put one finger along our nose to show that we were wise to the ropes.

"Mighty, mighty sorry, gentlemen," said the proprietor. "I'm afraid you've been misinformed. This Lakeland is in a dry county, you know. What's that drink? High something?"

"Highball," we said. "Rye or bourbon."

"That's liquor, ain't it? No liquor here. Maybe you boys'd like some ice cream? That General Lee Ice Cream Soda's mighty tasty."

Ice cream! And with a pass good only till six o'clock!

"Ah'm mighty sorry," continued the proprietor, "real sorry there ain't no way of accommodatin' you boys. This town is sure dry. But maybe you'd set an' rest awhile before you go traipsin' out lookin' for what Lakeland cain't give you nohow. Now you go take a cheer out back under the arbor — it's mighty restful an' I know you boys is tired."

Disillusioned, we went back under the arbor. We sat in rocking chairs and cussed out our friend. It was, we agreed, a mighty shabby joke. The minutes dragged. It was hot and the sun was flecking the ground with irritating patterns. A voice came out from inside the store. "How you gentlemen enjoyin' yo'selves. . . ?" And before we could make suitable response, the proprietor appeared, from a doorway that apparently led to the family kitchen. In his hand were two tall glasses of the kind the Bowery made famous years ago and known as "high hats."

Little beads of lavender moisture were already gathering below each brim, and from within came the gentle tinkle of ice.

"Ah'm hopin' these'll be somethin' you gentlemen won't mind partakin' of — it's a temperance drink, you know. We don't sell nothin' but temperance drinks. Law's against it."

It was, in fact, a marvelous temperance drink; it tasted exactly like a highball.

"You boys had me a bit puzzled when you said 'highball' — never heard of it. That a New York drink? This here is a — well, you might say a General Lee Ice Cream Soda, if anybody asks you. Or a General Miles Milk Shake. Anyway, it's a military drink, if you get what I mean."

Then he chuckled.

"Anybody in uniform can get any drink he wants — just let him ask for it and tell me what it is. I guess 'highball' must be a long drink from its name, and shucks, you said either rye or bourbon, didn't you? This's bourbon."

We agreed that this General Miles Milk Shake stood highest on the list of temperance drinks of any in our experience. Until a half hour before six we sat there under that cool and delightfully sun-flecked arbor and had another. Later we had some ice cream; plate after plate of it, between drinks. We loafed happily for four hours. Then we went out and sat on the front porch of the store and watched the luckless ones without passes being garnered in by the Provost Guard. They grinned sheepishly back. The proprietor joined us.

"Mighty sad sight," he said, pointing to three forlorn young men walking dejectedly before a cavalry horse that was surmounted by a "black bastard" from the Tenth Cavalry, "a mighty sad sight. If you would accept my hospitality and have another of those military temperance drinks, gentlemen, I should be happy."

We thanked him cordially and declined.

It was the end of a perfect day. We went back to our regiment, turned in our passes and sat down like good young men and watched the unfortunates as they dribbled to the guardhouse after being turned over by a poker-faced cavalryman.

We drilled in the palmetto scrub beyond Lakeland. Here, as I knew, were rattlesnakes and coral snakes, both deadly. And this menace in a dry county where snakebite remedy was proscribed! The perils of war had begun. Suppose one were bitten? The prospect of swelling up with venom and dying for lack of an ice-cream soda had no allure for us. So, for skirmish drill we adopted a method. When the order came and the bugles blew for "Right front into line — double time," we would rush forward noisily, giving all snakes notification to get out. At the command, "Lie down — commence firing!" we would fan the grass before us with the muzzles of our rifles and then flop forward into the space thus presumably cleared of rattlers and corals. It seemed to work, for not a snake was ever seen.

In the Civil War the ranks stood up, perfect targets, and blazed away at each other. There was a reason for this, foolish as it may seem in the days of modern rifles. A man lying down would have had difficulty in muzzle-loading his old musket, a long and complicated operation. We, with our breechloaders, could lie down. It was safer and far more comfortable. War had become much more relaxing at its most perilous phase.

Here in Lakeland, for the first time, we drilled as a regiment. It was an imposing procedure and every formation had its bugled directions. We would, for example, be out amid the palmetto scrub, the colonel mounted and in front of our array of three battalions in line, each battalion with four companies and each company with its bugler and drummer; each company with eighty-four men, rank and file. The colonel, majors, adjutants, and staff were all mounted.

The colonel would face us and order:

"Form for attack — second battalion fighting line! First battalion, support! Third battalion, reserve!"

We could not hear him, but the majors and the adjutants could. Then the tumult began.

The major of the first battalion would order: "First battalion — stand fast!" Every captain of the first battalion shouted: "Company A" (or B or C or D) "— stand fast!" The major of the third battalion shouted the same, and his captains duplicated the order.

The major of the second battalion, in the center of the line, ordered: "Form for attack — forward!" and waited for the regimental bugle from beside the colonel.

"March!" the colonel would order. And his bugler, Gorman, would blow the single note that put us in motion toward the enemy.

The buglers of the second battalion would repeat the call and then, when the second battalion had advanced a suitable distance, the first battalion would move forward. After an interval, the third-battalion bugle would blow and the third battalion moved forward on the right flank, keeping farther to the rear than the support.

After another interval the second battalion's bugle would blow: "Commence firing!" Thereafter, amid the clicking of the empty rifles in a "fire at will," the first battalion would presume that sufficient men of the fighting line had been casualties, or the major on the fighting line would decide that he needed additional aid through losses incurred and would call to the major of the support: "One Company on the fighting line!" And One Company's major would command: "Company C — on the line, double time!" The company would go forward on the run to flop down on the line, regardless of rattlers, tarantulas, or scorpions. During one of these drills I was harpooned by a scorpion; it was like a very hot hornet sting, but there was none of the delirious pain so often credited to it.

This was the way battles were fought; nice, formal, punctilious, and with every move to the singsong of a bugle. It was half concert and half fight. Later, at San Juan Hill, all of us, infantry and cavalry, went into action in close order. Column of fours, fours left — a battle line in a clotted jungle of cowpaths. The Rough Riders' charge on Kettle Hill was an instinctive "right front into line" — and Kettle Hill was theirs.

At San Juan Hill itself, we executed a "line-of-companies-on-left-front-into-line" in the unmapped, jungle meshed, unpatrolled, and unscouted no man's land. Fortunately, the Spaniards knew no more of what we were doing than we did ourselves.

At Lakeland we also did open-order drill, a slight variation from the days of the Civil War. Then it was "Skirmishers out!" and designated men, one from each squad of eight, stepped out in front of each company and preceded in the attack, with massed companies following behind.

Then it was "As skirmishers — march!" and a whole platoon, or company, or battalion — or regiment, if desired — would fan out as they ran forward.

Then we were drilled in advance by rushes. Alternate squads, or companies, crouching and running forward — then dropping flat and opening fire while the squads behind rushed up to that line, or ahead of it; each squad lying down instantly and opening rapid fire to cover the alternate squad in its forward rush.

There is a fascination about drill. Long lines or columns of men welded into an instant and common action. A surge of scrambling, running units that seems to have no coherence, yet is under perfect control. A parade with a drum corps and the formal lines in formal maneuver is its symbol. But back of the parade lies a precision of imprecise individuals. This is war. Its payoff, its summation, is battle; and battle is bloody, cruel, merciless, and blind in its human destruction.

As will be noted, I am basically and deeply a pacifist. I believe in peace. I believe in law and the justice it codifies. But, together with Cromwell and Jefferson and Washington and Lincoln, I can believe in peace and yet realize that peace, in this slow barbaric consciousness of our human era, can only be preserved by battle. Peace can only be achieved through justice; and justice, so far, has to be fought for.

7

Heat stroke paves the way to Tampa Heights. The plight of Jim the Cook. Payday at last. "Smooching" taught by an expert.

ONE day at Lakeland was much like the next. Our colonel, Francis Vinton Greene, was sent back to Washington and made a brigadier general, and Colonel Wallace A. Downs succeeded him, and the old routine went on. We slept, we drilled, and we heard rumors. The Spanish fleet had been located. No, it had not. We would invade Spain. We would not. We would be the first regiment to attack Havana! New York was attacked — we would go north! The Navy had attacked and been sunk — no, it was the Spanish fleet and Admiral Cervera. Rumor followed rumor, all of them canceling each other. They were bred in the ice-cream parlors or down at the freight platform where the swinging legs held regular sessions since there was little freight to jack. They were bred in the latrines. Bored as we were, we enjoyed the inner thrills that came with each rumor.

Then came news. Rumor again, we said skeptically. But this time it was true!

We were to be of the Fifth Army Corps, the corps that was to invade Cuba! We were to be First Division, First Brigade. Major General Shafter was to command the Fifth Army Corps. Brigadier General J. Ford Kent was to command the First Division, and Brigadier General J. S. Hawkins was to command the First Brigade. We were to move closer to the port of embarkation at once. With our brigade were to be the Sixth and Sixteenth infantry regiments.

It isn't much for a soldier to move; at least, it wasn't in those days. Five minutes would stuff our haversacks; not much more would fill our canteens. Not so our regimental headquarters. Details had to be rushed to pack the colonel's stores and the adjutant's outfits of books and papers. Dave Werdenschlag had to have the Buzzacot oven assembled in its nested form for transport. The company chest, half as big as a steamship's stateroom, must be packed with more kitchen utensils and the coffee grinder. The tents must be struck and tied up in bundles. Then the grounds were to be policed. At last, we could line up and go.

Admiral Cervera, the Spanish admiral, still had his fleet somewhere on the high seas, so until he was located our transportation for the invasion of Cuba must wait. But we were to move nearer the port of embarkation against the time which would come. We entrained for Tampa, which is slightly less than thirty miles and almost due west of Lakeland.

But we did not go to Tampa direct. We stopped and detrained at Ybor City, a straggling, shabby Spanish-and-Negro outpost of Tampa and, socially, very, very much south of the railroad tracks — even for the South. Off the train, we swung our Merriam packs, and the sun of Ybor City beat down on us. The railroad station was a siding and a tank; the sand was loose and dusty and ankle deep. We waited in the sun until the horses of the staff had been unloaded, together with the colonel's horse and the majors' horses, and until they had all been saddled and placed at the head of the regiment. It was only three miles, perhaps two. But no one could keep up with those damned staff horses who set the pace for us foot sloggers.

Did we march crisply like soldiers into our new camp on Tampa Heights?

We did not.

Our regimental ambulance was soon full of heat cases. The route was lined with men who had dropped out, muddy with perspiration and dust, faint with heat of exertion. They leaned against their packs by the side of the road and Ybor City residents rushed out with pitchers of cool well water. Not one-half of the regiment arrived behind the first battalion. Men straggled in and kept straggling in until long after tattoo, and even taps. But the shrewd ones who had recovered from the pace, stayed out for supper in Tampa. They arrived later, fresh and piquant, and commiserated us novice freshmen who had tried to do an impossible march and did it.

Our camp in Tampa Heights, just beyond the end of the trolley line, was out in the full glare of the Florida sun. The Heights were about fifteen feet higher than Tampa itself — a veritable hill! We dug new latrines, and the area of palmetto scrub was so barren of habitation that they did not need to be screened.

The next day, we got passes into Tampa, which seemed like a metropolis; even the short trolley ride in seemed to savor of New York and Brooklyn. The main street was filled with soldiers — regulars — and with some of the Second Massachusetts that had kept close company with us from our days on the *Seneca* in New York Bay. They had been on the *City of Washington* anchored just south of us. (The *Washington* had been struck by some fragments of the exploding *Maine* while she was in the harbor of Havana.)

Camp life at Tampa Heights was the same as it had been at Lakeland. Only, the camp was hotter. But it was here we got Jim. Jim was a tall and gangling Negro. Jim was a cook — the first hired cook since Chumbum had come into our ranks. And Jim's ma had taught him well.

Jim was the humblest Negro you ever saw when he was taken on. Somehow, he got a blue uniform blouse and wore it, hot sun or no hot sun, in a fullness of new Army pride. Like enough, it was the first time he had ever owned a coat all in one piece. Under him our fried eggs came out fried eggs, with no curled celluloid fringe on their edges. The Buzzacot was no mystery to him. He had been brought up on open cookfires in a back yard, and the Buzzacot responded affectionately to his subtle attentions. We had hash and we had stew that was honest stew under Jim's artful prodding.

At first Jim was puzzled by our kitchen details — white folk doing nigger work! We men of the ranks clearly were white folk; but white folk with a difference. We had many bosses — sergeants, corporals — and yet they were not quality folk, either! Jim adopted a method of common address: "Hey, you, please suh." This worked fine. To the kitchen details he directed: "Hey, you, please, suh, clean up them pans." By degrees, the "suh" dropped off and Jim consorted with sergeants as equals, and they with him. "Hey, you" was enough.

It was just about as Jim got settled in this groove that one of the Southerners in our company came in after guard duty, late for supper. Jim, thinking it was one of the kitchen detail, called over his shoulder without turning: "Hey, you, clean up them pans — I'm a-needin' of them."

The Southern black-and-tan dictionary of objurgation exploded in his face. Jim, of course, knew that he was a "black bastard," but it is doubtful if he had known all the other things that he was too.

"Yessuh," said Jim. He knew when he was talking to quality white folk.

"You hear me?"

"Yessuh," said Jim.

"Now you talk. What did you say?"

"Yessuh, suh. I say, please Mister Smith, suh, might I han' you a ration, suh, Mister Smith, suh?"

"Right! And what was it I told you?"

"Mister Smith, suh, never to forgit the Mister, suh, never. Not to nobody, suh."

And Jim did not.

Thereafter, everyone in our company was pointedly spoken to as "Mister, suh." Except, of course, the kitchen detail. Sometimes he forgot and addressed them as "Mister, suh, please." Dave Werdenschlag was puzzled. He heard Jim as he dished out the Buzza-cot pan with his running "Mister, suh" to the mess line. "What the hell is this mister business all about? What's got into Jim?"

"Yessuh, Mister, Yessuh," said Jim. He never could pronounce "Werdenschlag."

Payday came at last, and we lined up before a little portable table at which sat the paymaster and his clerk. I stepped forward when my name was finally called, and received a slim wad of money. It was $10.35, for I had not yet officially been in service one month.

That night, out of approximately a thousand men, there were only eighty-five privates left in the camp. We eighty-five were all there were to send on Provost Guard to round up the others, who were in Tampa drinking it dry. So, commanded by officers, we marched out of camp in column of twos, down into Tampa. Every saloon brought forth its amazed prisoners. With fixed bayonets, we formed them in a column of twos. The column grew and, as we turned back to camp, it stretched away down into the darkness of the scantily lighted street. All told, prisoners ran up into the hundreds, and we took only those of our regiment.

The Regulars, far wiser, sent out no Provost Guard. They shut their eyes on paydays, and until the night after. I think that without a doubt we made ourselves ridiculous. However, we did what the military bible said we should do.

And I profited by it. For, under my eye, and, in fact, abreast of me in the line of prisoners, was Jimmy Shortell of Brooklyn. Jimmy was a prize fighter who had a brother, Tommy, a chap of some eminence in the arena. Jimmy was quiet, self-contained and pleasant. As we reached the end of the trolley line we halted. There was an orange orchard across the way. Adjoining it was a fair-sized barn, newly built and with the boards still a fresh sawmill yellow. Known as Noah's Ark, it was a gambling house and offered chuck-luck, keno, roulette, and faro. The barn was packed to the doors; not an officer could get in. But here, at the trolley terminal, under flaring gasoline torches, was an ice-cream and soda fountain forty feet long. Here were sold soap, coconuts, souvenirs, oranges, lemons, writing paper, and sandwiches. On the counter, soldiers were playing chuck-luck and craps.

Jimmy Shortell looked at it and then leaned to me.

"For the love of Mike," he whispered, "let me over there. I'll come back — honest!"

My virtuous soldierly instincts instantly recoiled. To let a prisoner escape! I could be court-martialed.

"Nix!" I said.

"Look," he pleaded urgently, "there's candy and cake — all sorts of things — half yours — go on, just a minute?"

"Nix," I repeated monotonously. "We're going on in a minute."

"I'll join you. Just holler — honest!"

"Nix," I said loudly. "But," and I lowered my voice, "if you go *when I ain't looking* . . . get back for God's sake!"

"I will," said Jimmy. And swiftly, deftly, adeptly, Jimmy was over at the counter wriggling through its jammed fringe of men.

We halted only five minutes — maybe it was three. Jimmy was back before we moved on.

He had a box of smelly soap inside his blouse. He had three coconuts, a box of candy, six oranges in a bag, and, in one hand, a half-consumed glass of ice-cream soda.

"Take it," he said of the latter. "I've had one already."

"Trash," I said. "What do you throw money around like that for?"

"Money?" said Jimmy. "This didn't cost anything. They gave it to me. Honest they did."

"It's like this," Jimmy explained as we marched on in the darkness. "A crowd like that just jams up.

Everybody hollering for soda and ice cream and candy, or whatnot, and everybody reaching up and grabbing what's poked at them. Somebody behind the counter says, 'Oranges? Who ordered oranges?' and holds up the bag. I just reach up and take it. Who knows whose hand is whose in a mob like that. It's a cinch. Not a cent. And I come back like I said I would. I'm an honest guy, I am. You can trust me."

And I could. Jimmy was a good soldier.

"It's like this," he said. "When a fellow needs something — here in the Army, I mean — if he goes creepin' and smoochin' around, everyone's on to him to see what he's up to. You got to act like you belonged. Make a thing look like it belonged to you and everybody thinks maybe it does."

What I learned from Jimmy made me, in Cuba and later, the official smoocher of the company. Once the captain even assigned our second lieutenant to be under my command, as a front for a raid on the headquarters in Siboney.

8

The horse-collar pack and striking camp. Ptomaine. The transport Vigilancia. *The sporting sandbar of Port Tampa — soldiers only.*

NOW that we knew we were destined for Cuba and would be among the first in the actual fighting, daily after drill the men began to line up before the chaplain's tent. We could see, from our distance, the chaplain baptizing various members of the regiment.

We knew from Tampa civilians that the transports were swarming in the bay, and that some were even tied up at Port Tampa and taking on stores. That they were definitely Army transports was proven by the fact that there were huge, fifteen-foot-high numerals painted on each bow. The fleet was some fifty-five vessels.

Also, we had received an order to turn in our Merriam packs and our overcoats and, at the same time, were given instruction, a drill, and inspection in making the horse-collar blanket roll. We were issued our dog tents — officially "shelter tents" — and their pins and socketed, take-down poles. We were also issued ammunition for our cartridge belts. Each cartridge was as big as your finger, with a .45-caliber slug at its front end. It could, properly directed, knock down two men, the one it hit and the one who fired it. For the kick was tremendous. The first instruction in firing it was a direction for placing the legs apart and well braced for the recoil. It had seventy grains of old-fashioned black powder and, with each discharge, there burst forth a cloud of white smoke somewhat the size of a cow.

In the business of making a blanket roll, you lay the blanket on the ground, put into it your tent pegs and your half of the two tent poles — for each man carries but one-half the tent — and then arrange your towel, socks, shirt, and extra underwear and roll up the blanket. Then, turning your attention to your half of the tent, fold it lengthwise. This you lay on top of the blanket roll, fasten it at the ends and the middle, much as if reefing a sail, then bend it until it takes its horse-collar shape, fasten the two ends — and there you are, ready to stick your head through and sling it. It is excellent. But — and this we learned on our first march to the transport — the blanket roll must be made sloppy, not neat. A hard, neat horse collar will bear into the shoulder like a steel bar; so roll it loose and floppy for the part that lies over the shoulder and with no baggage inside the center section — just at the two ends. It looks like a clumsy, amateur sausage lying out straight, but it is soft on the shoulder. In Cuba our horse collars made us look like a bunch of hobo blanket-stiffs; hobos know this trick too — if they can get a blanket!

There was now no doubt of our getting to Cuba and starting the fighting. We were envied. Hence, too, the rush for baptism; there had been none from Camp Black to Lakeland. The chaplain's tent had no fly, so the candidates stood lined up before the tent in the open sun while the chaplain, a portly man, administered the sacrament from the shade of the tent.

The next few days were days of industrious letter-writing home. The country road before our guard-house had become one long, dusty train of baggage wagons passing and repassing. Everyone was on some detail or other: freight cars to unload, spare stores to be stored or carted and inspections to be made.

Then came the order: The "general" would be at six o'clock, when we would strike the tents and pack them. Striking camp is a pretty sight. One moment there is a long, wide and orderly array of tents. From in front of the colonel's tent begins the "general," one of those bugle calls, six bars with its up-and-down, staccato phrases. Then, the last lingering note, the only half-note in the call. With this final note, three acres of white canvas sink to the ground and 600 men are pouncing upon their folds, bundling them, lashing them, and hurling them upon the company baggage wagons at the end of each company street.

Then came the last supper in Tampa Heights. But it was not for me. I was on detail jacking freight. So was Jim Booth. When we were dismissed to return to our company, supper was long since over. Even the guard detail had been fed.

"Mister, suh — there hain't no supper," said Jim, for the Buzzacot was nested, all except two pans — and those had been lying in the sun since noon, unwashed. But there were fragments of the noon dinner along the bottom and in the corners.

"What's that?" Jim Booth and I both pointed at them.

"Mister — suh, that's all that's left."

It made no difference. Jim and I both scraped the bottom of the pan; then we had some cold coffee. As we ate, the company assembled in full kit.

Jim and I fell into rank a little late and we all waited. There was a delay. Somewhere at regimental headquarters some red tape was being woven or unsnarled. It began to grow dark. And then, suddenly, as if by signal, Jim and I were both engulfed in pain. It was a shrill, keen agony. It was colic — or worse, if there is worse — and it descended with a violence that dropped us to the ground in a cold, gray sweat, and drew our knees to our chins. We could not pretend. As we lay on the ground there was a bugle from headquarters, then a battalion bugle. The company swung into fours-right and they were off to Tampa and to Cuba. A sergeant was left to take us to the hospital — or where our regimental hospital tent had been.

We staggered, crawled almost, and every crawl pulsed like one of Prometheus' vultures at our belly.

We were bent like cripples. A hospital sergeant looked us over.

"Medicine's all packed up," he announced. "Nothing doing. You boys go to the general hospital." This was the Army general hospital in Tampa.

Our company sergeant moved off. His job was over, and he left us on the ground. A baggage wagon was taking the last of the hospital supplies, including the hospital blanket rolls.

"Put us on the wagon," we pleaded. "We'll be all right in the morning."

"Nope. Can't be done," said the hospital sergeant. "General hospital for you!"

"Where's Captain Stafford?" we groaned. He was our battalion surgeon.

"Down in Tampa," said the sergeant.

We announced that we had been well up to a half hour ago.

"The more reason for hospital now," responded the sergeant. He turned back to his packing of the medical field trunks.

The wagon driver passed behind us.

"If you two go down the road a piece, you kin get on — I'll be lookin' for you."

Get on — we couldn't have climbed a chicken runway! We could not even stand. The pain had doubled us up again, knees to chin, like the spring of a jackknife.

It was at this moment we heard a voice we recognized. It was Major Wells taking a last inspection and wondering why in hell that hospital outfit wasn't yet on its way to Tampa.

With the desperation of despair, Jim and I yelled, and managed to get to our feet.

"Major," we said, "we're just a little sick — but we've got to get to Cuba!"

"They're real sick men, Major," said the hospital sergeant, "and they want to get on the baggage wagon, but it's against orders. The general hospital is the place for them."

"The hell it is," responded the major briskly. "I hear they need men in Cuba. What's the matter with them?"

We answered before the hospital sergeant could mix in with some learned diagnosis.

"Just a stomach-ache, major," we said. It was a stomach-ache to end all stomach-aches.

"Can you ride the baggage wagon?" asked the major.

"Yessir!" We didn't tell him we couldn't climb on.

"Put 'em on!" said Major Wells. And he was off in the darkness.

With the driver and the sergeant, we got on, and lay up back of the driver among the bundles of lashed tents. It seemed endless hours that we jolted with the wagon over the rutted roads down to Tampa. Yet it was, in fact, only a short distance. We had thought the pain was bad before, but now it grew worse with every griping spasm. The driver was sympathetic, but we apologized for being two groaning invalids be-hind him.

"Don't you mind me — grunt if you want to — or holler. I'll bet what you got must hurt." It did.

We were in Tampa a little after midnight. We saw a drugstore, dark, but recognizable. Jim's instincts as a pharmacist came to the fore.

"Morphine's what we need," he said, "and I'm go-ing to get some! This fellow's got a night bell some-where." With matches held by the driver Jim wrote out a prescription for morphine. The driver helped him down. A few minutes later an upper window lighted up, then a door opened and there were voices — one of them Jim's. He came back.

"Got it!" he said, and climbed back with the driver's help. "Told him I was a doctor with the Army — had a sick man up back in the wagon outside. We'll split it," he added.

Carefully, he opened a little paper in the darkness.

"You lick and I'll lick," he directed.

So he took a lick and I took a lick, alternately, until the powder was gone. It seemed sort of mildly bitter-ish, as I recall, but with a red-hot crab gnawing at your stomach, all flavors fade. I said that maybe it was not morphine and the druggist was just fooling.

"No," said Jim, "he wasn't fooling. He was mighty nice about it. If he wanted to fool, he would have been mad, wouldn't he? He made me sign the paper and I signed it 'Dr. Smith.' "

Whether it was morphine or not, I shall never know.

But I do know that the pain began to lessen. I found myself in a doze. The wagon had stopped.

"I don't go no further, Jack," said the driver. We were alongside a freight car. Jim and I climbed down.

"I feel better," said Jim. "How are you?" I was much easier, too. Vaguely, in the darkness of the midnight, we could see some sort of house. It had a porch. We went over there and lay down. The pains were eased — or at least numbed.

When we awoke it was daylight and the hearty Negro tenants of the shack had long since been up and about, but they had not disturbed us.

We were beside a railroad track that led down to Port Tampa. Wagons were rolling down in that direction. So were trains, mostly flatcars with troops or cannon, or case after case of sowbelly and beans and canned goods, with all of which we were thoroughly familiar.

We hopped a freight car — that is, we were helped on by willing hands. For we were all in and looked it. Then there came a waving and halloing far up the track. A train was approaching, and in the open door of a boxcar was Teddy, Colonel Theodore Roosevelt, grinning as his car passed our lines of flatcars. His khaki uniform looked as if he had slept in it — as it always did. He wore the polka-dot blue bandanna that was the hallmark of the Rough Riders. The rest of our army wore red bandannas.

Teddy's was a long train; it had flatcars, too, and one held the odd dynamite gun that later was bought by the Khedive of Egypt. Also, there was Lieutenant Tiffany's privately bought Colt machine gun — a very recent development of the Colt Company, and of which much was expected and hoped. The dynamite gun was a pocket-sized edition of the great dynamite guns of the USS *Vesuvius*. But, whereas the *Vesuvius* had herself completely crammed with air-compressing machinery so that the muzzles of her three guns merely peeked out of the deck, to which they were firmly fastened in immovable positions, the Rough Riders' dynamite gun was completely self-contained and on wheels, with a trail and spade. It had two barrels, upper and lower. The lower was larger and into its breech one thrust a blank cartridge. When this cartridge was fired it pushed a piston, the piston compressed air, the air was released by a valve behind the dynamite projectile in the upper barrel, and the dynamite winged on its way somewhere up to a mile or so.

Jim's and my first job was to locate our regiment and company. As our flatcar came down the long dock at Port Tampa, we could see the line of transports alongside. Men, mules, horses, and stores were going aboard. I saw Captain Rafferty and reported. "Hunt up some breakfast," directed the captain. We were opposite No. 23, the *Vigilancia*, our troopship and transport.

But how were we to forage breakfast — milk, warm milk, if possible? Something suitable for badly bruised and spavined stomachs. Then, almost opposite the *Vigilancia*, I saw a street that stretched off in the distance at

right angles to the wharf. I could see umbrellas stuck in
the sand, under which would be a fat black mammy with
a little Cuban clay stove, like a plumber's brazier, before her; and I knew she would be frying chicken. Beyond were booths, or tents, that looked like eating
shacks. Most certainly I could get a breakfast there.

"Too late for anything on board," said Captain Rafferty. "Take your time. Doubtful if we even pull out
today. Sleep on board is all, probably." He pointed
down the sandy street.

So Jim went on board and I went down the heavy,
deep sand of that street of Port Tampa. The old black
mammies had fried chicken, sure enough, sizzling
in hot grease and dripping succulently for each cus-
tomer. But my stomach was as sensitive as if it had
been scalded or kicked into a mass of black-and-blue
bruises. There was no milk.

Farther down the street, still no milk. I came to the
line of tents with tent flies before them that made a
sort of porch. Under each fly was a counter made of a
couple of planks laid across a pair of barrels. A gent
in a white shirt and no collar was the general run as to
bartenders, and behind each bartender was a woman,
maybe two. One at least was always outside. You
could get a drink or a damsel, or both.

Up and down this street, which had so plainly sprung
up overnight, were soldiers, nothing but soldiers. It
was a street solely of tent saloons, with one exception,
a large two-story house of lumber still in its first
glare of raw, yellow boards. Maybe, somewhere, some-

one had some milk. I didn't care where I would get it.
But down the entire street there was whisky and beer,
nothing else; an occasional wagon from Tampa kept
them fairly supplied with ice. This was Last Chance
Street — last chance for a drink or a girl before Cuba.
Beer was too slow for action; whisky got you there
quicker. So only two drinks — whisky first, beer for a
chaser. The girls drank cold tea from a whisky bottle
— it looked like whisky and their vis-à-vis never knew
the difference. But no milk.

On the raw-lumber building was a porch and above
the porch a sign RESTAURANT. Now a restaurant should
have milk! I plodded up the porch steps, not noticing
the line of men that paralleled my weak footsteps as I
climbed; they were contentedly motionless. A voice
called, "Hey, git on line!" But it made no impression.

Inside the restaurant there was not a chair, not a
table. The room was utterly bare, with its walls of unpainted boards. At one side a steep stairway led to an
upper floor. I suddenly noticed the atmosphere of suspicion from the line of men. Oh, hell, I thought, maybe
I'll have to wait my turn for a table — and I needed
food and strength. Perhaps the dining room lay beyond. "Hey, Doc, git in line!" came scattered commands. "Hey, Four-eyes, who the hell you think you
are, hey?"

Mighty uncivil to a sick man, I thought vaguely. I
spoke politely.

"I want the dining room."

A roar of raucous laughs was the instant response.

And, before I could ask again, a door at the far side of the plank wall opened slightly and a naked feminine arm was thrust out and upward with a beckoning movement. The leading man in the line vanished, and the line closed up one pace!

I was amazed that I could have been that dumb, even sick as I was! I know I was still pale from the painful contortions of my stomach, but I am certain that my blushes as I crept back past the line imitated roseate health to those twenty-five or thirty sophisticates waiting patiently in line.

Yet all were not so patient.

Two men secured a ladder from somewhere, and it was placed softly against the sill of an upstairs window around the corner. Those who were in a position to see it looked on with a sporting interest. Cautiously, the pair climbed up the ladder. The first man went through the window, and then the second. The next instant there was the most gosh-awful uproar. Words of objurgation could be distinguished — and it could be discerned that the feminine vocabulary was entirely at home in Army usage. Then the uproar faded and became muffled as it descended into the interior of the establishment.

A moment later, the two doughty aspirants were bounced across the porch to land in the sand. The line sent up a cheer for them. Then all became calm and the slow siege of patient, and more pacific, amorists continued.

I never did get any milk — or eggs. Or, in fact, anything. Perhaps it was as well. Both Jim Booth and I recovered handsomely. That it was ptomaine is probable. That it was really morphine is also likely, for, after all, Jim was a drug clerk and knew the ropes. And, moreover, the excruciating agony of those cramps began passing almost immediately. We were dopey and weak all the next day.

Food, any food, was grateful. It needed to be, for aboard the *Vigilancia* we were bereft of the Buzzacot, which was stowed in the hold. Each company of the regiment cooked on little individual messes of their own. Cooking on the *Vigilancia* was simple. Dave Werdenschlag dumped the required number of cans of corned beef into a wash boiler, broke some hardtack into it, and then, on deck, turned a steampipe from the engine room into it. It was not bad; the steam seemed to soften the hardtack, and perhaps it was the boiler scale from the fire room down below that gave a tang to the corned beef.

Coffee was made the same way. The estimated number of bags were dumped in, water from the water butts added, and the same steampipe turned on it until the coffee boiled. The process involved a vast bellowing and gurgling of the steampipe and the water butts, as they battled to produce coffee. When we had hash we did not have coffee; for we had but one wash boiler. Each company had its turn at the steampipe; this made for friction. Quartermaster sergeants developed bad tempers. Yet the bugles punctiliously sounded mess call.

The hash was carted down to each deck in the wash boilers — down a companionway that was steep as a ladder. It took two men to carry it and this was no small or easy job. Once, a wash boiler of coffee was dropped; once a wash boiler of hash. Each time there arose from 'tween decks the classic yell: "Hey, do it again, I didn't see you!" No one could be really mad — hell, we were off to Cuba, weren't we?

Some men bought food from the ship's stewards, the same chow the officers had, at a dollar a meal, or whatever the traffic would bear. We even bought water.

The water butts were forward, great casks in rows, lashed to the forward deck and filled with a sluggish fluid mixed with particles of charcoal for health's sake. It looked like muddy glycerine and tasted like bilgewater. And it not only looked and tasted revolting, but it stank. Four rows of this barreled abomination was our drinking-water supply until we reached Cuba. It had been barreled six weeks before, the crew told us, and in barrels that had held anything and everything from pickled fish to kerosene or worse. The crew gave us some of theirs or we bought it from the stewards of the officers' mess. In a final resort, we dosed it with the lemon drops we had laid in through the kind of advice that inspired our bellybands. That made it worse.

There is no monotony equal to that of being tied up alongside a wharf and with nothing to do. Drills would have been welcome; but there was no space on the dock for drill; it was a clutter of freight cars, wagons, details jacking endless stores, and rambling mules or picket lines of horses that were to embark. There was nothing to do, yet all about was the panorama of endless activity and bustling industry.

There were passes, of course, but for what? No one strayed far — no one knew at what moment we might pull out. And not a man would chance missing the boat for Cuba! The sandy street of tent-fly porches still did business; here and there along the wharf would come a drunken soldier — but not many and not often. The "street" kept them there until they sobered. Occasionally, some soldier barred by lack of pass from coming aboard, climbed along the hawsers that moored the transport to the dock, cheered on by cordial friends. No one minded. The officers looked on idly — if the soldier made it, okay; if not — and he dropped into the bay — okay, too.

Sometimes a mounted orderly would ride down the tracks. That meant orders — or at least we would think so. And, thinking so, we could speculate. And the rumor committee, that standing element of cannon-fodder life, helped pass the time with its speculations.

9

Landing drill. The tin-can transport fleet moves. We're off to Cuba! The night's sing-song and the day's monotony.

IN SINGLE file along the Port Tampa dock stretched the long line of transports. All of them stubby, single stackers from coastwise service. All of them jammed with men, and each with its big painted number on the bow. And nothing to do but wait.

We were waiting for Admiral Cervera and his fleet to be located. At sea, this flock of tin-can transports would have been an easy mark for the flimsiest Spanish destroyer. Of course, we would have a Navy escort, but Washington nevertheless thought it safer to wait until Cervera could be discovered. Where he was, no one knew.

The newspaper correspondents waited at the Tampa Bay Hotel, with ice water, steaks, eggs, ice cream, highballs — and Scotch whisky, which was just becoming fashionable. To us doughboys, it tasted too much like creosote. We were very common folk. Richard Harding Davis was busy conning his *Social Register* on

the cool hotel porch, until he knew the élite of the
Rough Riders from Teddy on up or down, and keeping
himself and his silk undies in perfect condition for the
rigors of the coming campaign. Trumbull White, from
Chicago, was probing into the ranks and writing specu-
lative stories about the vanished Spanish fleet; Stephen
Bonsal of the New York *Herald* was becoming the
heavy intellectual, whose dispatches knew more than it
was humanly possible to know. And George Kennan,
who was to write the only fair, decent, and un-vain-
glorious account of the war, *Campaigning in Cuba,*
distinguished himself by writing about mere men and
brass-hat bungling.

Kennan had been foreign correspondent for *Century
Magazine* throughout Russia and Siberia, where he
had studied the Russian convict system of Siberian ex-
ile. He was a great reporter.

Eventually, we moved out into Tampa Bay for landing drill. Tampa Bay has channels, and interspersed
among the channels are little sandy bars, swarming
with scuttling masses of one-claw soldier crabs that
move like the ancient Roman and Greek phalanxes:
forward, sideways, right oblique, left oblique, to the
rear, and always in a huge, solid mass of thousands,
with their one claw valiantly held aloft like a ruddy
two-pronged lance ready for instant action.

Out in the bay we lowered the lifeboats, clambered
down the companionway, and stepped in. We had our
rifles and nothing else. As a matter of fact, the landing
drill was nothing but a disguised opportunity for a

swim. Each company had its own landing drill; there
were not enough lifeboats to land the regiment. Any
man who said he could row was given one of the long
lifeboat sweeps. We rowed like centipedes out of step.
But we got close to the sandy island the captain had
picked out.

"Overboard!" shouted Captain Rafferty. "Line of
skirmishers — fire at will!"

"Whaa-oo-ee!" we yelled, and went overboard up to
our middles, soaking our pants-pocket chewing tobacco, clicking our rifles at the imaginary enemy on
the sandy key, and charging across the defending phalanxes of soldier crabs. This, *this,* was soldiering! We
captured the craven enemies without losing a man.

That night few slept easily. Three men were in the
hospital amidships with sunburn. Worse, they had hospital diet — which was no compensation for any form
of sunburn. They got a sort of biscuit of tangled shreds
of wheat moderately sluiced with diluted condensed
milk of pale blue. Our usual canned corned-beef hash
was to be preferred. One man who had to stay four
days in the hospital traded his wire biscuit and blue
milk for our rugged hash, and a friend threw the bis-
cuits overboard.

For myself, I was not badly sunburned. I had copied
some of the wise minds and had sat drying on the sand
with my shirt on. But even my mild sunburn was
enough. I slept the uneasy sleep of the partially parboiled in my bunk below decks.

These bunks had been hastily built — so hastily that

the earnest contractor in his effort to speed the war along, do his bit, and make, perhaps, a little margin of tidy profit, had put two boards twelve inches wide into the bottom of each bunk. Thus he saved one board for himself out of the three he was paid for. Each bunk was thirty-six inches wide, so the occupant had the choice of twelve inches of open space on which to sleep. The open space he could put in the middle, or divide half-and-half on each side. Also, these bunks were four tiers high in each hold. Wise men, not knowing what a seaway or a storm might bring forth, invariably chose the topmost bunk; the innocent chose the bottom berth.

For ventilation, the side cargo ports were left open. There were two cargo decks, and the freeboard of the lower one was but three feet above the water line. In the one-minute seaway we had, the waves slopped up and over and into the hold. A sentry was posted at each end of the lower cargo ports, with instructions to call the guard in case of storm or high waves. Also, we had canvas ventilator pipes leading down to the lower holds. These were long canvas tubes, about two feet in diameter, strung from the rigging on the upper deck. They were open at the top, where two huge, batlike wings stretched wide to capture any vagrant breeze that might be about. Below, directly under one of these canvas tubes, there was a lovely blast of air when the ship was under way. But it must have blown right out of the open cargo ports, for below decks and amid the bunks the air was as stuffy as ever.

Life was a peaceful routine. A routine of hot days

and lovely twilights on Tampa Bay, and soft, cool nights — if you spent them on deck. From the deck we watched the burning of that sandy street in Tampa, that street of bartender-and-girl tents, together with the greater blaze made by the raw wood "Restaurant." How it started, no one knew. Perhaps, like the great fire in Alexandria during World War I, it had been started by angry soldiers. Perhaps by an over-turned lamp in some brawl. The little tents flared quickly and were gone like the puffed-out candles on a birthday cake. But the "Restaurant" blazed and burned in the night breeze like an irritated torch. That it was rebuilt and re-operated I have no doubt, for there were some thirty thousand soldiers left in and about Tampa; thirty thousand soldiers who would have another payday, and another embarkation from the long wharf on which this sandy city of the Last Chance would re-establish its soiled dovecots and warm whisky.

Then there came a startling rumor. Admiral Cervera's fleet had been located!

Our fleet would attend to them and we would be under way at last. The Spanish fleet had been located within the Bay of Santiago, in that huge expanse of landlocked water that opens out so suddenly from the narrow passage leading from the Caribbean. No view of the fleet could be had from the sea end; it was sheltered by the crooked passage and also by the high hills that rimmed the southern shores of Cuba. Cuban spies saw the fleet, and it was from them the news came.

On the fifty-five idle transports swinging in Tampa Bay were more than fifteen thousand men, four batteries of field artillery, and four Gatling guns.

As we left our anchorage, we could see the bustle on shore. The few mules and horses were rounded up and loaded at the last minute; they had been held on shore until then so they could be kept in condition. From the *Vigilancia,* with her number "23" high on the bow, we watched the others slowly swing away from the dock, with the little harbor tugs puffing alongside or shuttling out to assist. Our own first mate was up in the eyes of the ship scanning our mooring chain. A wave from the captain's hand on the bridge and the steam winch began clanking in the chain. Two of the crew leaned over the side, washing the chain with a hose as it reeled in.

The first mate turned to the bridge and waved: "Hove short, sir."

Down the bay and disappearing in the distance ahead was a long line of transports and cruisers. Far ahead, we knew that a battleship was heading the line.

The *Vigilancia* began to throb, slow and slight. From the pilothouse the captain waved to the bow. The first mate shouted and the winch again began to clank.

"Up and down, sir!" called the first mate.

The captain waved again. The winch began its grind; the anchor was coming up. From down below there was the muffled clang of a gong. The ship's throb increased to a quiver, then down to a heavy, steady vibration. The Tampa Bay dock was changing its position. The crew was catting the anchor.

We swung around and found ourselves part of the long column of ships. We were off. The invasion of Cuba had begun. Behind us was everything familiar and routine. No one could know what tomorrow would bring forth. The aspiration to survive was there, of course, but it was not a condition. The dice would be thrown, but we could not throw them. We were a fragment of destiny.

At sea we knew there was a screen of Navy ships fanning out ahead and to the rear. Sometimes we caught sight of them — a cruiser, perhaps, but hull down. All day long, swift little torpedo boats dashed up and down the column in a lather of foam, giving orders and latitudes and longitudes for various possible emergencies. Amidships of our column were two scows being towed; one broke loose one night and was never recovered. The other, a continuous cataract of spray over her blunt bow, reached Cuba and became a landing dock.

At night, the torpedo boats came up with final orders as to our course. Sometimes they came across the water by wigwag, for we had a Navy signalman on the bridge; sometimes there was shouting through a megaphone. Some of it was in code, but in general it was plain English with final orders if we should be dispersed during the night by storm or enemy — where to gather, what to do. Also, what the magnetic north was at that particular moment.

It was the afternoon of June 4, 1898, when we swung into a column of ships and passed out of Tampa Bay. We kept on heading eastward, rounding Key West and steadily pointing into the dawn of each day. Santiago was our goal — and that was all we knew. We were to be two weeks, less one day, aboard the transport before we landed in Cuba on that little sandy beach at Siboney, which lies just to the east of the narrow entrance to the expanse that is the Bay of Santiago.

Perhaps two weeks on one of those old single-stack transports might be boring to some. I did not find it so. We soon settled into a routine. There was some poker, but the wind made dealing difficult. Down in the holds, where there was no wind, it was too dark to see. Men who smoked pipes began carving them with skull and crossbones, or the Cuban flag. Rifle inspection in the morning, as the companies lined up on deck, became somewhat more rigid. We had a bit of oiled rag stuck in the muzzle of our rifles, and another wrapped around the breech. The ship's carpenter began making Jacob's ladders by which, perhaps, we would clamber down the sides to abandon ship and swim ashore. But there was no boredom. The mornings were beautiful. The marvelous sapphire blue of the warm tropic seas, the flying fish that never lost their novelty, the occasional porpoise or dolphin, or perhaps some lazy turtle slowly paddling as we passed him, had a never-ending allurement. The cool and fantastic clouds slowly coiling up from the hot lands just over the horizon took odd shapes as they eddied among the cooling geysers of air rising from the ocean.

Twice we saw waterspouts, but they were far off to port and did not perform very well, for they faded into clouds of mist and, presently, were gone. We speculated on the clouds and what they resembled — Uncle Sam was very plain in one, full profile, chin whiskers and all. One enthusiast saw what he claimed was the Virgin and spread the rumor of victory as a certainty. Another saw a cross. You could see anything in those marvelous masses of slowly coiling cumuli and brilliant masses of vapor. Once I saw a long shifting cloud bank boiling up in the afternoon sun that reminded me of Edouard Detailles' *The Bivouac* in the Luxembourg of Paris — flags, marshals, and the massed press of cavalry and infantry, as in one of Napoleon's vast charges, all rising above the sleeping forms of French soldiers in their dreams of glory.

Every moment, from dawn to the short twilight that faded rapidly from the superb glow of a molten sunset, was a thrill of color. In the darkness, until taps, we gathered on the upper deck and sang. Some companies had song leaders, like Roby of C Company. Mostly, we followed him; all sang what they liked. Sometimes a song would start — a favorite like "The Banks of the Wabash" or "Sweet Marie" or "I Don't Like No Cheap Man" — and from stem to stern, everybody on the ship would join in. Not to know the popular songs of the day, whether one could sing or not, was the mark of an illiterate.

In any moment of silence, we could hear the transport ahead of us singing the same songs we sang, for at night the ships closed in. Not five hundred yards ahead of us was the next transport, and there was another the same distance to the rear.

We ran without lights, and smoking was forbidden unless you first got your light behind a bulkhead or in the hold. At the stern was a soapbox, its single open side facing astern. In this was a lantern, and by its glowing wick the transport behind us kept direction and the proper position in the fleet.

Below, each open cargo port had a sentry. Down two decks, past the rows of foul water barrels, over endless sacks of potatoes beginning to rot, off in the dimness where the four-tiered bunks held loafing men in the daytime or snoring figures in the blackness of night, was my tour of guard duty. Resting comfortably on a sack of potatoes, with the open cargo port before me framing the mystic blue of a star-spangled night, I found the sentry-go a pleasure. It was, in the first place, something to do besides loaf. During the day, the brilliant blue with the endless review of marching, coiling clouds, and the shimmering flicker of flying fish, furnished unrivaled entertainment. At night, the soft swish of the waves alongside, the occasional phosphorescent flash of one rising to slap itself inboard through the port, the pattern of the stars and the inky blackness of the hold, with the knowledge that you were one part of a thousand men on their way to kill or be killed, combined into a feeling that was poetry — a poetry without words, yet pulsing with rhythm. Even the sickly odor of spoiling potatoes lent a sordid accent of drama to adventure.

The orders for a sentry were, first, the standing orders, such as No. 1 : "Walk to the post in a military manner, observing everything that takes place within sight or hearing." It could hardly have been done in a military manner; one cannot parade-step over bulbous sacks of potatoes in inky blackness. Even the corporal had to post his men in complete blackness since, being in the presence of the enemy, he was forbidden a lantern.

In addition to the standing orders, my special orders were to report the presence of any strange vessel, or vessels, on the horizon or closer; to challenge them if they came too close, and to call the corporal of the guard and to open fire if my challenge was not heeded. This probably applied, I reasoned, to swimmers as well, since it might well be presumed that any swimmer now rambling about the Caribbean would surely be Spanish. The matter of opening fire bothered me. I had been given no ammunition! But I had a bayonet — a rod bayonet — always in place on guard duty, and I resolved to sell my life, and the life of the *Vigilancia,* No. 23, as dearly as possible. But the night passed peacefully and the ship and its regimental contents were still safe at dawn.

The routine of another day began.

10

FOR me there was not an uncomfortable moment. I loved the sea. Then too, I was well provided — through a pleasant arrangement with the chief engineer and his staff — so far as meals were concerned; and this included drinking water, ice cold and at any time. I was lucky.

I was an artist, or in the throes of becoming one, and the chief engineer had seen me sketching. Could I do a portrait of him? Of course! Then I did another of him. Then I did one of his assistant. Then I was invited to dinner — down in the engine room, where it would not be conspicuous and where I sat with my back against a bulkhead while the pistons plunged steadily above and the ponderous crankshafts rolled just beyond my nose. It was first-cabin fare — roast beef, French fries, and fixin's, with apple pie and coffee to follow — coffee with cream, and in a china cup! The

chief and the chief's assistant were entitled to seconds
or whatever they wanted. When I did not dine as the
chief's guest I dined as the guest of the chief's assistant
— for I made portraits of him too.

However, I did subject myself to the regular Army
breakfast of hardtack, hash, and tin-cup coffee. But
this was due to the fact that the hours of the watch-on
and watch-off of the engine room did not correspond
with the regimental breakfast hour. Later, in the engineers' cabin with the louvres hauled up for privacy,
I had a snack of oatmeal and milk, and ham-and-eggs
with wheat cakes fresh from the griddle.

I gave fair value to the engineers. There was a
sketch, "Chief in the Engine Room," with the chief's
hand upon the wheel of the throttle; there was a "Chief
in His Cabin" with its slatted window and his carafe of
ice water at his elbow; there was a "Chief Looking
Out to Sea" just forward of his cabin door and with
the davits and their lifeboats just as natural as life.

Nor were the slow afternoons without their interest.
I loafed on the floor of the chief's cabin, where it was
nice and cool, and presently would appear the afternoon snack of tea and crumpets, jam or marmalade,
and ice water that was the sea custom for ship's officers.
I lived the highly nutritious life of the socially elect.

It was occasionally noticed that I missed our mess
call.

"Hey you," Sergeant Dave Werdenschlag would
say. "Where the hell were you last mess?"

"Not very hungry, Sergeant," I would say. "Don't keep it waiting for me."

"Waiting, hell!" Dave would respond scornfully. "Maybe you got a little seasickness. Don't worry, Jack, we won't wait."

Corned beef and hardtack hash, breakfast, dinner, and supper! And me with ice water and roast beef and French fries and pie and coffee!

I got plenty of it, but water was at a premium for the other soldiers. Sailors gave it to them whenever they could, or swapped some for a cigarette or a chew of plug. The crew had plenty of water, and were generous in sharing it.

Then came an order from headquarters. No more buying of water. Whether this order came from the colonel, or the ship's captain, or from a Navy spriglet, we never knew. Possibly it was intended to toughen us for the rigors of war. This theory of war is generally born amid flowery beds of ease. Kipling — who knew his army from all angles — wrote something very much apropos:

> The toad beneath the harrow knows
> Exactly where each tooth-point goes;
> The butterfly upon the road
> Preaches contentment to that toad.

But did the order stop the buying or trading of water? No. We could still get water, but now it was on the sly. The stewards that served the regimental officers'

meals now sold water for five cents a glass, sometimes
a dime; they passed it out through the dining-saloon
ports into a passageway that ran thwartships, where
the transaction could be concealed. Before this they
had, not infrequently, passed out the leavings from
some officer's plate, and taken a tip. It had developed
into quite a little trade, in fact, but it was always a tip,
never a charge. This order of "no buying" of food or
water made the stewards indignant too. And but few of
the regiment's officers approved the order. I do not
know of an officer but who turned his back if in the dining saloon, or if outside hurried by the thwartship companionway so as to save embarrassment and see nothing illegal. Except the chaplain!

One day the chaplain happened to be passing while
two soldiers were buying a leftover plate from an officer's lightly touched meal; the other was buying ice
water from another steward. The chaplain called the
sentry and had the men placed under arrest. The chaplain filed the facts, and justice started on its way. Justice
gave the men a nominal sentence, for sympathy was
with them. Later a couple of men were lying on the
crowded deck, in the space allotted to officers — although no officers were on that side of the deck, nor
had been. The chaplain called the officer of the guard
and directed that the men be ordered to move. He, the
chaplain, had ordered them to move, and they had not.
Under his breath the officer of the guard made a few
statements to the chaplain to the effect that he, the officer of the guard, was in charge of order on the deck

and the chaplain was not. Then he ordered the men to get up and go lie in the sun, or they would be put under arrest. The men moved from that vacant portion of the deck into the sun.

By sunset the story was all over the ship. There were no two opinions in regard to it. Maybe it was the confinement on shipboard during the voyage, or maybe it was one of those sudden situations when everything is tinder, but in those two days the chaplain laid the foundations for a bitter resentment that gave itself to open and jeering expression even after the regiment's return to the States. Unfortunately, the chaplain added other blunders in his career in Cuba and in his devotion to the "pride, pomp, and circumstance of glorious war."

Ever since leaving Tampa we had been out of sight of land. The fleet of transports kept as far from the shores of Cuba as possible. They held to a leisurely speed — about eight knots — and, once in a while, far off, we could see one of our Navy cruisers hitting it up to us with a bone in her teeth until she could get close enough to the head of the transport column to blink signals or wigwag messages, for this was long before wireless. All we knew was that there would be some landing place at or near Santiago, the only city of consequence in that eastern section of Cuba.

One lovely morning a thin, distant, and darker haze appeared off to the south. The shadows on the deck began to shift and we knew we were changing course to round Cape Maisi. We were in sight of Cuba at last!

Steadily now we held to the south, until Cape Maisi

dropped below the horizon. Again the shadows of the deck began shifting, and we headed west. A long blue ridge came over the horizon. We moved in closer and the mountains, now delicate blue and green, rose in gently flowing tiers that lost themselves in the amethyst blue and lavender of the mountains beyond.

It was a rugged coast, and in those mountains Cuban soldiers and Spanish troops were fighting. We could see some little settlements on the beaches — from one of these, perhaps, centuries ago, buccaneers had put forth in their crude cockleshells to board a Spanish galley and plunder it for silk and rum and doubloons.

Presently we approached the shore, coming close to a little dock which we later found was Daiquiri, where the Rough Riders were to land. Then, farther on and nearer to Santiago, we came to a little bend in the coastline, sheltered under a hill. This was the cove of Siboney where we were to go ashore. Above the little village and on all the hills and ridges that surrounded it were the little Spanish *fuertes* — blockhouses — that were always built in sight of each other for protection against the Cuban troops in the field. A little farther to the west, we passed the narrow entrance to the Bay of Santiago where Admiral Cervera's fleet lay at anchor. The entrance was almost indistinguishable from the green jungle that rose above it on each side. We could see the pinkish ocher of the ancient forts that guarded it. They looked like the toy forts made for children, or like picturesque defenses of the old-time barons, but Washington knew that they had modern guns as well as the olden bronze cannon. We were three miles off shore, wholly safe, and we gave the Spaniards a review in force — some fifty ships and transports in single column, while our battleships and cruisers fringed the line. Not a shot was fired; it was a demonstration.

We turned slowly back to Guantanamo, and drifted lazily along the coast with the tide, with only here and there a transport turning her engines occasionally to keep her place in the column.

Then we steamed back to the entrance to the Bay of Santiago. This time, the cruisers and battleships began the attack on the forts that guarded the bay. Our transports lay about three miles off, and we had good seats for a perfect panorama. The air was as clear as crystal.

Slowly the battleships and cruisers steamed past the entrance, perhaps two miles off; sometimes it seemed closer. Their turrets would burst into a vast billow of smoke as they scanned the hills with their fire; and occasionally they would turn one into the ancient forts that would burst forth in a blast of shattered brick and dust. We could see shells burst in the jungle. The cruisers steamed slowly from Daiquiri, past Siboney and on past the Santiago forts and into the west, bombarding as they went, and then came back again. The little Spanish blockhouse above Siboney seemed to be hit — yet later, when we landed, it was intact and without a trace of damage. For fifty miles the coast was bombarded, a maneuver to mislead the Spaniards as to where we would land.

The battleships were more stationary. They hovered

off the entrance and played their heavy guns on the Morro forts. They took turns as they circled the entrance. It was target practice, for there was very little return fire from the Spaniards. The cruisers were under steam and always moving. But, closer in, and to the east of the entrance, was one sluggish little low-lying craft not altogether unlike a monitor. She had three big pipes that protruded slantwise and parallel from her forward deck and a small bridge and superstructure aft of them.

This was the dynamite cruiser *Vesuvius*, invented and developed by Lieutenant Zalinaki of our Navy. His first gun — which looked somewhat like a pile driver laid on its side — was mounted on Governor's Island in New York Harbor, and its air-compressing machinery was concealed in the little round fort that later became a military prison. Dynamite is too sensitive to be fired from an ordinary cannon; the jar of its sudden impulse would explode it before it had left the muzzle.

The *Vesuvius* had three dynamite guns, each a part of the cruiser's structure, and to aim the guns one aimed the ship. Each of the three pipes protruding from the deck was the barrel of a dynamite gun. Almost the entire hull was filled with machinery for compressing air and releasing it behind the dynamite projectile of the guns.

We could see the *Vesuvius* as she moved in, head-on to the coastline. One might, by watching carefully, see the faint haze at the muzzles of the pipes as she fired and the compressed air was released. Then, after a pause there would come a blast from the jungled hills beyond. It was like a blast from a quarry and a whole section of the hill would be torn off; the dynamite shells were very effective. The whole problem lay in landing on the target — to aim a ship is a problem in itself.

It is doubtful if this bombardment had any effect, other than perhaps to delude the Spaniards. They had the whole coast and Cuban mountain range to retire behind — and they did.

Then we prepared to land.

We steamed back to the bight of land where a little beach stretched down from the village of Siboney. Then we drifted with the tide, waiting our turn to land. We watched the little steam launches of the Navy towing strings of ship's boats packed with soldiers and their horse-collar blanket rolls. We envied them. Great Scott, there wouldn't be any Spaniards left by the time we could get ashore! Impatiently we lined the rails and looked at these boatloads of lucky men. We could see the troops form up on shore and then lose themselves in the green that fringed the foothills of the mountains beyond.

The horses and mules were jumped overboard and swam ashore. And not a colonel or a wagon master had the power to tell a ship captain how close in to shore he should come. The transports were under charter merely, and it was the ship captain who could tell the colonel what he, the skipper, would or would not do with his ship. The horses and mules were jumped overboard from a half to a quarter mile off shore —

depending upon the skipper's digestion or his judg-
ment — and then swam. Horses by the hundred were
drowned.

A horse would be led to a cargo port and shown the
view of Siboney. As he looked, a blacksnake whip
stung him from the darkness behind and he went overboard in a wild plunge. Then he struck out for the
beach, where buglers were blowing the calls to which
the horses had been trained: "Stables," "Boots and
Saddles," "Fours Right, "Charge," and the rest, to
give the animals their direction to shore.

The deep blue of the Caribbean became dotted with
the bodies of drowned horses and mules. Once we saw a
frightened horse turn back and try to make the transport from which it had jumped. The transport had begun turning its screw to get steerage way. The horse
was caught in the slipstream; it plunged and splashed
in the wake, and was swept into the stream of the following transport and brushed alongside until it vanished in a bloody cascade astern.

Teamsters, mule packers, and artillery drivers
rowed out in boats and talked to the horses, patted
them, or tried to keep their muzzles out of the water.
The sea was calm, with only a slow rolling swell, but it
was enough to obscure the coast from the swimming
horses. Animals become dazed and hysterical. Suddenly a horse would begin to splash with its forefeet,
and a boat would race to it. A tow rope would be fastened to the halter and the horse would lose its panic

and swim steadily after the boat. Sometimes five or six animals would be swimming behind one of the boats, with the teamster or cavalryman talking encouragement to them. Some did not make it, and were drowned before they got to shore. Sometimes an animal would begin swimming in circles. In one case, a horse was found two miles out at sea, heading for Venezuela!

I have been told by some authorities that if a horse gets water in its ears the animal feels all is lost and will drown. This may have accounted for the heavy loss of horses and mules in the landing.

It was this loss of horses that left each field battery with no spares. Later, when Captain Best's battery was on San Juan and had to be withdrawn, they did not dare risk the horses up in the open on the hill. Two infantry companies were sent over to screen the withdrawal of the guns by the cannoneers. Over twenty infantrymen were casualties in three minutes, though only one artilleryman, a sergeant, was killed. Also, two generals went into the battle of San Juan on foot — an unheard-of thing for those days — and one of them reached the battle line from his headquarters riding on a cargo mule. Horses were reserved for orderlies and messengers and for the immediate staff of General Shafter. Colonel Teddy Roosevelt had a horse but left it behind when the fighting began at Kettle Hill, and fought the rest of the day on foot; but Teddy had a certain way with him. All cavalry had been dismounted and left their horses in Florida. The horses that swam ashore and those that were drowned were almost entirely artillery horses, wagon teams, and pack mules. General Shafter had his own horse, a special animal that could carry his great weight; but he used it only when necessity compelled and more frequently rode about in a buckboard that bent beneath the weight of its single passenger, for he drove it himself. Nor was there room for another beside him on the seat. The picture of General Shafter in his buckboard inspecting his lines after the victory of San Juan Hill is an outstanding memory.

We were on the alert all night, each company in its own group, ready for the word to go over the side and into a lifeboat. Time passed slowly. It grew lighter. Line after line of ship's boats passed the *Vigilancia,* towed by the Navy launches. Then one launch, with a string of empty boats in tow, hailed our bridge. It was for us.

The bugle blew and the regimental adjutant took his place at the head of the gangway that had been lowered over the side. Some company jostled past us — the first to go into the boats. We cheered them and jeered them, the lucky stiffs, first of our regiment to go ashore. The boat was filled, tight, with barely enough room for the four sailors and their oars. Our turn came at last.

"Company F — attention!"

It was Captain Rafferty at the gangway. We were counted and checked off as we shuffled past. At intervals down that gangway was a sailor who told us to take it easy and was ready to grab a man if he stumbled. A horse-collar blanket roll, a bulging haversack, a canteen, a beltful of ammunition, and a rifle are awkward to manage on the narrow and steep steps of a gangway. Down on the grating of the ship's last step, two more sailors grabbed each man and steadied him into the heaving side of the lifeboat. There was no sea; it was as gentle and slow a rolling swell as has ever been; but the little boat seemed to dance compared with the steady deck of the transport. Two men had drowned at Daiquiri, where the Rough Riders had landed. They had fallen into the water when stepping from the lifeboat to the dock and, with their gear and ammunition, had stayed down.

I got in the boat. Men squatted on the floorboards, packed tight. There was room for a few on the seat that ran around the sides. Sailors at bow and stern held the boat to the ship's side. In the stern a coxswain bossed the loading of the soldiers. It was the first amphibious landing in which troops from New York State had taken part, and one of the few in our nation's history up to that time. If one counts Washington's crossing the Delaware and the landing at Veracruz during the Mexican War in the 1840's, this would be the third.

The four sailors pulled us away from the transport and hooked us into line with the boats already loaded, and in the next moment we were headed for the beach and Siboney. As we neared the shore the steam launch cast off her line, and the sailors pulled in until the deep-laden lifeboat grounded a hundred feet off the beach. The surf was light — it was hardly a surf, merely a heavy ripple from the slow Caribbean swell. A few ragged Cuban rebels and some ragged children — ragged to the point of mere fluttering nudity — formed an amiable welcoming committee.

On shore, we formed a column and marched down the railroad tracks to the machine shop that was to be our camp. In this short march we learned one thing: that our narrow, woven haversack strap cut in and hurt. It had been different when we marched down that sandy street in Ybor City; then we did not have five days' rations and spare ammunition in them. Our first search in that machine shop was for leather belting for our shoulders to ease the cut of the haversack. But some unscrupulous soldiers in the earlier boats had already looted and cut up every leather machine belt in the shop.

Before disembarking we — at least I — had breakfast. Double ham-and-eggs with compliments of the chief engineer; also, compliments of the assistant engineer, wheat cakes and sirup, and coffee with condensed milk and sugar. I was to need it, for shortly I was at work heaving boxes of ammunition out of lifeboats and wading ashore, and then jacking the same down to pile them in the machine shop. Those who had labored most faithfully with the ammunition had the reward of being allowed to choose any box they wished for the trip to the machine shop. The boxes all weighed the same: they were fifty pounds when you started and

gained in weight to about two hundred pounds before
you reached the shop.

This detail was still in progress when the bugles
blew. All down the little rambling lanes of Siboney,
regimental bugles were blowing and first sergeants
were shouting: "Fall in — fall in, rifles and belts and
canteens!" This meant business.

It seemed that the Rough Riders and the cavalry
brigade that had landed at Daiquiri and then come on
down to Siboney had decided that the war was proceeding too slowly. So they started off on the road to
Siboney — a march of eleven miles — and then struck
inland, where the Spanish troops suddenly met them at
Las Guasimas.

We saw them as they passed through Siboney and
started into the narrow jungle-bordered lane that was
regarded as a road. I was jacking ammunition and
stopped near a Regular Army major who was also
watching their column. He turned to me. He was exploding and he *had* to say something to someone.

"Goddam it — they haven't even got a point out!"

A point is a solitary soldier, or very small group,
that goes some distance in advance of the main body of
troops in order to draw the fire from first contact with
an enemy. It is an elementary and ordinary provision
when advancing into unknown enemy territory.

The dismounted cavalry, headed by the Rough Riders, was in column of fours, solid, and only lacked a
band at its head to give it a thoroughly festive and in-
consequential air. It walked into an ambuscade at Las

Guasimas.* And the cavalry brigade sent back word that it needed help!

It was for this hasty assembly of all the available troops in Siboney that the bugles were blowing. Amid the shouting and the bugles, men were falling into ranks and all Siboney was a tumult.

---

* In a frank letter to his family from Richard Harding Davis, war correspondent for the New York *Times* and London *Times:* "July, Santiago, 1898: Dear Family, This is just to reassure you that I am all right. I and Marshall were the only correspondents with Roosevelt. We were caught in a clear case of ambush. Every precaution had been taken [*sic*] but the natives knew the ground and our men did not. It was the hottest, nastiest fight I ever imagined. We never saw the enemy except glimpses. Our men fell all over the place, shouting to the others not to mind them but to go on. . . ."

11

The Rough Riders ambushed at Las Guasimas. We rush to their aid. The sounds of combat! The wounded trickle back. Every man a cook.

THE Spanish troops were, according to information in General Shafter's possession, but two and a half miles beyond Siboney, to which point they had retired after abandoning that coast village — after an effort to set fire to it. It was the proper business of the cavalry, which was entirely on foot, to find out where the Spaniards were. They immediately set out to do so.

As I have mentioned, in an advance into enemy territory where the enemy is not yet definitely located, an army sends out a "point." This point keeps anywhere from a hundred to three hundred yards in advance of a following group, the support. Then, some seven hundred yards behind this follows a still larger group, the reserve. About seven hundred yards behind the reserve is the main body of the advancing column. Between these groups are single soldiers whose function it is to call back from the point any information about the enemy that the point may discover. Also, on each side of the column, if possible, flankers are posted to warn against flank surprise. These are elementary precautions. Hence the amazement of the Regular Army major and his explosion as he saw the Rough Riders start down the jungle-bordered trail with the main body leading the advance from our village.*

The two leading correspondents with the Rough Riders, both devoted admirers of Colonel Roosevelt, have left their record in history that the colonel walked into an ambuscade; although Marshall phrases it quaintly: "So it is well to say here that the battle which followed was not technically an ambush, although it is true that the American troops met the Spaniards before they had expected to."

Richard Harding Davis, a brilliant and superficial writer to whom glamour was always gold, and an intense worshiper of Colonel Roosevelt, published the story that Roosevelt was ambushed — and Mr. Davis was with him when it happened. Thus it was that emergency messengers rushed back to Siboney with the word

---

* In his book *The Rough Riders,* Colonel Roosevelt called this fight "General Long's Fight at Las Guasimas," although he describes the Rough Riders as being in the advance. He differs with Richard Harding Davis and Edward Marshall (the latter badly wounded in that fight), both of whom were, by Roosevelt's own statements, up front when the action suddenly began. The writer, after careful search, has been unable to find any map or battle sketch of the battle of Las Guasimas, although such map-sketches are definitely required in Army reports of actions. The bravery of the men is clear, but the tactics are shrouded in vainglory and mystery. There is no official report of Las Guasimas from Colonel Roosevelt.

that the Rough Riders were caught and needed help,
urgently. The Seventy-first Infantry was summoned by
the urgent bugles and rushed up the hill, past the little
abandoned blockhouses, following the same path taken
by Colonel Roosevelt's cavalry, such a brief period before.

No formation was ever made more quickly. There
was no roll call. "Fall in — fall in! Count off! . . .
Fours right!" And we were off. All through the straggling lanes of Siboney, bugles were blowing. Popeyed
and silent, the population watched us go. For all they
or we knew, the Spaniards might have been just on the
outskirts of the village.

Other regiments were falling in. Columns of troops
were marching over the ties of the railroad tracks or
over the worse footing of the ground alongside. "Take
it easy — take it easy — you'll get there!" I heard a
Regular Army officer say to the hurrying troops. A
sergeant grunted cadence, just as sergeants have always done since Caesar's time and before. "No use getting to a fighting line when you are all in — steady
there, o-o-onph, ho-omph — hasty men are useless
men. Keep something for the last mile. It's all down in
the book." The bugles stopped; no more need for them.
There was the steady slog of marching men.

News and rumors began to trickle down the column.
Soldiers left behind called it to the men as we passed.
"Wheeler's sent for help — they got Teddy in am-
bush!" The official record later showed that General

Wheeler *had* sent a rush message at half past eight that morning, saying that he was engaged with a large force of the enemy and needed help.

Beyond Siboney, on the path taken by the Rough Riders, the ground rose steeply in a narrow ridge that sloped away on either side. We passed a little block-house that the Spaniards had left. Below us and fading into the Caribbean we had a brilliant view of the transport fleet, with the battle fleet beyond, and an occasional torpedo boat streaking its way with some message. It was still morning, with the tingling opalescence of a fresh day. But our bodies sweated under their blue flannel Army shirts, from the rapid march and the pressure of climbing. The trail grew steeper.

Soon the first wounded began coming in. Two Rough Riders, astride an Army mule, had been shot in the legs, and their trousers glistened with fresh blood. Another Rough Rider, shot in the shoulder, led the mule. Farther on, a few casualties rested by the side of the trail. Several with arm wounds had used the big slings from their first-aid packets. They were bloody and silent. Some talked. Some swore obscenely at the Spaniards who had got them. "G'wan up — get there — they need you," one man said as we passed him.

"How'd you get yours?" I asked of another, who was astride a mule. He had been shot in the thigh, and his khaki trouser leg was soaked with blood. He was angry.

"Damn near stepped on the sonofabitch — then he

got me. But I got him. I got mine. Now you go an' git yours."

Another, farther on, grinned at his luck. He pulled open his shirt. "Got me in the belly," he said, almost with pride, and there were two bloody little holes about six inches apart just below his navel; between them was a purple welt where the bullet had passed just underneath the skin. "Kinda stings is all," he said.

Another passed. "You can't see 'em," he said.

Here and there other casualties were resting. Of the first-aid packets, it seemed as if only the big arm-sling was used; the other things were too complicated.

The hill and ridge had not looked too steep when we saw the Rough Riders go up it that morning. But, after we passed the first blockhouse, it rose like a railroad bank. The sun was hot; the trees and jungle began to close in on either side and, if there was a breeze, the jungle growth climbing above the ridge on either side screened us from it. Just a rifle and belt of cartridges and a canteen had seemed such a little load at the start; and now it weighted like the burden of Atlas. Yet, from far ahead, repeated and echoing down this tunneled jungle hill were the steady calls to close up — dammit, close up! We had left the village in column of fours, we had broken into column of twos, and now we were in column of files — just one man ahead of another. From behind us came orders to move on — get a move on, close up — *get on!* There was no doubt as to the emergency. We climbed and panted, and then climbed some more, and faster. There was no pause and no rest. Once at the top — for I knew my regulations — there would be a pause and a rest, brief perhaps, but a rest.

We reached the top. Here was another abandoned Spanish blockhouse. Around it was a little patch of cleared ground with some sweet potatoes, tomatoes, and peppers and some tropical vegetables planted by the Spanish soldiers. And there were two or three rows of flowers — from their blossoms, they looked like four-o'clocks — but both vegetables and flowers were low so as not to obscure the line of fire from the banked and loopholed blockhouse or the little rifle trench that surrounded it. Ahead there were ragged gaps in our column — we were forming fours again, for the trail had widened — and one had to run to catch up. "Form fours — double time!" We could hear the command coming down the line and a medley of sergeants echoing it. We formed fours, double time, and sweated.

Now would come a few moments' rest, to catch our breath. The book said so. But from far ahead came the regimental bugle: "Double time!" We swung into double time. Alongside the trail there was a surgeon and a couple of hospital corpsmen. A man had gone down under the pressure, but only one! Double time! Then a change to quick time, the normal march. Our bodies quivered with the heat and steamed with hot sweat that would not evaporate. Yet, curiously, there was a thrill in the very exhaustion and the greater effort that was demanded.

By the trail taken by the Rough Riders from Siboney to Las Guasimas it was approximately two miles. We made it, half double time and half quick time.

Then, from the distance, there came a dull, soft boom. It was a gun, a heavy gun, not a rifle. Then a distant crackle of rifle fire. A low whine sounded above us — our first bullet. We were marching now in quick time. Again there came a long-drawn, seething whine above our heads — another bullet. And again a distant popping that came in little spats and died down raggedly and then burst forth in a sudden gust. It was dead ahead of us. We were under fire!

There was no danger as yet, but the thought of actually being under fire was a thrill in itself — the thrill we had come for. Perhaps it was the safety that furnished the glow for the thrill. But we were under fire! And when we returned to Siboney we would be veterans! Those were my thoughts, and I looked about me and wondered if the others were having the same. The popping fire was a little louder now, and there were more long-drawn notes from overhead.

From the head of the column came the regimental bugle: "Column right!" The head of the regiment moved into a large abandoned field where scattered second-growth already had some sizable saplings. Our second battalion turned, column right, into the same field. We knew the formation from our drills. It was "Form for attack, first battalion fighting line, second battalion support." We were forming for action. Yet we could see nothing; the jungle was all about us. From somewhere beyond, the popping continued. From farther off came fainter reports, and these, we knew, must be Spanish. We hoped, and we feared; and we hoped we would not fear.

Finally the order came: "Rest." We sat down; we lay down; we opened our shirts to any vagrant air. And steadily the exhaustion evaporated. The popping grew fainter; then there were no shots at all. Only an occasional rifle, and that at a distance. We realized that the fight was over.

Presently the bugles blew "attention" and we formed up for the return march. Out on the trail once more, we now and then passed a wounded Rough Rider. We hailed them, and they answered. "Yeah, we knocked hell out of them," was the response. The march back was all gaiety. A slight breeze sifted down into the trail and the tops of the jungle swayed with it. There was no hurry; we took our time. The breeze fanned our contentment. The trail we had climbed so laboriously now slipped easily down. Here we passed some of the wounded we had seen on our way up. They had not been able to make it down, and lay on the ground waiting for a stretcher. In the little lanes of Siboney more wounded strolled about in their arm bandages and asked us if it were all over. Cuban insurgents looked at us, and we felt that now we were their equals — we too had been under fire! We could feel ourselves swelling with satisfaction. We were in a foreign country; we had met the enemy, and he had retreated. We were veterans!

Back in our machine shop we rustled our own midday dinner — canned corned beef, or sowbelly, as we might choose; and hardtack and coffee. No Buzzacots had come ashore, so we made our own little fireplaces with a few rocks and with a fishplate or so to make a grid. The shallow mess tins and tin cups were our only tools. We might have bought chickens from the villagers, except that the Spaniards had commandeered all the chickens before they left Siboney, and the few that had been left had already been absorbed by the unscrupulous soldiers who preceded us, or by the ones who had not been rushed up that hot trail to Las Guasimas. So we cooked what we had.

I traded my ability as a maker and maintainer of fires for other duties that were apt to be onerous and laborious. Later, by adding a little cooking to this, I even lessened the fatigues of soldiering. For example, I only had to take out the sixteen canteens of water detail for my section when I chose; sixteen canteens can become heavy, and it was simpler to loll about a little fire and boil or fry something while someone else, less gifted in cookery, performed the section's arduous tasks.

12

The Cuban rebel troops arrive — ragged but heroic men. Cuban prostitutes and Spanish cartridges for rebel rifles.

ON THE afternoon of that first day in Cuba we loafed. That run up to the fight at Las Guasimas had been a day's work.

Cuban troops kept arriving from scattered points throughout the Santiago Province. We all traded with the ragged insurgents. Their rebel battalions looked with awe on our vast resources of food. We found a ready market for trade in our sowbelly or canned corned beef or hardtack. They had mangoes, the sweet, rather turpentinish flavor of which fascinated us. And they had platanos, a fruit that looks like huge, green bananas with coarse skin. The platano is an acquired taste — and we never acquired it.

For haversacks, the ragged insurgents had jute sugar sacks or, in better cases, Pillsbury's flour sacks. There were always platanos in them and a few sticks of sugar cane. As mess cups the Cubans used half a coconut shell; and often their canteen was an old cognac bottle. We traded for the sugar cane; and learned to shave off slivers of it and chew them instead of, as at first, trying to gnaw on the whole stalk.

The war correspondents sneered at these Cubans and ridiculed their rags, their rifles, and their fighting! The correspondents knew nothing of it. Some years later I met and became acquainted with General Frederick Funston, who was with them, shoulder-to-shoulder, as chief of their artillery before the United States entered the Cuban revolution after the sinking of the *Maine*. Their revolution had to be fought with guerrilla tactics; there was no quarter on either side. Jungle hospitals were massacred; and only in the cities and fortified towns were the Spaniards safe. No troops ever received warmer praise than that which came from General Funston for these tattered troops with their varied rifles and scanty ammunition. Barefoot, or only in rawhide sandals, they could outmarch any of the professional armies. I have seen them, and side by side with our column when they had to make time. They swung along in single file over the narrow trail, in an easy stride that had the suggestion of a lope in it. When they came to a shallow brook, they splashed through it. Some, thirsty, fell out of the column and knelt to drink their fill. Others shuffled on through without losing their place in the column, and as they moved they scooped up water and lapped it from their cupped hands.

General Funston knew their courage, their heroism, their stoicism, and their idealism. He was one of that growing group who understood our Latin neighbors, who knew them as fighting men and soldiers. Cubans, perhaps, know us better than we know them. It should be mutual. For the Cubans in their series of rebellions for freedom from Spain had much in common, in the campaigns and in their aspirations, with our own soldiers of the American Revolution against the fattish autocracy of King George. They had Calixto Garcia and Maceo, and scores like them. We have only to recall the days and the troops of Marion, the Swamp Fox of the Carolinas, to be able to picture those *insurrectos* in the province of Santa Clara and its village of Siboney.

I had known one of them in New York. Alfredo Poey, of Havana, was a Harvard graduate who volunteered for the *insurrectos*. He lived in New York and he loved its life, but he put his name down in the roster of the Cuban Junta and began studying military books. He practiced in the little shooting galleries on Third Avenue. He had his instructions: he was to be at his rooms on East Thirty-fourth Street every night between six and eight o'clock. He was to have a big dinner before six. Many nights I sat with him for company while he waited. Nothing happened. Then one night I went up there, and he was gone.

After the war he told me about it. With only a paper parcel — he was forbidden to take anything else — he went out with a man who had the countersign and, joined by three others, went down by train to Barnegat Bay. There they boarded a little sloop, crowded with the other parties that had joined them. They lay just out of sight of land, presumably fishing if anyone saw them. Then along came a small coastwise freighter and took them aboard. All down the coast little sailboats were sighted and more rebel volunteers came aboard.

Somewhere off Florida, they were landed on a little key, a tiny island, and told to wait there until a boat from Cuba came. Poey still had his paper parcel, as did the others. Tinned food was left with them, and fish lines. This would keep them alive until the gun runner would appear, but no one knew when. The mosquitoes were frightful. And there were no mosquito nets. So they made a long tunnel of palm leaves, and built a smudge fire at one end; in this tunnel they slept and lived, though not entirely free of mosquitoes. Here and in this way they waited for three weeks. One night the gun runner appeared and gave the signal lights, and they were taken to Cuba.

Poey served under Funston in the *insurrecto* artillery. It was not much, as artillery, but it was enough to batter towns and their Spanish blockhouses before the rebels went in with a machete charge. Poey, a neatly fastidious man, became amazed at his own indifference. In one town they captured, they found a keg of new sugar-cane rum, *canassa*. All the *insurrectos* got drunk. Before Poey passed out he recalled that his men were playing some sort of soccer football up and down the village street. Three or four balls were used, and each ball was the hacked-off head of a Spanish soldier who had been killed in the engagement. It was not a nice war.

All day the Cuban troops came marching in. Their officers were mounted on what were little more than scrawny ponies; and it was difficult to tell an officer from a private in that army. For months they had been out on guerrilla warfare, laying ambuscades and avoiding pitched battles. Used to the hill trails, or to no trails, they came in a column of twos, and each man carried his rifle as best suited him.

These Cubans were a curiosity to us. We spoke no Spanish, and they no English. But, when we gathered with them, they would rub their stomachs and say *"Hambre."* And this means "What have you got to eat?" in any language.

Their uniform was but a jacket and breeches; the jacket ragged and in some cases a mere lacework of tatters. Each carried a machete and one or two cartridge bandoliers of denim or sacking. Over his shoulder was a gunny sack or canvas hammock, in which he carried, among other things, his rawhide sandals, or the fiber-soled *alpagatas,* for when the going was easy he went barefoot. Some wore hats, the straw Cuban sombrero, but rain-soaked and shapeless. Here and there in their column would be a commissary mule straddled with two huge baskets or bags, holding the heavier supplies of the regiment and its officers, including a few iron pots; the rest of the space was filled with platanos and bundles of sugar cane.

There was no ammunition train; there was no ammunition except that which each man carried. And there were empty bandoliers in that column too. Those with

full bandoliers generally carried a Spanish Mauser rifle
— a sign of valor in action; it meant a dead Spaniard
— but most of the Cubans were armed with Reming-
tons and Winchesters.

Duty in the little chains of outlying blockhouses was
definitely disliked by the Spanish troops, for the jungle
was all about them from the edge of the little vegetable
garden which each blockhouse tended. And beyond the
edge some Cuban scout might be lying in ambush. If the
Spaniard was unarmed, as a precaution against losing
his Mauser, he lost his life in a machete stroke. Pursuit
in these jungles or their trails was dangerous. The *insurrectos* often tried to bait the Spaniards into pursu-
ing them — and running into an ambuscade. The blockhouses dotted all of Cuba; they were within range of
each other, and technically in support, but in fact they
became little isolated garrisons patiently waiting their
turn for relief.

The Mausers the *insurrectos* captured were excellent weapons, but there was no ammunition for them —
beyond the beltful unbuckled from a dead Spaniard.
Ammunition was precious. Never was there enough in
any rebel command to fight a pitched battle, even if that
had been good strategy. Curiously, it was Havana —
stronghold and main citadel of the Spanish commander
in chief, General Weyler — that became the chief
source of the *insurrectos'* supply of Mauser cartridges.

It was the prostitutes of Havana and other cities
who supplied the rebels, as I learned later from my
friend Alfredo Poey.

From an ordinary private soldier of the Spanish Army, *soldado raso,* they would demand 100 Mauser cartridges. From a noncommissioned officer, the demand would be for 200 cartridges or more. With an officer the demand rose steeply — a box of 1,000 cartridges. It was, said Poey, an amiable arrangement all round. The Spanish soldier's pay was small and luxuries were expensive. But cartridges — *Mira, hombre!* they are the issue of the government, they cost nothing, *Vamanos!*

At night a friend of the prostitute would call. He had a load of wood or charcoal or sugar cane, or some wine. When he left, his saddle pads would be lined with Mauser bullets. Thus the *insurrectos* kept themselves supplied with a frugal ammunition. For their artillery, and for rifles other than the Mauser, they depended upon the gunrunning little steamers or the fishing boats that, every now and again, were caught by the Spanish patrol boats fringing the Cuban coast. I have no doubt that various of the Mauser cartridges I saw in Cuban bandoliers had come through the underground by way of Havana's ladies of the night.

13

*Ed Marshall, Hearst's man, gets shot. "Shafter's Dock."
Mule packing. I become an official smoocher and get frustrated.*

BETWEEN the beach on which we had landed and
our machine shop a general hospital had been
established, but it was not much — a few rambling
buildings with corrugated iron roofs that had been a
Cuban home. It was ringed by little groups of soldiers,
all curious like myself, and scattered among them the
mildly wounded from Las Guasimas.

I started to sketch the hospital and a group promptly
surrounded me. I asked questions — they were almost
all cavalry and Rough Riders. What did you do?

"Me?" said one. "I jest dropped. What else was
there to do! You couldn't see nothing."

"Well," said another, "maybe even if you couldn't
see nothing you could let go whenever you heard a
Mauser. I did."

"They say Ham Fish got killed?" one asked of me. I
was from a New York regiment; Ham Fish was a ser-

geant in the Rough Riders and in the *Social Register,* twenty-four carat. It was quite a compliment to be asked that. I didn't even know who Ham Fish was, then.

"They got Ed Marshall too," chimed in another. I knew Ed Marshall. I had worked for him when I was in the art department of the *New York Herald.*

"He's out there yet," he went on, "but I hear they're bringing him in."

They were. But Ed Marshall was not dead, though he had been shot in the spine. Roosevelt pays a tribute to him in his book, and to his bravery. He had gone along with the cavalry wearing a white linen coat, ideally adapted for tropical wear, but not for battle. Some Spanish sharpshooter got him; the *soldado* probably thought he had bagged a generalissimo at the least.

Marshall was brought in on a stretcher just before sundown. His white coat was flecked a little with blood, and he was pale with pain; but his teeth were clamped in a smile. There were encouraging murmurs from the little lane as they made way for him. I was in that lane. Once he said "Thanks" in response to the sympathetic murmurs. He was inside the hospital for some fifteen minutes. Then an officer appeared in the doorway and, behind him, a surgeon with bloodied hands.

"Volunteers," said the officer, "to take him down to the boat?"

There was no lack of volunteers. He was paler, and

the examination had evidently hurt. A hospital sergeant took charge and we carried him down to the beach and put him on board one of the landing boats to be taken to the hospital ship. Marshall recovered, but he never had the free use of his legs again.

I ran across the man who had been shot through the belly. The purple welt was darker and a little bit of lint stuck out of each end. There was no other dressing.

"What did they do for you?" I asked.

"They took something and poked a rag in one hole and out the other," he explained. "Then they pulled it out and stuck in another — and pulled it back and forth. And Jee-sus, did it hurt! Don't hurt now though, much. Then they asked me if I had anything else. I said no. But they made me take off my clothes and damned if they didn't find I'd been shot in the backside too. They fixed that up and I'm walking around — can't sit down though. They stuck a rag in that too. Think of that — a feller gets hit twice and only knows about one."

Making camp that night was easy. We laid the dog tents as mattresses on the machine shop floor. One of our men, who had never swung an ax in his life, was sent to chop wood. He was brought back with one foot half off. The campaign was over for him, and this troubled him more than the foot.

The next morning they pulled in the scow that had not been lost and beached one end of it. It was decked over and a gangway led to the shore. It made landing supplies much easier; no more wading through the surf. This scow was promptly named "Shafter's Dock" on the unfounded rumor that General Shafter did not come ashore until the dock was in place.

Life was again delightful. Everything was running smoothly. At reveille the morning was lovely. A fresh breeze off the Caribbean gave no hint of the heat to come. Inspection was held, with the officer of the day strolling around to see how we were quartered, followed by the mounting of a heavy guard. Inspection of the guard was no formal ceremony; every rifle was examined for oil and action, and we stuffed rags in the muzzles to keep the dirt out. We were ordered to keep the big brass buckles of our cartridge belts unpolished and turned to the rear so that, in a fight, the brass would not heliograph our location to the Spaniards. There were details — wood-chopping was one, and jacking ammunition up from the new wharf was another. But there was a tap in the machine shop that came from some spring up in the hill back of Siboney, so no water detail was needed.

But the branches of the service other than us doughboys were busy. The wagons were coming ashore and teamsters and artificers were busy putting things together. Horses and mules were being sorted out and a supply for our advance was being organized; the animals that had been drowned were a serious loss. The cavalry brigade was up in front near their fight at Las Guasimas; they were between Siboney and the Spanish forces. They made their camp not far from where they had fought; and they were running out of rations. So the first pack train started. Mule trains could get through the narrow trails, but roads were to be built for our army wagons. The engineers started to make a road that would lead to Santiago, and we found that the engineers could call on the infantry, or anyone else, to supply the brawn that did the work of shovel and pick. These details were made up and announced at morning roll call, and they were not popular. Before my turn came we moved out and were on the way to Santiago.

But in Siboney I learned how a mule is packed; I watched the packers sling the cargo so that it balanced with equal weight on both sides, and then wind the pack rope under the mule's belly and back and forth across the back, the loops settling down almost as if they were automatic. The final swing and sway brought the whole rope up in the diamond hitch that made the cargo a part of the resentful mule, himself.

I also rejoiced that fate had not made me a mule packer. I only had to walk. While a mule packer is supposed to ride, and has a horse and saddle assigned to him, it is a meaningless gesture. He is on foot a good part of the time, relashing a pack, getting a mule back on its feet — for mules get tired — and hauling a mule out of the mud, but first throwing the pack so that the animal can struggle up, and then loading it all over again.

My prowling with a sketchbook was not all for art. I

was on the lookout for some nice leather belting. As I have mentioned, all the belting in our machine shop had been looted before we got there — and we needed pads for the woven-web haversack straps that cut our shoulders. We had been issued two hundred rounds of ball cartridge with no place to carry it but in the haversack — and this alone weighed about twenty pounds, besides our rations. We had fifty rounds in our belts, and our belts were full.

Since we were camped in a machine shop I knew that, somewhere, there would be a company tool-and-supply room. I found it, and glory be, saw it was being used as our own regimental adjutant's office! I also saw, on shelves in the dusky inner room, behind the barrier of the sergeant major, some beautiful rolls of brand new oak-tanned leather belting. Evidently it had been overlooked.

When I saw that belting, my duty was clear. The roll would be enough for our whole company and some left over to trade with. And so I tried, in the most natural and businesslike way, to pass beyond the rail that separated the common doughboy from sergeants major. I opened the gate boldly, as one having authority and official responsibility. A sergeant major barred my way.

"Nix!" he said brusquely. "Out!"

It was just as well. For I had no blanket under which to conceal the belting even if I had been able to get my hands on it; and furthermore, if I had such a roll under my arm out in the open I would have been murdered for it before I could get to my company. I asked myself what Jimmy Shortell would have done. Then I went back to Captain Rafferty. He listened with interest.

"Well," he said thoughtfully, "how can we get it?"

"If," I replied, "the Captain will detail a lieutenant under my orders, we can get it."

I explained. The second lieutenant of the company was a good man and quick in his head. He would have some official business in the adjutant's office; I would be his orderly, and his business must have plenty of talk — the more complicated, the better. Just get me past that rail and its sergeant major, that was all!

"Suppose you get caught?" asked the captain. "That's regimental headquarters. They'll chuck you in the guardhouse."

"Not if the lieutenant gets mad enough at me, *his* orderly. He'll drag me out and be too mad to talk, and off we go. Then we'll try some other way."

"Suppose I just go and ask the colonel for it?" suggested the captain.

"Yes," I said, "and he'll be so damned fair he'll give it to the regiment, share and share alike, and this company'll get about eight pieces and the noncoms'll grab them. I'm pleading for us common folk, Captain."

The captain laughed, and nodded. "Lieutenant Roberts!" he called.

Lieutenant Roberts stepped over.

The captain outlined the plan. "Mr. Roberts," he concluded, "you are under command of Private Post for special duty. Good luck!"

This is probably the only known case — short of

mutiny — when a private was given command of an expedition over a commissioned officer. I was making military history.

We reached the regimental headquarters and the adjutant's office. The sergeant major was at the gate of the inside railing. He stood up to the lieutenant. "Regimental adjutant?" demanded Lieutenant Roberts.

"He's busy, Lieutenant," said the sergeant major. Lieutenant Roberts had been a sergeant major himself only a short while back.

Off in the far distance I could see the regimental adjutant, Abell. Battalion Adjutant Fisher was nearer.

"Never mind," said Lieutenant Roberts briskly. "Hello, Harry," he called.

Adjutant Fisher looked up. "Oh, come on in," he called cordially. Lieutenant Roberts entered, and as I started to follow with my blanket under my arm the gate slammed shut. "Nix," said the sergeant major, eying me coldly.

Lieutenant Roberts turned haughtily. "My orderly!"

"Sorry, sir," said the sergeant major, "no soldiers allowed inside the rail."

"Harry," said the lieutenant, "my orderly —" He pointed at me.

"Against orders," returned Harry, "not inside the rail —"

"But I need him," said Lieutenant Roberts, which was quite true.

"Oh, dammit, let him in."

The sergeant major opened the gate with an icy glint in his eye that marked me for death before a firing squad. Sergeant majors boss the job of policing the camp; it is they who can detect imperceptible cigarette butts or bits of paper or twigs and require one to go to the other end of camp to dump them in a designated waste can. It ruins their character for any job, I think, but that of housekeeper and, someday, such training will undoubtedly make someone a good wife.

I was inside the rail. The moment had come. I was on my own in a one-man commando raid. I seeped through the turbid mob of sergeants and shoulder straps unnoticed, because I was not furtive. I drifted down the aisle to the shelf where lay the beautiful oak-tanned belting that would protect my shoulders from the cutting haversack strap. Ah, here it was, golden and shoulder-soft in the dim light of the shelf. I looked around. The blanket was over my arm, neatly folded. My arm stole gently to the golden roll.

But something was wrong! It was chill to the touch, and with the hard dustiness of rusty iron. It was iron! It was an eccentric strap for a locomotive. Well, I would take it for a trophy. I grasped and pulled. It could not be moved. It weighed somewhere around a hundred and fifty pounds.

We went back to camp, Lieutenant Roberts resuming command.

The captain was kind. "It was a good try," he said. "Rusty iron eccentric straps look exactly like rolls of oak-tanned leather."

The captain had not lost faith in me. Later, when I came in with a twenty-pound sack of brown sugar — worth its weight in gold, if we had had gold — I felt that his confidence had been justified and his patience, too. Then I picked up a poncho — for mine had been stolen when I was on guard — and he remarked that it was a better poncho than the one I had lost, and so it was. But this was merely private enterprise and was to my personal advantage without any factor of social responsibility.

14

The Merrimac *is sunk. We jack ammunition. Making our first camp.*

FRIDAY, the 24th of June, 1898, brought news. Lieutenant Hobson had sunk the *Merrimac* in the narrow channel that led to Santiago Bay, and Admiral Cervera's Spanish fleet was bottled up! We of the infantry could now capture the Spanish Navy, and the feat would undoubtedly make imperishable history! It was good news. The *Merrimac* lay sunken in the channel not five miles away as the crow flies — even less. She had been sunk on the night of June 3, and it had taken the news three weeks to travel to us.

This was something to write home about, and we did. But back home they already knew it. News was what had been happening to Hobson. What we were doing was just commonplace, unimportant routine!

The next day, Saturday, dawned in a gorgeous splendor that turned to a slow, white heat. More unloading at the scow dock. Some field guns came ashore. More Cuban rebels trickled in in uneven columns, and we had a chance to trade for more sugar cane. The com-

pany's camp became better organized; the first sergeant
chalked off his quarters on the machine-shop floor.
More supplies were landed and stacked under tarpaulins. The supply of hardtack and sowbelly seemed
endless. The hospital that had taken in the wounded
on the day of Las Guasimas now seemed a trifle
more scoured and sanitary. All the wounded had
been taken off to the hospital ship, the *Olivette*. General Shafter was coming ashore tomorrow. This
looked more like the business we had come to Cuba for.
It would mean action.

The chaplain came rambling through the regiment;
at various companies he would stop and then move on.
He knew me slightly, and at our company he stopped
and spoke. Tomorrow was Sunday and he was going to
hold service. Would I help him organize a choir? I
knew nothing about music; I did not even know why he
didn't use the choirs he had organized back in Lakeland and Tampa. However, I was willing to help — we
are always more flattered when asked to do something
for which we have neither knowledge nor capacity. I
hunted up Roby. Nothing doing. I spoke to some others. Nothing doing. They reminded me of the arrests
on the *Vigilancia* of the men who bought drinking water from the stewards; they recalled the incident of the
shade and the soldiers ordered into the sun. They all
said they'd be damned if they'd sing. And they didn't.
Let him sing himself, if he wanted singing, they said.

That Sunday, at one end of the machine shop, there
was a church service; but no choir other than the few

straggling voices of those who comprised a very lean congregation. Officers were almost wholly absent.

That night there was a rumor that we were to move. At the dawn roll call we were ordered to hustle through our breakfast at full speed. By this time we had several little fireplaces made with railroad fish-plates and rocks and could cook fairly comfortably. Breakfast was corned beef, hardtack, and coffee. The coffee beans were still issued already roasted; we pounded them to a very coarse powder in our tin cups, and then boiled them furiously. It suggested coffee — and later we were to make coffee from green beans that would not do even that.

The coffee was not even boiling when the sergeants were around our heels. Pack! Roll your pack — get a move on! Hurry! Get on — sling your pack — fall in! Roll call — right shoulder arms — order arms as your name is called — hey, you, get in there! All present or accounted for. The captain drew his sword and waited.

Far down the line toward regimental headquarters the bugle sounded assembly. Fours right — and the single staccato note, *march!* There was no column; companies had been brigaded or camped here and there in a helter-skelter pattern over the western section of Siboney, in rambling lanes, in a foundry, in the machine shop, and in the storehouses. But each company knew its place in the column of its battalion, and each battalion knew *its* place in the regimental column. Where the bugle blew was the colonel and his staff. Out of a mass of confusion of companies and shouting of company commands a column began forming; elements flowed into it smoothly and suavely and gave it form.

Where our first camp would be no one knew. At any rate, it would be nearer Santiago; and this was a happy thought. We passed the battlefield of Las Guasimas and looked over the trodden grass and the blackened blood where the wounded had fallen or the dead had lain. Here were bullet-scarred trees and the little spurts of shredded bark where the bullet had smacked through. It was somewhat like an abandoned orchard except for the cactus and the land crabs and the feather-duster palms against the hills. We had been under that Spanish fire. The little glade, the jungle weeds, and the scrawny trees were commonplace — except for what we knew had happened here; here men had crawled and killed and been killed.

A man kicked at a bit of broken grass over a blackened puddle of blood. "Sons of bitches!" he said, and he was referring to the Spaniards. Men talk like that. It was his tribute to the man who had fought and fallen there.

It was a little further along in the march that our column of fours turned off the road to the right and into a large field — or what had once been a field — that had a scattering second growth of shrubs and cactus and a harsh, tough grass. The bugles blew. Interpreted, they meant: "Column of battalions on first battalion; first battalion fours left!" And there we were, each battalion nicely behind each other and ready to stake down our dog tents in an orderly array. "Ri-i-ight dress!" We dressed right. "Pitch tents!" And the camp was made.

In an hour it was as nice a looking camp as one could care to see. It was the first time we had used our tents. We tramped down the long grass into a mattress. We had not had a real mattress since we left Long Island in the chilly North. We had forgotten that there could be such a thing as a soft bed. Water had already been located — a cold brook fresh from the mountains just to the east of us. We filled our canteens with the first cold water we had had in weeks; and then we had a chilly bath — also the first in weeks. There had been but little bathing at Siboney, for the only beach was a narrow sandy strip on which supplies were landed, and at either end began the low, ragged, rocky cliffs of no use for bathing. Also there was enough supervision to see that no time was lost in frivoling on a silly little beach. In the Army it is not necessary that one keep on doing something useful, but one has to seem to be.

Then came an orderly from our headquarters. Colonel desired to see the captain. When the captain came back he picked out a section, sixteen men; he was to scout our eastern and northern flank for signs of Spaniards — for we were now on the front line and must scout and picket both of our own flanks. Ahead were the dismounted cavalry and the Rough Riders and, beyond them, the Spanish Army of Santiago. So we scouted for any prowling band of Spaniards that might be lurking in the hilly, jungled slopes of these foothills.

15

"With ball cartridge — load!" We scout the right flank. On picket, left flank. The shooting starts — land crabs repelled. Spanish bugles just across the valley. We draw five days' rations and move out.

ONCE we were clear of the camp and in a little glade in the jungle, the captain halted us.

"Load!" he ordered.

Once before we had loaded with ball cartridge, but that was on the target range back in Lakeland, five cartridges and five shots to prepare us for the Cuban campaign. This was the real thing. The cool, heavy cartridge, about as big as a man's little finger, held a human death. We had no lust for killing, but we felt a tingling in the fact that we had the power of life and death over another human being. Also, in the back of our minds was a not too subtle consciousness that somewhere — in that jungle or beyond — was someone who had the same power over us.

We divided into squads, the squads to keep within reach of each other. We moved cautiously or thrashed

The Rough Riders with their famed dynamite gun on the dock at Tampa — Teddy Roosevelt on the left.

through the undergrowth; often we had to go around it. We prowled up and down the mountainside. We saw nothing; not a sign. Then we returned to camp. But before we could get settled for even a smoke, the battalion bugle blew.

Break camp, down with the dog tents, and sling our packs. We were going on heavy outpost duty, out to the left. Where we had scouted had been *away* from Santiago; this outpost was between the regiment and Santiago, with Spanish troops somewhere in the middle. The sun was fading into the mellow sunset when we pitched our tents on the flatness of a hill where the palmetto scrub and jungle was less dense, and where a few gnarled and stunted trees gave the effect of an abandoned apple orchard. The hill rolled down toward other hills and a rolling jungle that faded into the distance where lay the city of Santiago. The little Spanish blockhouses that dotted every hill and ridge silhouetted slowly into the blues and lavenders of evening and turned to violet and purple in the far distance as the valleys became dark below them. We could see the tiny flickers of Spanish campfires at outposts like ours, far off, and beyond those our minds pictured a city with people passing to and fro. We wondered if the Spaniards drank beer and if there would be any left when we got there.

The whole battalion was on outpost guard, a picket. One company was posted as an outer line on double guard — two men, back to back; one hour on, two hours off; ball cartridge; challenge and then shoot.

Down in the valley by the Aguadores road on which we
had come, we heard the regimental bugle blow retreat,
and then taps. Far across the rolling jungle below us we
could hear the Spanish bugles, lovely in the strange
cadences. The stars turned on their lights in the black
sky, and all was as peaceful as peace itself.

Double guard was interesting; it meant that there
was imminent danger in the darkness. Bayonets were
fixed and, back against back, we peered into the black
mass of jungle and listened for something that might
be different from the ordinary sounds of night. There
were all kinds of crickets and chirpy things rubbing
their legs together in shrill amorousness, and the occasional sound of some night bird clearing its throat.
Then, of course, there were the land crabs. During the
day we laughed at them, and the sounds of the day covered over their clawing among the dried debris of the
jungle floor. At night they sounded for all the world
like battalions of Spaniards hell-bent upon surprise
and massacre.

For my partner in double guard, I had drawn a
sailor. I wished I had drawn Jimmy Lowe; for Jimmy
knew every sound of the night made by fish, fowl, or
pad-footed quadrupeds and would, I knew, have mastered the land-crab clatter. My partner and I discussed
these noises, in whispers. I gave him my theory that we
should start shooting only after we saw something to
shoot at. He disagreed thoroughly. We sat back to
back and argued over our shoulders so as not to lose
sight of any of the 180 degrees of jungle darkness that

was our share. We had been told to sit so as to make no silhouette against the night sky.

Then down the line of the doubled sentries there came a shrill challenge and *Bang!* Mingling with the bang was a buzzing overhead — it was a .45 bullet and American.

Up along our line of doubled sentries someone had heard a Spaniard. I think he was a city man with his first taste of the country at night. "Corporal of the guard!" The call was high on the night air.

Halfway between our line of sentries and the battalion camp was the guard; we could hear them turning out and the hoarse orders as they were lined up. We could hear the corporal of the guard and his squad crashing through the underbrush on the double.

"Halt, who's there?" The challenge came from where the shots had come, the post next to ours.

"I'm the captain, goddamit," was the answer. "Don't you know my voice?"

Back in the battalion camp we heard a bugle blow; men were turning out and lining up in the darkness under arms.

Out of the darkness to our left there came another *Bang*. And somewhere in it was a challenge; both bullet and challenge had issued concurrently.

Far to the right another *Bang!* Then another!

Down in the valley the first-sergeants were waking up the men. Not that they needed to be awakened; they sat in their company streets with their rifles across their knees and their cartridge belts on.

Up and down our line of doubled sentries the captain and the lieutenants stumbled and crashed wherever a *bang* was heard. The story was all the same: I seen a Spaniard, Lieutenant — I seen him — well, I heard him — yeah, I got him — down there — I seen him just as plain.

My sailor side-kick and I sat there in the darkness, silent. We could hear the captain now and then, and in a calm way. Men were put there to hear things and see things; the orders for sentinels say so in the book; you break men for shooting when they are supposed to shoot and maybe they won't shoot when they *should*. But underneath the calm voice it was apparent that the captain was seething. One could hear him crashing through the brush.

"Halt — who's there?"

"The captain, goddammit! Who you shooting?"

Then an excited explanation in a hoarse whisper. And then another *Bang,* and the captain was off again to the new alarm. Yet it was all perfectly correct, according to the book. I was thinking how the bird sounds had stopped and even the crickets stopped rubbing their legs against their abdomens when — *Bang!* and my sailor side-kick had let go. And his breechblock clacked as he reloaded and snapped it shut. The captain came crashing down.

"Who fired?" he demanded.

"I did," said the sailor. "I challenged and then I fired. I heard him — right there," and he pointed.

Well, he *had* challenged, I recall; but it was at the

same time that he fired. "I seen a Spaniard, Captain. I could hear more."

The captain turned to me. "Did you see him?" he demanded.

"No, sir," I said. "I wasn't facing that way."

"I seen one," insisted my side-kick, "and I could hear the others."

"Yes," said the captain, "very good. Always shoot when you see a Spaniard. If you let a Spaniard through I'll hang you at daybreak. But have a heart for the land crabs." Another bang down the line, and the captain was off.

My partner was chafed. He turned his head over his shoulder to me. "I seen a Spaniard," he said, "maybe more — I heard 'em. You didn't see him?"

I said no, I hadn't.

"Maybe you was asleep," he suggested bitterly.

A few minutes later the sergeant of the guard came with our relief and we crashed back through the cactus and underbrush to the guard line. We lay down for the two hours' sleep as prescribed by the book, but we couldn't sleep. From a hundred yards away where our line of double-bitted sentries began there came another bang — modified by distance. The battle with the land crabs was beginning. The sergeant of the guard was among us on the instant. The rest of our off-duty was mainly standing in line in the darkness as we listened to the occasional bang of Springfields and a half-hysterical sergeant seething in hoarse excitement. What sleep we got, we got standing up in line!

All that night we did double sentry, one hour on and two hours off. When we were off we would lie down and then be routed up. Then lie down again, and again be routed up and counted off by the sergeant, who went along with a poking forefinger to prove our actual presence in the darkness. I recalled vaguely those lines of Swinburne in which he refers to that night in which "our bodies leapt or lay"; it was very descriptive of that tour of guard. What the Spanish troops across the folds of the little jungle valleys thought I do not know. I hope, vengefully, that at least we kept them awake. And, perhaps, when they had first landed in Cuba they had their own battle with the land crabs.

A land crab is entitled to more than this passing mention. For we became well acquainted with him. He is an armored spider surrounded by legs; the hub of these legs is a globular turret in the center of which is a pair of eyes on stems, like two periscopes. His total complexion matches the withered vegetation he travels on. His family name is *Gecarcinidae,* and his tribal badge is *Brachyura.* Most of the time he lives a solitary and misogamistic life of an anchorite. Then, like the famous monk of Siberia he leaps from his cell and becomes a ravening roué. From his cell in a hole in the ground he emerges and joins other emerging anchorites in a great caravan to the sea. He moves in vast hordes that crackle through the underbrush and, on the way, is joined by the ladies, the *vivandières* of his army. Or perhaps it is at the sea that he finds the bathing beauty of his choice. Once at the sea he awaits the arrival of his offspring, which arrive in due season, and then the family returns to the hinterland where he dons the garment of repentance and misogamy and lives a frugal life until it is time for another Legion convention in the Atlantic City of the Brachyura and the candles of love are again alight. When it is also realized that each land crab possesses five pairs of legs, the nightly clatter of Crabshooters Hill is more easily apprehended. The Spaniards, with but one pair of legs, could never have made such a clatter in the underbrush. Any military expedition to the tropics should be well briefed in this fact.

By dawn, the firing had long since died down and the captain had long since grown hoarse. The land crabs had retired to their holes.

Across the ridges that lay between our outpost and the Spanish lines we could see the distant wisps of blue smoke that marked their early-morning coffee, their *desayuno*. Doubtless they could see the little smoke from our fires where the hardtack and the sowbelly were frying. We had our bugles and reveille, and we could hear theirs. All was peaceful and calm — except that we were at war. The dawn was cool and fragrant with the deceptive gentleness of the tropics.

Conversation centered upon the night we had just passed. At first there were some specific denials, but then one curious man looked at the muzzles of a few rifles where the telltale black powder had left a mark. In an absent-minded way some men began rubbing the muzzles with a rag and the subject faded. We were still on double guard, back to back, and not a shot was fired. The major came up from the regimental camp in the valley below with questions from the colonel as to what-in-hell and who-in-hell were we shooting at. The major was urged to tell the colonel that not a shot had been fired and that it was all the hallucination of some dreamer down in their camp.

So the next company went on guard, double sentries, and we did a little catching up on our sleep. That night was peaceful and silent, and the Spaniards did not disturb us nor we the Spaniards. The new guard had been heavily briefed as to land crabs.

We lay in our dog tents and soaked hardtack for the next meal and watched it swell up; for there was nothing else to do. Or we scraped the bottoms of our haversacks for possible remnants of hard candy. So it came about that, from sheer boredom, I began to learn about Jewry and kosher. For one of my squad, Jesse Pohalski, came from a line of orthodox Jews who had been in this country since before the American Revolution. Jesse was liberal and joked about the sowbelly as he ate it; his parents were liberal — though not that far — but they were too close to his grandparents, who held every tradition as an ironclad rule and imposed it on their children and grandchildren. So I swapped my good old Presbyterian grandmother and her steely piety for his. I learned that his grandfather never went into a room without touching the *mizzuzah* — a little box with a prayer in it, which was fastened to the doorway of each room. Then I told about an

aunt who would open a Bible with deliberate careless-
ness and eagerly scan the verse her eye first lighted on
as a message direct from God. From Jesse I learned
that meat and milk could not be served at the same
meal — even milk in coffee — for, he quoted, "Thou
shalt not seethe the kid in its mother's milk." I learned
that his mother had a separate set of knives and forks
and spoons for a meal that had fish; and a separate set
when there was meat; and that a fish had to have
scales or it was taboo. He was interested when
I told him my Presbyterian grandmother did not
celebrate Christmas except with prayer and churchgo-
ing, because she had heard it was really the date of a
pagan festival; and her four children never had a doll
since dolls were graven images and as such came under
the prohibition of the Ten Commandments. Then we
crawled out from under our dog tent and began frying the swollen hardtack and the sowbelly.

Later, in the run over the hill to cover the withdrawal of a battery of field artillery, Jesse was
wounded, and went back to the States on a stretcher.
He got well.

The next day, the 30th of June, it was our company's
turn to go on guard again. We looked forward to it,
for now we knew the land crabs — in fact, we occasionally had to chase them out of our dog tents. But
there came a message from our regiment below. The
battalion bugle blew, and when the officers came back
we started rolling our horse-collar packs; we were to
rejoin the regiment.

Back in the regimental camp, we pitched out little tents in the same space we had left a couple of days before. We cooked a little hardtack and sowbelly. Sunset came and darkness. We loafed easily in our street and smoked an evening pipe. Again the regimental bugle blew. The first sergeants trotted over to headquarters and came back.

"Draw rations," they said, "five days."

That night, until half past one the next morning, we lined up and drew rations. The regimental quartermaster bossed the job and a special detail handed out the stuff. First we drew coffee — unroasted and loose — that had been measured for the five days' supply; a double handful. Then we went back and drew a double handful, maybe more, of navy beans, white, hard, and dry. Part we dumped in a sock, if we had a spare one — which was not often, because the spare socks had been used to carry the 200 rounds of ammunition that had been issued to us back in Siboney. We dumped the rest of the stuff, loose, in each of the two haversack sections, along with writing paper and chewing tobacco. The next issue was sugar, a moderate amount that could easily be held in our outstretched palms — and this went in with the coffee and the beans to mingle with the plug cut. Then came loose salt and pepper, both dumped in an envelope with a letter from home. Then came an armful of hardtack, a chunk of sowbelly, and one of the red-painted cans of "roast beef" that had been intended for the Japanese. One of these cans was issued to every two soldiers, with instructions

to share it with the next man when we halted for breakfast. You may compute the supply of hardtack: the ration was two per meal, six for each day, and a five days'
supply meant thirty hardtack. They went into the haversacks or were wrapped up in our blanket roll and
were mostly crumbs and bits when we needed them.

It was still dark when reveille was blown. We had
been asleep two hours and a half. It was before dawn,
though the soft gray in the east threw the Cuban hills
into relief. We were going to move; that much we
knew when the order to strike tents came. Then we
waited. Slowly the dawn mounted and outlined the
nearer hills and the little abandoned Spanish blockhouses. The colonel went to the head of the regiment;
the colors, covered in black oilcloth, were taken to
their place in the column. Daylight came. We ate hardtack. Rumors flew. We were off to Havana! We would
get 'em in the rear! Ha, five days' rations proved it!
(We didn't know that Havana was over 400 miles to
the west!) We were going to march through Cuba to
the sea, like Sherman. That sounded rather good —
we translated it in terms of sugar cane and cigars.

Then we waited some more. There was nothing to
see, nothing to do — just stand or sit in ranks, and
wait. The sky was blue and little birds were twitter-
ing and strange tropical birds were squawking. The
shade was still cool, and we told ourselves that waiting
was better than walking. Then came the bugle: "A-a-
ttttt-en-shun!" The clumps of loafing men stiffened.
"Forward!" The bugle was drawling its command un-

til the final note of execution — "March." The jumbled ranks of waiting men resolved into columns of fours, orderly and contained, and the day had begun.

We filed out of the chaparral and trampled undergrowth of the abandoned field where our camp had been. Ahead we could see the column turning to the right into what we called the Aguadores turnpike. Whether it was a turnpike or what Aguadores meant we did not know. It was not necessary that a soldier should. All we knew was that we were going deeper into the heart of Cuba and that, with our five days' rations in our haversack, the campaign was on. Down ahead on a slope of the Aguadores road we could see our colors encased in their black oilcloth; they were always cased on a march. In the sheer joy of the fresh morning someone started to sing "The Old Gray Mare," the obscene song that always marked a state of blissful contentment.

It was a pleasant morning and we were on our way.

16

A nice cool morning for a battle. Hearst reviews the troops at the front. Jungle fighting ahead. The balloon gives our range to the Spaniards. We go into the jungle trail to Bloody Ford.

THE Aguadores road led between hilly ridges, much like any lumber trail to be found in Maine or the Adirondacks. Cactus and undergrowth closed in on either side — evidence of fields abandoned during the years of the Cuban revolution.

Between these hills the smoky mists of early morning were rising and feathering off into the full dawn. The road curved gently and sloped up and down in easy rolling grades. Trees closed in overhead and then opened again so that we could see the column of blue-shirted men stretching far ahead. A mounted orderly galloped past to the rear and a staff officer trotted down the line to somewhere ahead. A battery of field artillery came up and we crowded over to the side to give them room to pass. The narrow road was filled with troops. One of the cavalry regiments passed us on foot. We knew they were cavalrymen by the stocks and exposed barrels of their short carbines. From the distance far ahead came the dull boom of a cannon — or was it thunder? For the first time it dawned on us that there might be fighting ahead.

"Halt," the order came — each time with a bugle up where the colonel was, and repeated on down the column, battalion by battalion. Then "Forw-a-a-rd" and we started again. It was the same with the other regiments; once we were three regiments abreast. At one halt, sitting in the shade of a large, thick-leaved tree we saw a man on a horse. The horse was not big but the man was, and tall: his legs and white socks hung well below the horse's belly. Dressed in black civilian clothes as if he had just stepped over from New York, he wore a jaunty flat-brimmed straw hat with a scarlet hatband and a scarlet tie to match. It was William Randolph Hearst, who had fanned the flames of emotion in his New York *Journal* with tales of a beauteous maiden helpless in a cruel Spanish dungeon, and who would later distribute medals made from the sunken *Maine* as awards for something or other. I had designed the medals for him.

His private yacht now lay off Siboney, with a printing press and outfit aboard. Later he would print a newspaper with both boiler-plate and original copy and distribute it to the men in the trenches. It was a little four-page affair, something like the tabloids that were to come later. It hadn't much news, but paper was scarce in the trenches and it was welcome. Also, since

Army stationery was exhausted, regimental orders were not infrequently written on its blank margins.

We hailed him joyously — he was someone we knew! "Hey, Willie!" The hail went up and down the column, and it was all friendly. Someone from New York!

He never moved a muscle. Always poker-faced, he never cracked a smile. If he thought we were jeering he was wrong. We were just glad to see someone from home.

James Creelman, the correspondent, came galloping back from ahead and conferred with Hearst. One of the men recognized him. "Hello, Jimmy!" he yelled. And we all joined in with "Hello, Jimmy!" He waved in response and grinned a white smile through his heavy black beard. Then came the bugle and the shouting of company commanders and the column began to move ahead again.

Creelman turned in his saddle and called out to us: "Boys, you're going into battle. Good luck!" Then he turned and spoke to Hearst. Hearst made a gesture in our direction with his scarlet-banded hat. He almost smiled.

"Good luck!" he called mildly. "Boys, good luck be with you," and then he stiffened again.

From where Hearst sat on his horse the road sloped gently downward. We saw our colors in their black cases dip and disappear and then rise again with the banners floating open in the fitful breeze, brilliant against the tropic green of the sun-flecked trail. Now we knew. Hearst and Creelman were right — we *were* going into battle. In those days, troops went into battle flying their colors. Battle fronts were formed on them; they led charges, and on them troops reformed; they were the leading point and the rallying point.

Now we knew. Battle lay somewhere ahead. And not too far ahead either. For, a few hundred yards from where we left Hearst and Creelman, a field gun behind a jungle-screened bank let loose with a blast that stung our eardrums. It was one of Captain Grimes's battery, Second U.S. Artillery. We could see the white smoke rising above the little trees. Then there came a mild *plop* not too far from where the gun had been fired. It was a Spanish shell; the Spaniards were opening up too. Unlike our artillery, they used smokeless powder.

Now and again we heard overhead odd little sounds not quite a click and not quite a whine, and now and again a *buzz* when a Spanish bullet smacked into a tree, its course deflected. We were under fire! This was what we had come for.

I felt a tenseness in my throat, a dryness that was not a thirst, and little chilly surges in my stomach that no red-flannel bellyband could warm. Presently we could hear a distant popping of rifle fire — like firecrackers before breakfast on an old-fashioned Fourth of July, before the day was in full swing.

Suddenly, from our right, we heard a terrific *crash-bang!* as another field gun of the battery let go, and another billow of white smoke rose above the under-

growth. Then another *plop* as another Spanish shell
burst at the battery. Howard Chandler Christy, the
artist, had perched himself in a tree back of the battery
to make a sketch. Years later he told me that he had
just started when the Spanish shell arrived. He quickly
decided to make the sketch from memory. The battery
also moved. Whenever they fired they pinpointed themselves as a target with the telltale burst of smoke. Our
guns could not locate the Spaniards' field artillery because of their smokeless powder. The target for Captain Grimes's battery was a little red-tile-roofed building at the top of a hill in the distance. This was the
blockhouse on San Juan Hill.

Halt and move forward; it never changed. The
Aguadores road was thick with men, columns of fours
and two columns abreast, mostly. Fortunately the
Spaniards could not see us through the interven-
ing jungle and they contented themselves with silencing
Grimes's battery.

At one halt the Cuban troops passed us. They were
to scout in force ahead of our troops. But more of
them had gone on the day before. It was they who
were drawing the opening Spanish fire. They passed us
at a rapid march — half walk, half trot.

One of the first wounded men we saw was a Cuban
officer. He was in a hammock slung on a sapling;
from the hammock there came a slow and steady dropping of blood; he had been hit in the groin with a shell
fragment. He was breathing hard and now and again
groaned in agony through gritted teeth. Relays of Cu-

bans were carrying the hammock. Behind it walked an *insurrecto* holding a shattered arm that had soaked his ragged cotton uniform with blood. They went on past, back to Siboney. A little farther along, two more wounded Cubans were resting under the roadside bushes, bloody in their tattered shirts, until they could go on again.

Overhead, the clicking and buzzing noises had become more definite. They were high — machine guns most likely, since they came in thin, seething flocks and with only scattered hisses between. The Spaniards were firing blindly through the jungle, and going high. They had eighteen Maxim machine guns in their army; we had but four Gatlings, and these not yet in action. A regiment and a brigade passed us. They too marched and halted and then pressed forward again. We saw the Rough Riders go by; as cavalry, they were to clear out any outposts that the Spaniards might have established to protect the hill and its blockhouse.

The sun was high and hot. No one had had breakfast, and we were hungry. We crossed a trickling brook and were swung into an abandoned, overgrown field on the left. Here we ate the Japanese-coolie beef; we had its gravy and its gristle, hardtack, and a little sugar. It was good. The bullets overhead were no longer a novelty. In the distance we could hear the popping of rifle fire; we could not tell if it was ours or the Spaniards'. But it was louder than before. We wondered how soon we would get into it; we talked little — there was neither bravado nor timidity. We felt there

was a job to do and get over with, and each one hoped
for the best. Around us we could see nothing but the
jungle. The Aguadores road was a ragged, enclosed slot
through it. The field battery had seen the blockhouse
and San Juan Hill; we had not.

All one could do was think — and try to steady the
thinking. The first high bullets had been a thrill. Now
the bullets were proof that someone was trying to kill
us, each one of us individually, and in a highly impersonal way.

We were all curious to know what it would be like
to be faced with the real thing. Men were about to test
themselves in their own eyes and in the ultimate terms
of life and death. It is a difficult test. But most men
seem to be able to make it on the battlefield.

After we had finished eating, we went back to the
Aguadores road. It was still crowded with troops
slowly making their way forward between halts. Forward. It was getting hotter. Halt — and we threw off
our horse-collar blanket rolls and left a guard over
them. The guard grinned sheepishly. Poor chap, he'd
never be able to say he'd been in a battle. We went on.
The crack of rifle fire was louder, much louder now.
Some of it was quite sharp and not far away. Up there
ahead somewhere was our brigade commander, Brigadier General Hawkins. He had ridden to the front
from last night's camp on a cargo mule. His brigade
— the Sixth and Sixteenth Regulars and the Seventy-
first Infantry from New York — had been designated
as the spearhead of the attack on San Juan Hill. Gen-

eral Kent commanded the three brigades of the First
Division of infantry, and he and General Hawkins had
gone ahead to a point just beyond a ford in the San
Juan River where they could get a view of the hill and
the blockhouse their troops were to assault.

Lieutenant Colonel Miley of Major General Shafter's staff joined them there. General Hawkins was of
the opinion that San Juan Hill should be assaulted and
captured. General Kent was against the assault.*

Nonetheless, the immediate instructions were given
General Kent by Lieutenant Colonel Miley, in the
name of General Shafter: "I am entirely of General
Hawkins' opinion," said Lieutenant Colonel Miley,
"and I will, if you have no objections, in the name of
General Shafter and with his authority, direct General
Hawkins to advance with his brigade and capture the
hill." †

It is rare in military history for a subordinate officer,
even though he is on the staff of the commanding general, to take authority over the general of a division.
That the emergency was great is apparent, and the
need for Miley to take the responsibility from General
Kent reveals two outstanding factors: the uncertainty
of Kent and the leadership in the emergency of both
Lieutenant Colonel Miley and of Brigadier General
Hawkins. It is to these two that the assault and capture
of San Juan Hill must be credited. General Kent's
share must rest with his having stated that he had

---

* See General Kent's official report, 1898, p. 164.
† See *The Fight for Santiago,* by Stephen Bonsal, p. 126.

"no objection" to Lieutenant Colonel Miley's assumption of authority and decision.

Thus it was that General Hawkins proceeded to head his brigade and form them for the assault. It was General Hawkins' intention to use the Sixth and Sixteenth Infantry to outflank the Spanish position on the hill, and to use the Seventy-first in a direct and holding action so that he could, possibly, mislead the Spaniards as to the point of assault and make the flanking attack of the Sixth and Sixteenth more effective.* He would, at the least, deceive the Spaniards as to where the main assault would be delivered.

In the Aguadores road we heard yells and cheers from the rear of our columns. An observation balloon came into sight high above the jungle. A four-man ground crew held its trail rope and kept the balloon under control. Signal Corps men followed with coils of the rope, which they paid out or took in according to the directions from the basket of the balloon above. Two heads peered over the rim of the basket and occasionally a little note would flutter down, to be rescued and brought to General Kent. No one knew that the balloon had gone up against the earnest protests of the chief signal officer in charge of it, under the command of Lieutenant Colonel Derby, an officer of the Engineer Corps.† The trail rope led directly down into the Aguadores road; it was a beautiful range marker

---

* See General Hawkins' official report, 1898, p. 164.
† See the official report of the chief signal officer, Brigadier General A. E. Greely, 1898.

for the Spanish artillery and infantry, and they promptly used it as such.

A note from the basket informed General Kent that Lieutenant Colonel Derby had discovered a break in the foliage indicating a trail that led to the San Juan River through the dense jungle on our left. This trail was at right angles to the Aguadores road, down which General Hawkins was proceeding to develop his assault. As this note was being read, the Seventy-first Regiment under our Colonel Downs was abreast of General Kent and following the Sixteenth Infantry.

Immediately General Kent detached the Seventy-first Infantry from Hawkins' brigade, without informing General Hawkins, and turned it into the jungle trail. Hawkins never knew what had become of one-third of his force, and he was stripped of troops for the holding attack which would enable him to flank the blockhouse! General Kent had added to his reluctance by dividing his force — a cardinal error in elementary tactics — and this on the fighting line while Hawkins' brigade was forming for assault on a battle plan agreed upon but a few moments before. The enemy on San Juan Hill was in unknown strength, and this suddenly revealed jungle trail was completely unmapped, unscouted, and unknown in all its factors. Meanwhile, the enemy had begun to pour a heavy fire into the Aguadores road, thanks to Lieutenant Colonel Derby's balloon and its trail rope.

The jungle trail into which we had been ordered was as narrow as a cowpath. On either side the undergrowth was laced together by vines and branches. The first battalion broke from a column of fours to a column of twos, and then into a column of files; and this slowed up the following companies. Outside, at the entrance of the trail, General Kent was wondering at the delay! Just before it was our company's turn to go in, three civilians left the road and started into the trail. One of them was J. Stuart Blackton of the Vitagraph Moving Picture Company, who was going to make a real picture of a real battle. His two men carried a black box about one-half the size of a steamer trunk. How far they got, I don't know, but in one minute they came out again. The balloon rope had given the Spaniards all the information they wanted, and they had concentrated all their fire power on that trail. Mr. Blackton was very wise to come out immediately; had he stayed in, his black-box camera would have become a sieve.

Then we went in, breaking into a column of files. We were aware of a coolness and a shadowy dimness freckled with sunshine. Yet this did not lessen the sense of those thin seething sounds that streaked through the jungle. We walked through a light shower of snipped-off twigs and leaves fluttering in lazy spirals to the ground. One instant your eye lighted on a twig and suddenly it was gone. It seemed that if one stuck out his hand the fingers would be clipped off. We huddled within ourselves and bent over to shield our bellies. Overhead, a shell burst — like the popping of a blown-up paper bag. Another shell burst lower, and

George Featherstone of my section caught a glancing fragment of iron that shattered his shoulder blade. He slumped into the brush and later made his way back to the field hospital. That shell, we heard, got twelve men, including George.

There was no panic. The men on the outer ring of the burst gave way and then closed up and went on. In places, the jungle grew across the trail, and we had to throw ourselves against the brush to get through. The head of the column reached the ford of the river. It had been ordered to advance to the river and then deploy! You could no more deploy a regiment through that vine-laced jungle than you could deploy them through a pile of fishnets. "Lie down," came the order; we would be less exposed. We lay down. "Forward!" We rose and closed up, crouching. Part of the regiment still extended out into the Aguadores road, where General Kent was standing. An order was shouted into the trail — no orderly could get through.

"General Kent directs Colonel Downs to advance as far as possible."

Battalion Adjutant Fisher, who was nearest to me, shouted it on. Other men were trying to pass it on, too; for it relieved our tension to help, even if the shouts only confused the message. "Shut up!" ordered Fisher.

Adjutant Abell shouldered his way down the trail.

"Colonel Downs's compliments, and please repeat the order," he yelled, and Adjutant Fisher relayed it. We could hear it echo its way back to the Aguadores road. And back came the order again:

"General Kent directs Colonel Downs to advance as far as possible!"

To this there was no reply. Colonel Downs, like General Hawkins, was on his own; and like Hawkins he did not know that General Kent had broken the plan of assault and deflected it into complete confusion.*

A regiment of the Second Brigade was jamming itself through the trail, and then came some of the Sixteenth Infantry's bandsmen. In battle, bandsmen followed a regiment and carried off the wounded. The band leader and the drum major were swearing earnestly. A soldier stumbled and dropped. His rifle fell from his hand. On the instant a bandsman darted forward, throwing his tenor horn into the brush. He grabbed the rifle and unbuckled the dead man's cartridge belt. It was this sort of thing that the drum major was swearing about — half the bandsmen had discarded their instruments and picked up rifles and cartridge belts.

"You hear me, pick up that goddamn horn! You hear me!"

The bandsman paid no attention.

"You pick up that goddam horn!" shrilled the drum major. "An' that's an order!"

The bandsman looked at him. "Not by a goddam-

---

* General Kent, later and as witness before a court of inquiry, stated: "I had virtually abandoned him [Colonel Downs of the Seventy-first Infantry] so far as I was concerned. That belonged to his brigade commander." *And Kent had detached Downs and his command from that same brigade commander!*

site, Dan," he said. "You think I'm agoin' to get shot at an' not shoot back!"

"Goddam!" ejaculated the drum major. He darted at another bandsman, who was unbuckling a cartridge belt from a soldier who had just been wounded — and who was helping him do it. The band had few instruments left; but for every missing horn or fife there was a Krag rifle and a belt of cartridges. A fortnight later I saw some of those instruments; they had bullet holes in them, they were dented and battered and roughly straightened out.

More men entered from the road, throwing their weight against the bushes to widen the trail. Officers were shouting at their companies, and sergeants were shouting at their sections. Here and there a man would sink to the ground and, often, crawl into the bushes.

Two Second Brigade regiments were now in the jungle passage — the Second Infantry with the Tenth Infantry on its heels. General Kent later complained in his report that he had had to send a staff officer back to hurry up this Second Brigade — the second order to hurry that he had given them.

The Twenty-first Infantry, the third and rear regiment of this Second Brigade, was directed along the Aguadores road to join General Hawkins.*

Three regiments were now in the trail, and it was jammed. Companies were mixed up. Officers and ser-

---

* That General Kent had blundered in breaking up Hawkins' brigade while it was forming for attack is obvious from his sending forward this regiment to try to make good his mistake.

geants were shouting to keep their units intact. "Company F — forward!" "Company C — here!" It was no march, it was a weaving, shuffling mass of men, crouching, halting, crouching again, and always pressing forward over the rough path of the trail. Now and again a man would seem to trip and then sink down, badly hit or killed. Another would give a sudden jerk and the rifle would fall from his grasp while he crowded into the jungle growth to get out of the way. Sometimes the men nearest would drag him aside, and go on in the press. I remember thinking that it was not like a battle as I had pictured it. Men did not get hit or die in a dramatic outspread of clutching hands and arms. They just sank down, crumpled and wilted, and lay still if dead, or crawled to one side. Here and there a man would limply drop. So few were hit, it seemed, in that press of regiments. I was struck by the fact that it seemed to happen so seldom. And those lightly wounded in an arm or leg would jerk and snap at it as though only stung by a hornet in some hayfield. It did not seem as if those seething bullets could miss so often and leave so many of us. And sometimes there would come the plop of a bursting shell from somewhere high in the jungle trees.

The flies buzzed through the bushes and the little birds chirped overhead as if it were an ordinary noontime. But through every minute my stomach was cold and clammy and rippled in little chills in time with my pulse. It was a comfort — almost — to bury one's nose in the rank vegetation of the jungle floor; anything to shrink in size. And then up again, crouching, to follow on. There was a company of Regulars alongside us whose captain was shouting: "F — F — dammit — F — keep together — forward — F — F!" He was captain of a Company F. Our company was F, too. Captain Rafferty straightened up. "F Company — forward!" he yelled. He merged in with the other F Company and we followed. Captain Goldsborough, of M Company, saw us move, and he followed. Company H joined in and we went forward with the Regulars. The trail was so thick with men that I found myself with M Company and with a couple of Ninth Infantrymen alongside. We were shoulder to shoulder and breast to back.

Just ahead of me a man stumbled and dropped, dead. We stepped over him. The man beside me lurched a little and sank down: "Je-e-sus!" he grunted. Four bullets had caught him between knee and thigh; he was a Company M man. Harry Carpenter, next to me, and I grabbed him and hauled him into the bushes, and went on, for somewhere ahead we could hear Captain Rafferty's voice shouting to his company: "Keep together, F — keep together!" Then the press of mixed soldiers closed in and I was in the M Company column. Captain Goldsborough was yelling too: "Close in — M Company — keep together!" Ahead and behind, all along the trail, captains were yelling the same thing. And we all jostled along together — three regiments of us in that one cowpath!

By now the trail was a little wider — it had been

trampled so. From beneath the broken bushes on both sides a pair of shoes stuck out; dead men. Just beyond a soldier was hunching himself back into the brush to get out of the way of the trampling feet. On this side another pair of boots stuck out, motionless. Beside me I heard a dull muffled *chonk,* and a man clutched his knee and grunted; I had heard the *chonk* of the bullet in the bone a fraction of an instant before the straight-line hiss of the bullet. Bullets travel ahead of their own sound; this gives conviction to the standard Army saying that you'll never hear the bullet that gets you. Harry Carpenter started to drag the wounded man into the bushes. We heard a command, hard and sharp. It was an officer: "Go on — go on!" he said. "Don't stop for wounded — get on — they'll be taken care of!"

Sitting beside the man who had just been shot was another man; his blue shirt was open and he had on a red undershirt. The officer glared at him. "What the hell you doing here?" he shouted. "Get on!" Impatiently he grabbed the man by the shoulder — there were scrimshankers in that trail too, unwounded men crawling aside for safety — and the man screamed. His undershirt was soaked red with blood from a wound in the shoulder. "Sorry!" said the officer. "Sorry, old man."

Even in this slight delay there were men that had crowded between us and our company. Again we were pressing forward. There were more motionless shoes sticking out of the brush on either side. Here there was a little glade, a tiny open spot in the jungle. It was lined with wounded, who stared at us dully. Sprawled on his back, his shirt open, was a young officer fresh from West Point. His glazed eyes were staring at the trees overhead and ants were already crawling over his eyeballs. The open shirt revealed a yellow silk undershirt, with a little bloody stain in its breast. And in that little glade, no bigger than a hall bedroom, was a Regular Army major. Where his battalion was, he did not know or care. He was half shouting and half sobbing with hysteria. The body of that young lieutenant, staring, sprawling, had filled the major's blotted mind, and nothing else mattered. Yet it was not the death; it was the lack of respect for an officer that disturbed him.

"Cover him up — goddammit, cover him up," he was shrilling hoarsely. "He's an officer, goddammit, cover him up — he's an officer!" He wrung his hands in despair over the indignity. "Cover him up — he's an officer!"

He plucked at a passing soldier, who shook him off; he plucked at the man next to me. "Somebody cover him up — he's an officer." It was almost a chant. The man next to me, a Regular, flung him off.

"Cover him up yourself, you sonofabitch!"

The major gave no sign of having heard him, and kept up the hysterical chant.

From ahead we could hear more distinctly the sound of our own rifle fire, and the faint popping of the Spanish rifles beyond. Off to the right there was a heavier volume of fire, irregular, but heavy. Was it ours? Through the tunnel of our jungle trail we could see the water of the creek. Beyond, we could hear the louder reports of our own men who had already crossed the ford and were sheltered by a little bank back from the farther shore. But these were only glimpses; where we were was a crowded mob of men pressing steadily forward. My foot slipped, and I looked down. The trail underfoot was slippery with mud. It was a mud made by the blood of the dead and wounded, for there had been no showers that day. The trail on either side was lined with the feet of fallen men and the sprawled arms of those who could not quite make it.

This was Bloody Ford.

Because Lieutenant Colonel Derby's balloon had told the Spaniards we were in that cowpath, they turned all they had upon it and its approach. Over four hundred men were killed or wounded in that trail and at that ford, in an area that was, perhaps, a city block in length — some eight hundred feet — in a path not as wide as a city sidewalk.

From somewhere across the jungle there came a sudden burst of rapid fire. It was our four Gatlings, under Lieutenant Parker of the Thirteenth Infantry, and came from the direction where General Hawkins and his two regiments were. Then we heard from that same point a cheer, distant but distinct. The cheer spread to the ford. Back in the trail men heard it and cheered too. They didn't know what they were cheering, nor did we, but it was something to do and it relieved the tension. As if a cork had been pulled from a bottle, the ford was crossed and the pressure on the men still in the trail eased. An army of men, companies, squads, and sections of all the regiments in the division were pushing, ducking, and running to scramble up a hill as steep as a railroad cut to join those men of the Sixth and Sixteenth — Hawkins' men — who were already there.

With two regiments of his brigade Hawkins had done what had been planned for three.

The San Juan blockhouse immediately after capture.

Dinnertime on Misery Hill

17

Brigadier General Hawkins the spearhead at San Juan.
Lieutenant Ord leads the charge that captures San Juan.
Ord dies on the crest. The Gatlings.

BACK on the Aguadores road that morning the dismounted cavalry and Rough Riders had been abreast of us for a time, and then pushed on ahead. Acting as infantry, they were to go ahead and clear out any Spanish outposts that might have been set out. They went past the point where Generals Kent and Hawkins would view the blockhouse on San Juan Hill and where Lieutenant Colonel Miley would order the assault. The Spaniards had established a strong outpost on Kettle Hill, a small hill that would flank any troops coming down the Aguadores road and past the ford. The cavalry and Rough Riders took Kettle Hill with a rush which brought them beyond the blockhouse and fronting on the San Juan ridge. While little has been written about it, the Ninth and Tenth Cavalry, Negro units, were in the brigade with the Rough Riders and shared in the attack and capture. Had this outpost not been first destroyed it would have enfiladed General Hawkins' brigade before the attack on San Juan blockhouse could have been formed. It was strong support for that hill.

General Hawkins later told me the dilemma General Kent had forced upon him by detaching one-third of this brigade while it was under heavy fire and forming for the attack. I was in Switzerland, on the terrace in Lausanne, when I met General Hawkins two years after the war. The general was interested in the experiences of a private in his brigade, who had been in that tragic trail and at Bloody Ford, and I was keenly interested in the fight from the angle of my commanding general. The injustice was as fresh in his courtly mind as it was in mine. What I have written about General Hawkins is on the authority of his own description. It was he who told me of Lieutenant Ord.

"The fire," said General Hawkins, "was heavy — as heavy and, I think, heavier than any in the Civil War — at least in any of the engagements I was in. We could not go back into that jammed Aguadores road. The attack had been approved by General Kent. My brigade was to make the assault with my first two regiments of regulars; the Seventy-first was to make a direct and holding attack so we could outflank the Spaniards, perhaps. But the Seventh-first had been deflected and was entirely beyond my control. No messenger or orderly reached me. I did not even know where it was. It had disappeared by General Kent's order."

Lieutenant Ord was on General Hawkins' staff. He

was the brigade quartermaster who had issued us the
sowbelly, hardtack, sugar, and salt and pepper the
night before. We knew him; he was easy to know. He
had joked with the details as they arrived for rations
and as they left. He was one of those men who fit in
anywhere. Lieutenant Ord was with General Hawkins
as they crossed the ford and waited for word of the
deflected regiment that was to open the assault on
San Juan Hill. Hawkins was ready to put his two regiments in movement, but he wanted a covering fire to
mislead the Spaniards.

There was some cover on this fringe of the jungle,
but the Spaniards knew they were there and were
pouring in a heavy fire. General Hawkins realized that
something had happened and that he was on his own.
To order a charge across that open scrubby plain,
unprepared by preliminary artillery, and with but little
more than one-half his brigade would be a desperate
tactic. But he had been left in a desperate situation.
It was a crisis — and a crisis is often measured in less
than minutes. Lieutenant Ord knew what was going on
in the general's mind, and he spoke:

"General, if you will order a charge I will lead it."

Against that fire, with but a fraction of a brigade,
and with no knowledge of the strength of the Spaniards in the trenches of the Hill or reserved under the
shelter beyond! The military lessons of Pickett's
charge at Gettysburg were history; not enough men
reached the Union lines to capture them. Around General Hawkins wounded men were crawling through the

brush, every minute more would be counted. It was then that he heard the drumming of Lieutenant Parker's Gatlings and could see the dust spurting in sudden jets upon the Hill as the guns sprayed it.

Lieutenant Ord spoke again.

"If you do not wish to order a charge, General," he said, "I should like to volunteer. May I volunteer? We can't stay here, can we?"

"I would not ask any man to volunteer," said General Hawkins gravely.

"If you do not forbid it," said Ord, "I will start it."

General Hawkins listened to the drumming of the Gatlings. (Two of them were later to jam or burn out with the rapidity of their fire.) The fringe of dust lined the Hill in front of the blockhouse, and the Spanish fire seemed to have slackened. The Gatlings were doing it!

"I only ask you, General, not to refuse permission," added Ord.

"I will not ask for volunteers," said General Hawkins. "I will not give permission and I will not refuse it. God bless you and good luck!"

Lieutenant Ord jumped forward from the brush in a running crouch with his saber in one hand and his pistol in the other.

"Come on — come on, you fellows!" he yelled. "Come on — we can't stop here!"

In the next instant the scraggly undergrowth burst in a ragged fringe of blue-shirted men, crouching and running, with Ord in the lead. There went up what the academic histories call a cheer, but it was nothing more than a hoarse scream of relief from scores of men and the yell that soldiers give those whom they wish to honor. It was Hawkins' brigade, its two regiments, the Sixth and Sixteenth running in a pack, unleashed from the jungle, and hell-bent for the red-tiled roof that crowned San Juan Hill. It was a running spearhead. There was no nice order, no neatly formed companies crossing that plain or mounting the slope. It was more like a football field when the game is over and a mess of people are straggling across it, except that these men were on the run, yelling, and with no time to lose. At their head, Lieutenant Ord, in the lead, scrambled up the steep hill.

The Gatlings stopped firing when the charge neared the crest. As a matter of fact — wholly unknown until the charge revealed it — the Spaniards had constructed their trenches on the actual crest of the Hill instead of at the military crest; the military crest is the hip-roof angle of a hill, or the rim where troops may fire down on the enemy as he reaches the foot, which cannot be done if the trench is dug at the actual crest. Thus, when our men were at the foot of the Hill, the Spaniards were unable to see them, and from the base to the military crest Lieutenant Ord and his men were as safe as if they had been back in Siboney. From the military crest to the actual crest was but twenty to thirty feet and no charge can be stopped within such a distance.

Thus it was that there were no casualties once the climb had begun. The rush over the military crest was swift. The Spaniards were already leaving — those that could. Lieutenant Ord, in the lead, jumped over the trench and, as he did so, a wounded Spaniard shot from below and Ord's hat flew off. He landed in a crumpled heap and lay still, dead. That evening I met two men who claimed to have killed the Spaniard. One showed me the bloody butt of his carbine with pride. Ord, Ord, that evening the name ran along the trenches that we had captured. All the Sixth and the Sixteenth knew it; he was the man.

That afternoon, on the heels of the charge and the capture, General Hawkins was on San Juan Hill and looking over to the city of Santiago whose tile roofs could be seen in the distance. For the Hill was the military key to Santiago. Later that afternoon General Hawkins was wounded. And, one week later, General Kent reported that General Hawkins' regiments had not taken San Juan Hill alone but had assisted along with the regiments that General Kent had deflected into the useless trail of Lieutenant Colonel Derby! He would have been called a liar to his face if he had made that statement that evening on the Hill. And by men who knew.*

From our trail in the jungle we had heard the drumming of the Gatlings and the cheering, in which we had

---

* General Hawkins said we could hold the Hill too. He did not know then that General Kent would vote for retreat the next evening, July 2nd.

joined. We had heard the Gatlings stop — though we could not know that it was for fear lest they hit Ord's men. We could hear the shouts ahead and from our right, "Cease fire — cease fire!" though there had been little firing from our side; there was a bare hill with men in trenches, and but little to shoot at. Bugles took up the call to cease fire.

Harry Carpenter and I went up with M Company. We were not the only strangers in it — there were Regulars and cavalry and men from other companies in our regiment. Men reported to Captain Goldsborough or to Lieutenant Hutchinson. "I'm here, Captain, don't forget me." "Say, Lieutenant, I'm here." It was a precaution against any charge of hiding in the bushes.

We were at the ford. A wounded man was wading ashore. We waded across; it was knee deep, sometimes a little more. The current was sluggish. We went into it under an arch of bamboos and had a full view of the blockhouse on the Hill, with nothing but some coarse grass and little bushes between us and the beginning of the ascent; it was, perhaps, 120 feet high. On the far bank of the creek a log had fallen into the stream and across it two bodies were lying, their feet in the current on one side and their heads half covered on the other with the current rippling across their ears. A bullet smacked into the water as we waded, but it was only a stray, for there was very little fire now and that was chiefly from some jungled hills ahead and on the left flank of the hill. It could not have been an aimed shot, for the jungle was too dense.

It was just one of those that were poured in, as from a machine gun, as — in all likelihood — had been those that turned on us in the trail.

Beyond the ford there was another little bank that marked the narrow river's brim during high water. Against this were the wounded and dead of the men who had crossed and done the shooting that we had heard back in the trail. Men were wading in a steady flow across the ford. On the far bank officers were trying to get them into commands and sending them on up San Juan Hill. Formation was secondary to getting them up there. It was here that Colonel Wikoff, commander of the Third Brigade, was wounded. He died on the way to the field hospital. His men had found an abandoned Spanish chair, and he was placed in that and carried back. We passed him. He was conscious and waved to our company feebly. He spoke: "Get on up, boys, they need you — hurry!" His head drooped weakly on his chest.

Captain Goldsborough had a fair-sized company and more, with the additions of men lost from other commands. Halfway across the plain he halted us; for we had been marching more than raggedly. "Right dress!" he ordered. We right-dressed. "Front!" We fronted. "Count off!" We counted off in fours. "Forward, guide right — march!" And we went to the foot of the hill in perfect order as prescribed by regulations. This, I wish to say, was under fire — for we had not yet reached the shelter of the Hill and the Spaniards were firing in from somewhere on the left.

To tell the truth, it was a very ineffective fire and high overhead. But I cannot forbear the mild boast that I am probably among the rare group of men who under fire have dressed ranks, counted off, and supplemented a charge in a formation that was nicely dressed to the right. I have often chuckled over this, for Goldsborough was a good captain in more ways than one.

In the shadow of the Hill the formation was lost. San Juan Hill was steep — the Ninth Infantry camped on it a few days later, and the men had to cut terraces to hold their dog tents; from each terrace to the next they built steps revetted with saplings or logs — and we scrambled up diagonally and clutched at tufts of the coarse grass for handholds, sometimes kicking a foothold in order to make the next step. It is no discredit to the men of Hawkins' two regiments, or to Lieutenant Ord, to say that San Juan Hill was defended by brave Spaniards and thoroughly incompetent Spanish military engineers.

Just under the crest of the Hill we halted. It was entirely safe there. But above that crest the Spanish bullets were coming like hail in driving gusts.

We looked down; not a body lay on the slope. No one had been hit on that climb. Along the ridge below there were a few wounded men, not badly hurt. Here and there a few casualties were making their way back to the ford. Coming up from the plain was a steady flow of men in little groups, or singly.

We knew where the battle front was at last.

18

On the Hill. Will the Spaniards return? "Everyone under cover!" We cover a withdrawal and lose twenty men. We sleep in ranks, and then dig all night. Our stragglers.

ABOVE the crest of the hill we could see the feathery tops of the palm trees scattering through the distance. We could see the blockhouse but a few paces off, its walls pockmarked from our rifles and Gatlings. The trodden yellow clay stretched before it and, hot in the sun, still glistened in a few places with dark splotches of blood.

A dead Spanish soldier lay slantwise before us, and beside him was his weatherbeaten straw hat. Next to us was an irregular line of other soldiers. There were no lines of companies, other than Captain Goldsborough's, which we had just left. It was a mixed lot from various regiments and companies. There was an orderly confusion but no excitement; it was as if there were a lot of men on the job, all waiting for a foreman to blow the whistle. Below the crest, the slope was thick with men. There were officers in plenty, and every man was ready to follow the nearest one. Though we lacked formation, we were under perfect control. We had the Hill; no orders were necessary, and there was no wild shouting.

Overhead the Spanish bullets drove like gusts of sleet, but we were safe below the crest. Our men returned the fire whenever they saw an enemy figure running from bush to bush in the distance.

Somewhere under the same crest was Captain Rafferty and our company.

"You," called Captain Goldsborough, indicating Harry and myself. "You two get out and find your own outfit. It's somewhere about."

Harry and I left. We crawled on to the top of the Hill and looked over. We had become more used to the bullets and their noise, and we could tell when they were farther off. And we were curious.

Now we could see the blockhouse close up, its stucco walls yellow in the hot midday sun. The red-tile roof had a huge ragged hole in its center where one of our shells had burst. The few little windows that faced us were loosely boarded up, with cracks left between the boards for loopholes. The blockhouse had been the suburban home of a wealthy Cuban or Spaniard who had chosen it for the superb view of the surrounding mountains and the city of Santiago. The earth had been banked window-high against the blockhouse and was held in place by poorly made revetments of saplings. On the left side of the building was the main doorway, from which an officer would emerge now and then and scan the terrain toward Santiago through his field glasses. Above the hole in the roof was a crudely made cupola or watchtower from which the Spanish had surveyed our approach and spotted the trail rope and its balloon.

A few steps to the left of the blockhouse was a corrugated iron-roofed shed, which apparently had been a sort of open-air mess hall, for there were two great iron pots against which a door had been propped. One pot was full of beans and still warm. We had been warned not to eat any food that we came across. Just beyond the shed, two dead Spaniards sprawled in their thin, blue-and-white pin-striped uniform — like pajamas to us — half covering the Mauser rifles beneath them.

One of our officers stepped out of the doorway and raised his field glasses, then turned his head to speak to someone inside. Then he crumpled. Two officers rushed out and carried him into the blockhouse. Later we heard that he was Colonel Mills, who subsequently became the commandant at West Point.

From under that mess-hall shed some of our men were calmly shooting with steady aim. They were using the door between the iron pots as a breastwork, shooting over it or across the overturned table. One man dropped, crouched, and, still crouching, ran to the rear and was lost to sight below the crest. A few yards from where Harry and I were watching, a soldier jumped up, crouched, and ran forward to the place behind the door where the wounded man had been. A few moments later another man behind the door crumpled and lay still. On the instant a soldier beside me darted forward, pushed the body aside, and began firing.

Harry and I looked at each other. We both felt we must pay for our curiosity. There was no bravado — Harry was not that type — and my feeling was that this was a part of the job. We knew that no one would order us — no one had ordered those other men.

Harry looked at me and said: "What the hell did we come here for! I'm going up next."

I believe I nodded. After only a few more seconds another man dropped. Up went Harry, crouching. Another man collapsed and crawled to one side. Now it was my turn. I crouched — so low I could have run through a drainpipe — and ran. It seemed an interminable distance to that door. It was as if I were running in molasses. I got there and shoved in. Harry was down at the other end of the door.

"What range?" I asked the man next to me as he was loading his magazine.

"Set her three hundred — any range is good — they're behind the bushes yonder — you'll see 'em run now and again — shoot the bushes."

Even as he spoke a jet of blood shot out of his neck, a spout the size of a lead pencil. He dropped his rifle and clapped his hand over it. The jet stopped; but the blood came through his fingers in steady, pulsating gushes. He half rose and began running back for the shelter. He didn't make it. In a moment his body was limply sprawled on the trodden clay, drained of blood, and dead.

Another man was beside me, loading. "What's the range?" he asked.

"At the bushes," I answered. "Any range — you'll see 'em run — shoot the bushes."

It was at this point that an officer jumped out from the doorway of the blockhouse. Another officer just before him had slumped over.

"Get back! Get back!" He pointed to the rear of the blockhouse. "You goddam fools aren't doing any good. Get back. They'll be coming back and we'll need you then. Get back!"

Take my word for it there were some who got up reluctantly to run to the rear of the blockhouse. I was not one of them. I think I got there first. Then we went back and under the shelter of the hill; the shed was left vacant except for the two dead who stayed there.

Behind the blockhouse there were dead and wounded as well as whole men like Harry and me. There were officers who talked about the Spaniards' counter-attack, and when it would come. A medical-corps man was shouting down the hill for a stretcher bearer, and none came; there was enough for them to do at Bloody Ford. A sergeant was breaking open a box of ammunition with a rock and his bayonet. Two others were slowly climbing up, each with a box that held a thousand rounds. The sergeant called: "Count your belts. How many you want?" Many men had not fired a single shot. One called out: "Twenty-eight, Sergeant." The sergeant flung him a box of twenty-five. It was the highest number called out; he was a Regular, a sharpshooter. Few men asked for more than ten or twelve. For these the sergeant threw over a box. "Divide 'em between," he said.

This hill and ridge of San Juan was the key to Santiago. The Spaniards could not afford to let us hold it. Yet no counterattack came! It was less than a mile to the first lanes of straggling, red-roofed houses of the city. It was two miles to the water front of the bay where lay Admiral Cervera's Spanish fleet. We were within range of his guns, and later we were under fire of a six-inch naval gun, or perhaps two, that had been put ashore. But this was to be a week later when we were in the trenches of Misery Hill over a mile to the right of the blockhouse.

To the right of us Sumner's cavalry and the Rough Riders had paralleled the charge on the blockhouse and captured the trenches. Bates's division had extended to the left. Had we men enough to hold the Hill? It was an officer's worry, not ours. We had no doubts, then or later. Down below, in the plain we had crossed, more men were straggling across and climbing the Hill. There was little order, but there were plenty of men.

Harry and I lay there under the crest behind the blockhouse. From time to time we peeked over and scanned the area to the right and left, looking for

Rafferty and our company. To the right of us was a skimpy, almost leafless tree; it had been in the direct line of our Gatlings. In it a bird held its headquarters, a small, excited, indignant bird. It fluttered about and chirped angrily as the Mauser bullets zipped by, and tried to chase them as if they were insects. Yet, occasionally, the bird would perch on a branch of the skimpy little tree and sing! I have read, since then, that a singing bird is chanting its war cry; so perhaps this one was hurling his sturdy defiance at the Spanish bullets.

It was then that we spied Captain Rafferty and our company just below and slightly to the right of the blockhouse. We reported. As I spoke to the captain, close to him, a bullet brushed between us, its wind fanning our cheeks. He ducked, and so did I. Squatting, the captain laughed.

"No use ducking 'em," he said. "You'll never hear the one that gets you!"

When a man gets that feeling, he is a veteran. Duck one and into another! If your number is up, ducking won't do any good. That night, taking stock of the day, I realized that the captain had made a veteran of me; I could not remember ducking after that moment. With Harry and Jimmy and the others, it seemed to be the same. Later, when we were in the trenches, no one ducked. Two days later, when we changed reliefs in the trenches to the right of the blockhouse, we had a run in the open of about 100 feet. The reliefs passed each other and no one ducked.

The officers had to swear at the men to get them out of a mere trot. And this time, I can admit, everyone was guilty of bravado.

As the captain and I rose up, another man came up to report. He was shaking, almost crying. The trail, the wounded, the Bloody Ford with its dead, and the steady seething of Mauser bullets had got him. He was slavering and his jaws were chattering. He was on the verge of a break and he knew it.

"Captain," he said with shaking voice, "I can't go on — I can't go on — I can't —" It was becoming almost singsong.

"Steady, boy, steady," said the captain. "Stick it!"

"I can't, Captain — I can't —" The voice was sobbing and the eyes staring without seeing. "I can't stand it — I can't stand it — for God's sake send me back to the hospital corps — I can't go on — I'll break, goddammit, I'll break — I'll break —"

"All right," said the captain. "Sergeant, he's detailed to the hospital corps."

Even before the captain finished, the man was halfway down the hill in plunging leaps from clump to clump. The reaction of the rest of the men in the company who heard this was of interest. Some said it took nerve to say you haven't got nerve, and it was to be respected. Most said, "Well, he couldn't take it, goddam!" There are many obscure factors that make for the persistent pride which keeps one going the tougher it gets. Courage, perhaps, is nothing more than a willful pride that is too proud to act ignobly,

much as it may envy it. Incidentally, this was the man
who later was sentenced to a life term in Dannemora
Prison for homicide. He was the one who had been
so dangerously drunk back in the yards at Long Island
City.

General Hawkins had come up on the heels of Lieutenant Ord's charge. He was near our company, a slender, well-built man with a white goatee and mustache,
vigorous and with no sign of age.

The Hill had been ours for, perhaps, half an hour
to an hour. Captain Best's field battery, the First
Field Artillery, of four 4.2-inch guns had come up and
taken a position somewhat to the north, or right, of
the blockhouse, where there was an open view to Santiago and the Spanish trenches in the distance —
about fifteen hundred yards away. Best fired a few
shots, and seeing the billows of white smoke, the Spaniards turned everything in his direction. This was at
about 2 P.M. Somewhere in the outskirts of Santiago
a five-inch naval gun began to fire. If the Spanish
counterattacked we could not afford to lose a battery
of artillery — we only had four of them in the whole
Fifth Army Corps. So Best decided to withdraw his
guns. But he could not bring up his horses in the heavy
fire, for they too were scarce and could not be risked.
So he asked General Hawkins for infantry support so
that, under its cover, he could withdraw the guns by
hand while his horses waited under the shelter of San
Juan ridge.

"Nearest me," General Hawkins told me later,

"were F and M Companies of the Seventy-first Infantry. They were the first companies to arrive on the Hill in formation, after the capture. I sent them over to windward of the battery to open fire. They provided rifle fire and a smoke screen behind which the battery was withdrawn by the cannoneers. Company H of the Seventy-first was the supporting line for F and M."

In company front, shoulder to shoulder, F and M doubled down to the barbed-wire fence that was to have protected the flank of the blockhouse. The wind was coming from the left. We opened rapid fire as we dropped to the ground slightly in advance of the battery on our right. It was the last action in which American troops went into battle in close order. With the first blast from our black-powder .45-70 Springfields, the front was clouded in an instantaneous white fog of smoke. Captain Goldsborough of M, as well as Captain Rafferty, stood upright behind the lines of their prone companies. Perhaps we were there three minutes, perhaps five. The first blast of smoke obscured everything and, from that one on, we fired through the haze at where we remembered the distant Spanish trenches had been. You jammed a cartridge in, snapped the butt of the Springfield hard against your shoulder — for the recoil was like a hurled brick — and pulled the trigger. The Spaniards instantly turned all they had into our cloud of smoke, including their Maxim machine guns. We heard no sound of bullets. The crack and bang of our Springfields drowned out all other sounds.

The man beside me quivered and his head dropped over the stock of his rifle; it was Frank Booth, dead, with a hole above his eye. He was an only son, an only child, we knew. On the run to the barbed wire my corporal, round-faced Corporal Scheid, was drilled through the stomach. He never had a chance to fire a shot. He died that night in the field hospital, and how he got back there no one knows. We heard that he and Jesse Pohalski, who was shot through the foot, had helped each other. F Company had one man killed and nine wounded in those few minutes at the barbed wire; M Company lost four killed and ten wounded at the same time. One hundred and twenty-five men went over in those two companies to that barbed wire, and twenty-four were casualties; over five a minute. It was a twenty per cent casualty list — and the books say that a ten per cent casualty is the point at which demoralization sets in. Then, by whistle, we withdrew; the battery had been withdrawn under the cover we made.

The battery? It lost one man, Sergeant McCarthy, who was killed just as the guns were being wheeled back by hand.

Back again under the crest of the hill! How safe it seemed. There were plenty of bullets whizzing by high overhead. Below, men were still streaming across the plain. They were mostly in company formation now. On the slope men were beginning to find their companies; we were getting organized. A field dressing station was established below us; wounded men trickled

into it and stretchers began to bring men in from behind the blockhouse. Assistant Surgeon Harry Stafford of our regiment was one of the surgeons up here
on the fighting line and I saw the hospital corps' Sergeant Froelich with him. One of the big sole-leather
surgical trunks, a big Red Cross on either end, had
been carried up.

Many soldiers had been issued first-aid packets, each
packet holding a small bandage and a big bandage that
might act as a sling for an arm or shoulder. The big
bandage had pictures all over it showing how it could
be used for different wounds.

Men died at that dressing station and were laid out
just beyond the ragged shade of a small tree. Other
casualties sat about and waited their turn for a field
dressing, or for a stretcher to take them farther back
to the field hospital. Those that could — the surgeon
made the decision — were told to go on back under
their own power. Some ambulances were reported to
be at Hell's Pocket, the ford where Hawkins' Sixth
and Sixteenth infantries had crossed the San Juan
River; at Bloody Ford the trail was too narrow for
them. And here, back at the field hospital, those cases
that were thought to be fatal were laid out under a
tree. Most of them died. Each wounded man who
reached the field dressing station had a small red-
white-and-blue tag hooked onto him by a piece of copper wire through his shirt; on it was a hasty diagnosis
to guide the field hospital. And, because the men laid
out to die wore these tags, the rumor spread that if

they tagged you, you were a goner! It was not true; but it gave many a wounded man a causeless funk.

One of the men of my squad, Earle Hall, an undertaker, had been hit. The Mauser bullet went in among his left ribs and came out below his right shoulder. It missed his heart, and that was about all. He got back to the field hospital and was laid out under the shade to die. But on the morning of July 2nd, Hall was still alive. A couple of surgeons passed by at dawn looking for the possibilities among these desperate cases. One of them bent over Hall. The other surgeon shook his head in negation. "Not a chance," he said. Hall, still conscious, heard him. "You're a goddamn liar!" he said. "I ain't going to die." And he didn't.

They put him aboard a springless baggage wagon that morning for the trip back to Siboney over rutted roads. Grass and palm leaves made a bed on the bottom of the wagon body and on this the wounded lay and grunted or occasionally screamed. Nine miles of agony; there were few ambulances, and those were for officers.

Two weeks later Hall was on a hospital ship on his way back to the States. He was bent over from his wound but was well enough to be assigned to "light duty"!

It was our army's first experience with the high-velocity Mauser bullets that burned like a cautery as they went through and left but a tiny puncture. In the Civil War, and earlier, a half-inch lead bullet hit like a brick and left a ragged path of shattered human tissue.

Under the safe crest of that hill we rested, as the incidents since dawn churned through our minds. We were tired. The sun mellowed into gold with violet shadows as evening came, and the rolling hills beyond us were lovely in the lavender distance.

Down at the front-line dressing station a man was having his shattered leg bone put in splints; the splints were palm fronds. Another, shot through the shoulder and naked to the waist, was gritting his teeth and saying, "Je-jesus Christ — go ahead, Doc — Je-esus Christ!" Two dead lay near him. Just beyond, another was dying — his first-aid bandage, over his face, was drenched with blood. He gasped in heavy, convulsive jerks that shook his body. I stopped a moment; a hospital man passed. "Goner," he said briefly. "Nothing to do." The man was unconscious, but alive.

Little columns of fours were climbing the hill. To our right were the Rough Riders. They mounted their private machine gun and dynamite gun in the trenches and called it Fort Roosevelt. There has never been any claim that these weapons were fired in anger against the Spaniards, or ever fired at all. The Rough Riders were the supreme of the élite; no regiment has ever received the newspaper space that was devoted to them. They were good men — make no mistake about that, even if some did admit it easily — and they could man the trenches or a cotillion with intrepidity. In addition to having Teddy as its second in command, this regiment had its own press agent in Richard Harding Davis, to whom the human beings not listed in the *Social Register* were merely varied forms of pollution.

Ammunition began coming up. I counted my belt. Eight cartridges were gone — few had more. The sun sank in molten copper beyond the western hills in the afterglow of evening, and, suddenly, as if a factory whistle had blown, the Spanish fire ceased. The sporadic crackle of our rifles stopped except for a lonely sharpshooter here and there until the bugles blew the formal "Cease fire!" Rapidly, the glowing sky darkened from a shimmering blue to green, to violet, and then to the velvet purple of dusk. The day of the battle was closed.

In the gathering dusk, officers walked down the front and marked off the trench we were to dig. But there were no shovels or picks. Captain Rafferty lined up the company and we counted off in fours. "In place," he said, "rest. Lie down, sleep, but do not lose your place in line — be ready and in formation." A water detail went down to the ford with his section's canteens; most canteens were empty, we had drunk them dry.

It was my luck to be next to a dead Spaniard, perhaps an officer; where his insignia should have been was a ragged gash. Souvenir hunters had been there already. His pockets were already inside out. His body was right between Harry Carpenter and myself as we lay down in the rank. He was inconvenient, for his arms sprawled out, and his legs too. It would have been easy to drag him out of the way, but we were tired. For two days we had been on outpost, and then this third day in battle and under fire since dawn. We debated the matter. Then, with one accord we shoved his arms and legs together and lay down and slept beside him. At least we thought we would sleep.

Sleep? We could not. Stray men passed up and down the line of the crest looking for their commands and asking who we were and what regiment. Cavalrymen, Rough Riders, Regulars, infantrymen. The jumble and mixture of the day was getting straightened out. One man was looking for his bunkie, a bugler. ("Bunkie" was the army term for "pal," in those days. To me "buddy" sounds the same, but with a cold in the head.)

"He had a gold bugle, too — he was good," the man explained. Later he found him, dead. But the bugle was missing.

Another came down the line looking for his bunkie. "He won five hundred dollars coming down on the transport," he explained. Later he passed back. "Yeah, I found him. Not a cent on him," he said. Another case was similar: a barber who had the regimental trade on the transport. He had made $250, net, but was dead without a cent when he was found. I would have been but a poor prize for any souvenir hunter. My pockets would not have tinkled — a single quarter cannot jingle by itself. And the pockets of Jimmy Lowe, my bunkie, were wholly empty!

It was about ten o'clock that night that the shovels and picks arrived. The whole line of the crest, disappearing into the darkness on either side, was one long line of rapid-fire digging. Ten minutes of furious digging and the men jumped up and out, and the next man caught the shovel on the fly and fell to. The earth was soft and crumbly on top, then it was a soft clay that cut like cheese. Picks were hardly needed. By dawn the trench was three feet deep with the banked earth in front. And as the flush of dawn spread over the distant red roofs of Santiago, the Spanish fire commenced. They saw our line of trenches with the new earth bright in the daylight.

It was the last of the digging on those trenches. Under the sun the soft clay hardened into earthenware; even a pick could only chip off little pieces. But shallow though they were, they gave adequate protection. And then came good news, by regimental order.

"All companies that have been digging trenches," announced Captain Rafferty, "have a rest of twenty-four hours from duty. You will rest in formation, your rifle always with you, and be ready for any attack."

We slept. The broad daylight did not bother us.

Later we sent a detail back and brought up our haversacks with their Japanese-coolie beef and the hardtack. And we were so hungry that for once these rations tasted good. No fires were allowed, for we were on the fighting line just below the crest. It was a grand day. At our age, recuperation was rapid. From above the crest came the varying spatters of Mauser bullets and the occasional bang by one of our sharpshooters. We watched a tall palm above the line of our company. Now and again there would come a tiny burst of pulp and sap where a Mauser bullet shot through the tree, and we could hear the *spat* as it struck and the *whuz-z-z* as it went on its way.

We had stragglers — every regiment had them. Two of ours came up. They reported to the captain.

"Well," he demanded, "where you been?"

"We been in the fighting, Captain."

"Yessir!" said the other.

"Where?" asked the captain.

"Over there, Captain, over there." They pointed to the left of the blockhouse.

"We was with the Rough Riders!" said the first. The other nodded. "Yessir, with the Rough Riders, Captain. We just left them — trying to find our company, Captain — we got lost so we went with the Rough Riders. We just left 'em."

"Where are the Rough Riders now?" asked the captain with interest.

"Over there, Captain — we just left 'em." They pointed to the left of the blockhouse.

The captain laughed, angrily. "You lying bastards," he said. "The Rough Riders are on our right!" The whole company line broke into a jeer, for we knew these men. They had been skulking in the bushes back in the trail.

Another straggler was a sergeant. He had not gone over the crest and down to the barbed-wire fence, but had turned yellow and welched. Someone had stepped on him and hurt his back. All day he had lain there with an occasional dramatic moan. Someone noticed that every time a noisy bullet seethed overhead or *whuz-z-zd* out of the palm that the sergeant perceptibly cringed. He was a mean little man, and we had despised him for weeks. He was fair game now. Someone imitated the noise of a bullet. It was a good imitation, and the sergeant cringed. Someone else tried it and added a pebble for realism. The company laughed. There was no mercy. It became a game; the pebbles grew larger. One as big as a man's fist bounced off him.

The captain walked over to the sergeant and touched him with the toe of his boot.

"Get up, you."

"I can't, Captain — I can't —" wailed the sergeant. "Someone stepped on me back — me back, oh, me back!"

"Are you going to get up and walk, or not?" demanded the captain.

"Oh, me back — ah, Captain —" said the sergeant.

"Get up — or get to the rear — reduced."

"I want to stick by th' boys, Captain — me poor back," the man was whimpering.

"Get up! Go to the rear."

"Me back, Captain —"

"Shut up," retorted the captain. "And get the hell out of here."

The sergeant rose slowly. He looked down the line

of the company, and did not see one friend. A smile of hatred crept over his lips, in which there was a suggestion of leering triumph. He walked down that rugged hill as easily as a man ever walked. He was safe. We jeered him in sounds and words that are common soldier vocabulary, and we prefaced every word with "yellow" and "yellow-backed"; thus there was no misunderstanding.

"Shut up," said the captain to us, and paused. "Good riddance," he added.

We grinned back. He was a fine captain.

The day passed slowly. We envied the men beyond the crest who were in the trenches we had dug. They at least could see something even if it was only the distant roofs.

Our twenty-four hours of rest had become boring.

19

Our errors in strategy. The blunder of Bloody Ford. Casualties at Bloody Ford reach four hundred. General Kent votes for retreat!

THUS it was with us on the fighting line. But no memory of that campaign should ignore the strategy of the higher planning. We were not all privates; there were generals too.

We privates knew that, somewhere, there were those who had given the orders that sent us into Bloody Ford and Hell's Pocket. Of course we knew that President McKinley had, in a manner of speaking, declared war on Spain for the sinking of the *Maine*. We knew that Major General William R. Shafter commanded our army of invasion. But all this was abstract and impersonal. It was all swept up in the chills-and-fever of invasion, of going into battle, of being on a fighting line, of pressing forward where there was more death, where the little twigs were snapping off more briskly, where we bent low to protect our bellies, and where every human urge was to stay intact. We knew vaguely that we were part of a plan, a strategy, a planned assault forged in the minds of the high ranks. But, primarily, we also knew that our business was to get killed in killing Spaniards. Later we would become historic statistics.

Two years later, when I had that memorable talk with Brigadier General Hawkins in Switzerland, I began to realize the higher facts. By this time I had become an officer; I had helped reorganize the National Guard of New York State from the white-pants-and-button-stick-polishing that marked the Peekskill picnic rigors of the annual encampment each year. And, in study, I finally understood the strategy of that Cuban campaign. It had none. It was just to slug, quickly and hard, and that may be a form of strategy in itself. But even the tactics got snarled up.

It was a commando raid long before even the term "commando" had been invented. It was a brilliant and inadequately equipped raid on the Spanish stronghold of Cuba; it struck at the furthest point from the central Spanish command in Havana. That was sound strategy, so far as maps and politics were concerned. But maps were lacking. A Regular Army captain later told me that he never saw a map other than an issue from a school geography. The Fifth Army Corps of invasion was equipped as for an Indian campaign; no one knew anything about fighting in the tropics. We wore heavy woolen uniforms. Our army was to land, fight, and win — or else. Politicians would be vexed. There would be deaths and promotions, and the bottleneck of promotion that followed the close of the Civil

War would be ended. Officers rejoiced. Soldier recruits did not have to pay for their own drinks. Patriotism was not merely aroused; it was in conflagration.

The social line between West Point officers and those who came up from the ranks to outrank West Pointers, was an issue not far behind that of the racial color line. Major General Shafter, commanding the Army of Invasion for Cuba, was from civilian life and the Civil War, and not from West Point. He was very fat, and very vulnerable. His rank protected him. But few, then or since, paid the honor due him. General Miles, his senior, had expected to be given the command of this spectacular Fifth Army Corps of Invasion. But General Miles was a most dashing figure, with white waxed mustachios and dramatic bearing. He might become a Presidential candidate. He was damned independent, and in politics too, where he was, probably correctly, suspected of being a Democrat.

Mark Hanna was in the saddle, with President McKinley riding pillion behind him. Hanna was a businessman who turned politician without losing the conviction that the United States was simply a somewhat larger form of business enterprise. Presidential possibilities — and war made them — must be limited to those whose potentials were wholly safe; and this meant well-tanned Republicans. No more unlikely looking Presidential candidate could there be than General Shafter. Thus General Shafter had the qualifications that would make him politically safe for the command of the army to invade Cuba. And General

One of our Gatling guns before the attack on San Juan Hill.

The death of Lieutenant Ord at the capture of San Juan Hill.

Teddy Roosevelt's Rough Riders join the assault.

Wounded being cared for on San Juan Hill.

Shafter gave both Mark Hanna and President McKinley a brilliant military victory despite the Secretary of War's embalmed beef and shoddy shoes and ponchos, and the all-but-utter breakdown in supply for Cuba.

Shafter could lay siege to Santiago and lose men by disease and caution. Or he could assault, and lose his army in battle. He decided to attack. He had been quoted as saying that he preferred, as a choice, to lose men in battle rather than by disease.

Events proved that his decision was sound. Unquestionably, we lost more men than the Spaniards; they were in entrenched and fortified positions. But we carried them against odds and in spite of blunders at the very battle line!

The battle of San Juan is one of the four epic battles in our American history in which an inferior force defeated a superior force. It is one of the two of these in which Americans inferior in number attacked and carried an enemy position that was entrenched on a fortified hill. Of these two, the first was the Battle of King's Mountain, North Carolina, in the American Revolution. The other was San Juan Hill in 1898.

We had something over 15,000 troops in Cuba. Of these some were left on shipboard as details; some were in Siboney guarding supplies, and others were teamsters and mule packers in charge of quartermaster supplies and transport for the front, noncombatants. It has been estimated that Shafter had, at the most, 12,000 men on the fighting line on that July 1st at San Juan and El Caney, and, in the field, four batteries of 4.2 field artillery (they were without shields in those days) and a battery of four Gatling machine guns.

Less than two weeks after San Juan and El Caney, the Spanish commander surrendered 24,000 Spanish troops and their side arms. Also, they surrendered 100 cannon, of which probably 50 could be considered as armament; 7 eight-inch modern cannon; 4 six-inch modern cannon; and 18 Maxim rapid-fire machine guns, each considered superior to our Gatling guns, which were practically obsolete. Together with this array of surrendered material were 5,575,000 rounds of ammunition, of which over 5,000,000 cartridges were small-arms ammunition.

In two weeks Shafter had done the military impossible!

General Joe Wheeler was Shafter's commander of cavalry, Fighting Joe Wheeler of the Confederate Army in the Civil War. General Wheeler, a frail old man, had first declined the appointment. "I am too old," he told President McKinley.

"We need you," said President McKinley. "There must be a high officer from the South. There must be a symbol that the old days are gone — you are needed."*

Wheeler was still reluctant. "It is a duty that only

---

* Told by General Wheeler himself to a group of men down in Cuba. Ziegler, private attached to Shafter as clerk from the Seventy-first, was in the group.

you are left to perform," said the President. "It is the inspiration of your name." So Fighting Joe Wheeler, late of Confederate gray, went out and bought a major general's set of buttons and donned the blue uniform.

Teddy Roosevelt became a lieutenant colonel from his Navy desk in Washington; and Dr. Leonard Wood was made colonel. J. Fort Kent, a West Pointer who had graduated from the Point in 1856 in the lower echelon of his class and in 1895 had risen to the command of one of the two regiments of Negro infantry, the Twenty-fourth, was made a major general of Shafter's First Infantry Division.

To Major General Kent was assigned the task of the assault upon San Juan Hill, the key position to Santiago. His First Brigade was commanded by Brigadier General Hamilton S. Hawkins, also of West Point, whose brigade consisted of the Sixth, Sixteenth, and Seventy-first infantry regiments. He had formerly been colonel of the Sixth Infantry. The Sixth and Sixteenth were Regulars. The Seventy-first was the only regiment of volunteers from New York State.

The plan of assault was simple. Just go ahead and attack. And this too is sound, provided the assaulting division reconnoiters the front before it; provided they have field maps and know the enemy — where he is and how strong his force, and what are his defenses. Kent had or knew none of these things. His plan seems to have been a sort of go-ahead-and-when-you-get-shot-at-why-dammit-shoot-right-back.

General Kent deflected the Seventy-first up the jungle trail, leaving General Hawkins with only two-thirds of a brigade to make the assault on San Juan Hill.

Kent's own official report, six days after the battle, gives an explanation that sets forth the proof of his blundering.

"General Hawkins," he writes, "deemed it possible to turn the enemy's right at Fort San Juan, but later, under heavy fire, this was found to be impracticable for the First Brigade, but was accomplished by having the Third Brigade coming up later on General Hawkins' left." The comment is obvious: Kent, in the rear, decided, because he was under fire, that the plan of attack he had reluctantly agreed upon with General Hawkins, and which Hawkins was even then developing, was "impracticable." As we have seen, General Hawkins, with his depleted brigade, *did* accomplish it.

Kent first accepted the report of General Hawkins and the statements of other officers that Hawkins with his Sixth and Sixteenth Infantry had charged and captured the Hill. But in a report six days later, he repudiated it. "Credit," wrote General Kent on July 7th "is almost equally due the 9th, 13th and 24th regiments of infantry." These regiments, fine regiments and as brave as any in Shafter's army, were the Third Brigade of Kent's division. He explains that the Second Brigade went through the trail at Bloody Ford and then deployed to the *left;* while the Third Brigade joined up with Hawkins' on the right! A regiment was one thousand men. General Kent, by his own report, had deflected seven regiments into that trail. And all this time General Hawkins was waiting at the ford until the Third Brigade could get through and join up with his left! In addition to patience Hawkins should be credited with a psychic sensitiveness to tell him where the Third Brigade was and how it would join him so they could charge San Juan Hill together! At least that is General Kent's story.

General Kent's report cannot stand up under analysis, and his charge that Hawkins falsely claimed to have captured the hill is not condoned by a few more kindly words later on.

General Kent had sent seven regiments into a narrow path which led an unknown distance to an unknown ford which his troops were to cross. Fords are not trivial affairs. The military textbooks state that they should be well reconnoitered — their banks, their depths, their bottom, and their relation to the disposition for attack or defense. None of these factors was known or had been scouted. General Kent had merely a brief note that there was a trail that led to the San Juan River: all that could be known from a balloon.

What Kent's blunder in deflecting those seven regiments into that narrow jungle path cost in men is easily computed from the official list of casualties. General Hawkins' Sixth and Sixteenth Infantry crossed the San Juan ford at the place we dubbed Hell's Pocket. The rest of General Kent's First Division went into action at Bloody Ford. Thus by noting casualties by regiments, we know where they occurred. Here is the official list of killed and wounded on that 1st of July, 1898 :*

Unit	Killed	Wounded	Casualties		Place
First Brigade					
(Hawkins')					
16th Infantry	14	115		129	At Hell's Pocket
6th Infantry	12	116		128	
			Total	257	
71st Infantry	12	68		80	At Bloody Ford
Second Brigade					
(Pearson's)					
2nd Infantry	6	53		59	At Bloody Ford
10th Infantry	5	40		45	
21st Infantry	6	31		37	
			Total	141	
Third Brigade					
(Wikoff's)					
9th Infantry	5	27		32	At Bloody Ford
13th Infantry	18	91		109	
24th Infantry	7	83		90	
			Total	231	

Hawkins' loss in capturing the Hill of San Juan was one-third less than that of General Kent's blunder into the futile trail to Bloody Ford.

There was only desultory firing on the day after the capture of San Juan Hill July 2, and in the afternoon there were showers. That evening General Shafter

---

* Taken from the report of Secretary of War R. A. Alger, *Casualties of the Fifth Army Corps at San Juan and El Caney, July 1, 1898*, p. 288. None of the regiments or companies of Kent's First Division were at El Caney or took part in that action.

called a council of war, at his headquarters, for seven
o'clock. The order was issued by Lieutenant Colonel
and Inspector General J. D. Miley. Present at that
council were: General Shafter, Lieutenant Colonel
Miley, Major General Wheeler, Major General Kent,
Major General Lawton, and Major General Bates.*

The discussion was general, and lasted for about
two hours. The methods of withdrawal, if such should
be decided upon, were discussed. Such discussions are
not public, but it was generally understood that the
proposition to retreat had been voted down. George
Kennan later wrote, in his *Campaigning in Cuba,* that
the events and the relative positions proved conclu-
sively that we could hold the San Juan ridge against
any attacking force that the Spaniards could muster.

But, following that council, a most remarkable
event occurred. It was described by Stephen Bonsal,
with a precision and keen sense of duty imposed upon
him by officers who were at the council. Who they were
he does not say, but perhaps it is not so difficult to in-
fer their identity. "It was my desire," writes Bonsal,
"to leave the details of what took place at this council
of war exactly as I wrote them at the time." (He had
written in quite vague terms, other than indicating
that a proposal to retreat had been the subject of the
discussion.) "It is certainly bad policy and most unmilitary to give the fullest publicity to such matters.
However, so much has been written concerning this
meeting, and so much that has been published is with-

---

* *In Cuba with Shafter,* by Lt. Col. J. D. Miley, p. 124.

out any foundation in fact, that *I have been requested* to modify my attitude and publish the following memorandum as to what was said and what did occur. It is *written by an officer who was present, and its publication is desired by a majority of those who took part in the conference.* [Italics added.]

"When the general officers assembled on the night of the 2nd, General Shafter said: 'I have called you here to have an expression of your opinion on the state of affairs at the front. I have been told by a great many this afternoon that we cannot hold the position, and that it is absolutely necessary for us to retreat in order to save ourselves from being enfiladed by the Spanish lines and cut off from our supplies, as an attack by the Spanish with a few fresh troops would result in our utter defeat.'

"The officers in turn, beginning with the one of lowest rank [General Lawton], expressed their opinions. They all talked at some length, and General Shafter finally said: 'Well, we will take a vote on this matter. Of course, I will assume full responsibility for any movement that takes place. But I desire to put the matter to a vote.'

"They voted in the following order:

> Lawton against retreat
> Bates against retreat
> Kent for retreat
> Wheeler against retreat

"After the vote was taken, Lawton was most vigorous and outspoken against retreat, making a long speech and doing almost all the talking and arguing against the step that was done in the meeting. General Kent told us that on that afternoon General Wheeler came to see him and was most emphatic and outspoken in his desire to retreat. We were convinced that he came to the meeting in this spirit, but as he had the last vote he was able to modify his views in accordance with those held by Bates, Shafter and Lawton.

"A few moments after the final vote was taken, General Shafter returned to his headquarters, saying that for the present the troops would remain where they were, and on the next evening he would meet the general officers again and confer with them further.

"General Kent explained his vote, saying that he was not in favor of withdrawing, but his brigade commanders thought it best."*

This document, obviously, places General Kent in a most unfavorable light; particularly since it is identified as having been first-hand evidence from a majority of those taking part in the council of war. Five were present, including Shafter; thus, Kent could be a minority of *one* or, at the best, himself and but one other. His defense is very thin. That he felt it necessary to pin on Major General Joseph Wheeler the responsibility for his desire to retreat leaves him in a poor position. A general in the Confederate Army who won the

_____
* *The Fight for Santiago,* by Stephen Bonsal, p. 256.

title of "Fighting Joe Wheeler" did not get it by yielding to inclinations to retreat.*

Nor has Kent's further explanation that he voted to retreat because "his brigade commanders thought it best" either professional dignity or probability. General Shafter stated that he took responsibility for his decisions. Kent passed the buck to his subordinates, all of whom were colonels or lieutenant colonels. If there was any talk about retreat in the trenches, no ear but Kent's heard it.

The authenticity of the memorandum quoted by Bonsal cannot be reasonably doubted. He took it from a source in whom he had implicit confidence, an officer who took part in that council of war; it was no lower-echelon clerk. General Kent, most assuredly, would not have given out any such statement. General Wheeler, old and frail and beyond desire for Army imbroglio, may also be ruled out. Lawton, a new major general and junior to all, would be extremely unlikely. Vigorous as he was, he would be unlikely to go over the head of his commanding general; and neither would General Bates. This leaves General Shafter, the commanding officer, as the final possibility. The motive?

---

* In his book *The Santiago Campaign,* General Wheeler does not give the slightest indication that our army was in a fearsome position on that 2nd of July. He made a careful examination of the Spanish defenses with a very powerful glass; he viewed them from our trenches "on all sides of the city," and estimated that an assault would cost us some three thousand men. He was not for assault. General Shafter estimated it would cost five thousand men. But this lends no support to the belief that Fighting Joe Wheeler was for retreat.

Lieutenant Colonel Miley was Shafter's most trusted aide. Miley had been with General Hawkins and General Kent during all the confusion and hesitation that had marked Kent and his "infirmity of purpose," as Bonsal characterized it. And what Miley knew, General Shafter also knew.

General Kent, in his official report, strews wholesale charges of cowardice, as if that would mitigate his blundering. Cowardice is an individual matter. Cowards do not organize — they cannot. There was not a regiment down there, or anywhere, that has not had its cowards. We had them in our regiment and were ashamed of them, and showed it. We were sympathetic to fear, for we had it too; but we were harsh with those who could not keep step with human dignity, be they officers or enlisted men. We idolized men like Captain Rafferty and Captain Goldsborough, as well as those of other outfits whose own men had given them the cachet.

In our conversations in Switzerland, General Hawkins spoke of Captains Rafferty and Goldsborough, and the covering of the withdrawal of Best's battery. "Theirs were the two companies nearest me," he said, "and they were the first that arrived on the hill in formation — you know how the troops got mixed up — so I sent them over. None could have done better. I recommended both for brevet."

I find no record in any volume of such recommendation. I have only General Hawkins' word for it, but that is enough. But I feel that there is logic in the thought that General Kent's report would have been even less credible had he mentioned a recommendation for brevet for men he had damned wholesale. In the absence of definite evidence the reader may choose his own opinion. Mine has been influenced by a first-hand knowledge of facts.

20

In the trenches. The night attack. We move to Misery Hill for the duration. Rations give out — except for hardtack. General Miles's Testudo! The fake bombardment of Santiago. Santiago surrenders and disease strikes.

WATER detail, that day of rest, was a pleasant break in the monotony of watching the little spats of pulp and sap burst from the palm tree. Going down for water, we passed two men laid out to await identification. Nearby was a dead horse, starting to swell. As were the two dead men. We could also see the two Gatlings that had been burned out and jammed by the rapidity of their fire the day before; their barrels were blue-and-straw color. Beside each lay a pile of spent cartridges as big around as an artillery wheel and a couple of feet high in the center.

We had a feast with our tins of Japanese beef stew. The sowbelly was raw, and the beans were raw and hard too. We ate, at intervals, all day long, and spread sugar on our hardtack for dessert.

Back in Shafter's headquarters, there were rumors

of a need to withdraw, though we did not know it.
We collected some Krag-Jorgensen rifles and carbines
dropped by the better-equipped casualties, and by
nightfall Rafferty's and Goldsborough's companies
were completely armed with them, and each man with
a belt of cartridges! (The next day we had to turn
them in, all nicely oiled and in good condition, and go
back to our Springfields.)

Fetching water was never uneventful. Scattered
through the jungle and up in trees over both Bloody
Ford and Hell's Pocket were Spanish sharpshooters.
Wagons, ambulances, any passing figure was their target. We sent out sharpshooter details to search for
them. Sergeant George Doyle, of our regiment, one of
the crack shots in the United States, was on these details. From the straight-line hiss of the bullet its direction could be determined. The bullet noise from another shot would be triangulated, roughly, and the
Spanish tree located. Then our men would close in.
One Spaniard tumbled out of the branches not fifty
yards from Bloody Ford — I had been under that tree
a half-dozen times. No prisoners were taken — at
least I heard of none. They had fired on stretchers
carrying wounded men and on anything that moved.
Up in their trees they were in a hysteria of desperation, for they were behind our lines and in terror of the
Yanquis. In about three days the snipers were elimi-
nated.

Bloody Ford was our nearest watering place. I was
in the ford filling our squad's canteens when a general

and his staff rode through. A Mauser bullet from a sharpshooter smacked into the stream not six inches from my dipping hand. It had just missed the general. "Didn't miss by much, did he?" said the general mildly. "Do you mind filling my canteen for me, my man?" He reached over his canteen. I filled it. I had never known a general, and I was curious.

"General," I asked, "do you mind telling me what general you are?"

"I am General Breckenridge," he answered.

And to this day I do not know who General Breckenridge is, or was, or what he was doing at that Cuban ford.*

With sunset on that 2nd of July came the end of our day of rest. At dusk we were lined up and counted off. Every man was to stay at his place in the ranks and sleep with his rifle by his side. The Spanish fire ceased with the setting sun, as it had the night before. Slightly ahead and above us under the crest was Company M. They too were to sleep on their rifles, with their cartridge belts buckled on. There was fear lest the Spaniards, not having tried to recapture San Juan by day, might try for it at night. And back at General Shafter's headquarters was being held the council of war at which General Kent cast his solitary vote that we should retreat. Of both companies only the officers and sergeants were to remain awake, in shifts, throughout the night.

---

* Lieutenant Colonel Miley lists no General Breckenridge in his official schedule of the officers of the Fifth Army Corps of Invasion.

The night came on, deep, black, and starlit. At least
that is as I remembered it when I fell asleep. Then into
that sleep there came a crackling blast of rifles. Over
the crest and from our trenches came a steady and rippling crackle of heavy fire. It was directly ahead, and it
traveled up and down the line of trench. Bugles were
blowing, here and there a whistle shrilled, and on the
instant we were on our feet and in place. Overhead we
could hear the sharp hiss of the Spanish bullets and the
smack and *whuz-z-z* as one would hit a palm tree. We
moved up in the darkness until our two companies, F
and M, were just under the low shelter of the crest.
From the trench just beyond there came one rippling
roar of rifle fire. We kept formation by feeling with
our elbows for the man on either side. The captains
were calling: "Don't load, men — don't load!" For
our own men were just beyond in the trenches. "Fix
bayonets — don't load!"

From the company ahead of us there came a sudden
blast of a Springfield rifle, and an instant shrill scream
of agony that, in the same instant, died down into a
gurgle. It was not ten feet from where I lay. One of
our own men, a Company M man, had died in that
blast. His own rear-rank man, half asleep perhaps, or
in hysteria, had disobeyed the order; he had loaded
and pulled the trigger. Almost in the same instant
Captain Goldsborough, wild with rage, had the rear-
rank man by the throat. Other officers came running
up. The rear-rank man was sobbing and gasping: "I
didn't mean it — I didn't mean it!" A silhouetted fig-

ure against the night stepped in between the captain
and the man. Goldsborough was saying, "I'll have you
shot for this — goddam you, I'll —" The voice of
Major Wells came through the darkness: "Shut up,
Goldsborough — or you will." The rear-rank man
was screaming. I heard the slap of a flat hand against
the man's face. The voice of Major Bell, our regimental surgeon, joined in. "Slap him, Major — he's out of
his head!" Slowly the panting screams sank into grunt-
ing sobs. And all became quiet except for the banging
rattle of the rapid fire from the trenches. We heard
Major Bell say: "He's dead; I'll send a stretcher.
We'll talk this over in the morning."

Who the M Company man was no one outside of
the company ever knew. The darkness covered him.
Somewhere in the tabulation of M Company's battle
losses is the name of the front-rank man, "killed in
action."

Perhaps the firing continued an hour, perhaps less.
Slowly it died down. Whistles began blowing and bugles sounded the "Cease fire!" in rapid succession up
and down the line. Again it grew quiet under the starlit
night and we returned to sleep. To this day no one
knows exactly what started it. Lieutenant Colonel
Miley investigated and held that the firing was begun
by the Spaniards. Earlier, a white mare had been seen
around the blockhouse; some held that she was wandering that night and had caused the outburst of firing.
Perhaps. But it is also possible that the Spaniards *did*
thrust out from Santiago in an attempt to recover in

the darkness what they had lost in daylight. After that night of the 2nd of July, there was no effort of any kind to assault our lines of trenches — although the Spanish General Toral received reinforcement troops to the amount of three thousand the following day.

The next day, July 3, we were back on duty. The trenches we had dug so easily were baked hard. We sat on the hard earthenware with our rifles laid across the embankment in front and listened to the Spanish bullets hissing away overhead. Once in the trenches, we were as safe as if we were home. But to get to the trench took a little risk. The captain of the company in the trench would blow his whistle to notify us that he was coming out; Captain Rafferty would blow *his* whistle to signal that our company, just below the crest, was also ready. At the second whistle from the trench both companies would leap forward on the run, and passing between each other, would reach safety, one in the trench, and the other below the crest. The instant the Spaniards saw these two lines of running men they would redouble their fire. Yet, on our front, never was a man hit. The two captains would have to damn their men into running, and yet they themselves always walked. "Dammit," said Captain Rafferty, "and I'd like to run myself!"

We never saw the white mare again. Whether she died between the lines or went back to her Spanish friends we never knew. But she lingered long enough at the famous blockhouse to become part of all the histories that have been written around the Hill.

If there was trepidation, it was not in the mind of General Shafter or his other generals, with the exception of General Kent. Shafter inspected his line of trenches in a Maine buckboard that sagged under his weight and was pulled by an artillery horse. That he was vigorous in mind and strategy there can be little doubt in the face of the record. The day following the council of war at which only Kent voted for retreat, General Shafter sent a vigorous letter to General Toral demanding the surrender of the city of Santiago under threat of bombardment! I have already mentioned our feeble resources in artillery.

Then began the series of almost continuous truces while the white flags passed back and forth between the trenches and the city. As the hour for each truce ended, the Spanish rifle fire began coming over. During the truce we squatted on the bank of our trench and looked across at the Spanish trenches, where a little line of pajama blues popped up at the same moment and stared across at us. The truces were so frequent, and getting shot at so infrequent, that monotony began to nibble at our heels.

Then, during one truce and while our company was not in the trench, there came a court-martial — a drumhead court-martial, literally. Below the bullet-spatted palm where we had made our bivouac some soldiers, Regulars, set up a folding table. A drum, with one head rain-soaked and the other rather dilapidated, was set down beside it. This became the clerk-of-the-court's desk. Sentries were thrown around the

meadow below us, and various civilians rode in and dismounted near the table. Some officers took seats on
camp chairs around the table; the civilians — including the British consul — stood. A guard brought in
two prisoners, Spanish soldiers in the light-blue cotton
uniforms; they were impassive. Our company had
front-row seats on the little slope that started at the
foot of the Hill. The trial was brief. We could hear
nothing. But we saw what was clearly the verdict being
read to the two prisoners. They were impassive because it was in English, and they knew only Spanish.
Then we could see it being translated to them.

As it was being read both prisoners sank to the
ground. One rose on his knees and was crying and
pleading. The other pleaded for a brief moment and
then fell on the grass, weeping and groveling. The
other straightened up, rose to his feet, and walked
off with dignity between his guards. The other was
lifted to his feet and half carried away, his feet drag-
ging on the ground. We were told they were Spanish
soldiers who had been in the trees firing on stretchers and an ambulance behind our lines. They were,
if that is correct, the only such sharpshooters taken
prisoner.

We heard the verdict was hanging, and that the con-
suls of Santiago had been requested to come out for
the court-martial to see that all was in conformity with
military procedure. And that was all I ever heard.
Later, when I searched the files of the Judge Advo-
cate's department, I could not find any record that cor-

responded to this case. But that the men were to be hanged or shot seemed evident.

By this time we had learned of the desperate effort of Admiral Cervera to escape with his fleet from the Bay of Santiago. The news did not travel fast. While we were in the trenches on the morning of July 3rd we had heard, far off to our left, what sounded like distant thunder. We thought it was very likely one of those tropical thunderstorms below the mountains that rimmed us. It faded quickly. We thought, too, that perhaps our left wing was having another scrap with the Spaniards down by the entrance to the bay where Lieutenant Hobson had sunk the *Merrimac* in the channel. But the thunder was so distant that it made no impression. It was not until the next day, the Fourth of July, that we thrilled to the news that our fleet had run the Spanish ships down the coast until, destroyed, they were beached. Admiral Cervera's fleet had been utterly routed.

On the 5th we left the trenches we had dug and went around to the left of the blockhouse. We dug no trenches but bivouacked in the open, for the rainy season was only beginning and the skies were fair. We did not use our dog tents.

That afternoon I picked up a sack of twenty pounds of sugar that happened to be unattended at the time. The canned beef was gone and we were down to hardtack, or the musty sowbelly, if you could stand its odor. I was so encouraged that I found another bag — ten pounds of salt! Salt was no premium.

There was no shade on this hill, other than the out-crop of a fair-sized rock. Dudgeon, the sailor who had been my partner that night back of Crabshooter Hill, picked this rock for its few inches of shadow. That night he was disturbed by rustling noises in the ground under his head. Rabbits, he thought; and slept. The next morning he poked a stick down the little hole his head had blocked during the night. He got results. Out slithered nine feet of snake, bushmaster or boa, none of us knew the difference. It was killed and skinned and Dudgeon abandoned his few inches of shade — we knew of the rumor that snakes had venge-ful sweethearts.

At sundown the next evening, orders came. And so did the rain, starting with a heavy drizzle and a rapid darkness. We slung our horse-collar packs and poked our heads through ponchos that were already begin-ning to peel and shred; their protection was light. The drizzle changed to unmistakable rain, a steady, relent-less wetting that lasted all night and well beyond the next dawn. We passed Hell's Pocket in the darkness, on past the blockhouse, and then could mark the greater darkness of the rim of the ridge to our left where the Rough Riders were in the trenches of Fort Roosevelt. Down here where we were slogging through a slippery mud was their private dynamite gun with its complex breech covered with ponchos and guarded by a sentry. Just beyond this we came upon the battery of the field siege guns with their high artil-lery wheels and 4.2 cannon rising above. And, among them, two little cannon that did not even reach one's knee — some kind of mortar; they looked like toys and could be carried under the arm.

From there on it was nothing but more mud and puddles through which we slipped and stumbled. The muzzles of our rifles were plugged with rag to keep the mud out of them. Silence was the order and even the tin cups that hung below our haversacks were muffled. Was it a secret march with a surprise attack at dawn?

Dawn came slowly. It was still dark when we scrambled and slipped up a rain-soaked ridge on our left. Here were trenches, already dug and left us by the troops that had moved still farther to the right in the encirclement of Santiago. There was four inches of water in the trenches, and the firing step had melted into mud. We sat on the near side and dangled our feet, sheltering our rifles with a fold of our ponchos. Smoking was prohibited, even if there had been a dry match in the company.

When dawn came drearily, we could see we were next to Battery E of the First Field Artillery, commanded by Captain Allyn Capron, Senior, and already outstanding in the Fifth Army Corps. Our battalion was in its support to the left. The battery was already in field fortifications in embrasures that were axle high and flanked with high mounds of earth. Before us the jungle rolled far across a little valley to the Spanish trenches, and beyond them we could see the roofs of Santiago. We were closer to them than before. There

were long, low buildings that might have been warehouses, or military barracks; and over each building
— or so it seemed from our distance — floated a red-
cross flag indicating hospitals. There were over thirty
of these flags — we counted them. We speculated: if
these were hospitals, all of them, we must have wiped
most of Toral's soldiers off the map. Far to the right
were the low swamps and marshes that marked the
end of the Bay of Santiago. Beyond Capron's battery
our trenches continued; we were laying out the lines of
the siege.

The rain slowed to a drizzle. The drizzle stopped.
Then the sun came out, and life began to look up. We
pitched our dog tents where we could over the uneven
ground that led up to our trenches. It was scandalously
unmilitary, by the book, for we should have been as
regular-looking as a military cemetery. But the Regulars were doing it too. That country had no level
ground; the Ninth U.S. Infantry, back at the blockhouse and on the hill, had to terrace like an Arizona
Hopi village, with steps from one level to the next.
And there was cactus. You can't chop cactus with a
rod bayonet.

"We'll be here some time," said Captain Rafferty,
"so make yourselves comfortable." He was right.
This was Misery Hill. And it is so known even unto
this day. The whole encirclement was Misery Ridge.

We gathered firewood, and found some that was
singularly uninflammable. Some pitched their dog
tents two together, and made a mansion. A few

brought in palm fronds and made a bower for shade; then the shade withered. We fraternized with the gunners of the battery, and with Captain Capron, whose son, Allyn Capron, Jr., a captain in Roosevelt's Rough Riders, had been killed in the fight at Las Guasimas two weeks before.

A scraggly little tree thrust up out of the earthen embankment of our trench, and another tree between us and the battery was the only shade. But there was, often, a nice afternoon breeze.

Then our food began to fail. We had used up the so-called canned beef, we had gone the limit with the sow-belly — it had not kept, and our haversacks reeked of its staleness. We were down to hardtack. Rations came through by mule pack trains; and there were two boxes of hardtack to each mule, with a box of ammunition riding on top. It was ten miles back to Siboney, our base in the invasion, and a mule train never reached the trenches without a loss in animals that were mired. Fifty mules was the standard pack train; and if thirty mules got through in one trip it was not bad going. When a mule was mired its pack was unlashed and the animal left to shift for itself while the rest of the train moved on. To get rations through was more important than to hand-nurse mired mules. Thus the country roundabout became a haven for mired mules when they struggled free. Anybody could have a mule who could catch one. They had rich forage in the Cuban grasses and would move gently off if approached.

Our company caught one, and we decided to use him

for water detail. He could carry all the canteens of the company. Water detail meant a trip to the Rio Purgatorio, a mile and a half each way from our trench, and ten or twelve full canteens get heavy. But our mule was as naked as the day he was born; he had neither pack-saddle nor halter, and his sleek hide was barren of hooks on which the canteens could be hung. So the water detail went on foot as it had done before.

But water detail was not too bad; we often asked for it. Tobacco had given out, and there was a cross-roads on the way to Purgatorio that was an informal meeting place of all water details of the army's left wing. It was a sort of Tobacco Exchange where men without tobacco could borrow a chew — for most men had taken to chewing as the most economical form of tobacco use there was. The Regular Army had learned that long before. You chewed, then you dried it out in the sun, and then you smoked it in your pipe. Also, neither plug nor fine-cut were affected by the weather or rain. They were always in edible condition. Old-timers chewed fine-cut; novitiates and the Negro regiments, plug. Piper Heidsick, Green Turtle, Black Jack, with their licorice and molasses base, were prime favorites; Piper Heidsick, rather blond and sweet, was regarded in some quarters as catering to effeminacy. But at the crossroads one could always ask for the loan of a chew; and I never heard such a request refused — unless the decliner was waiting to borrow one for himself. You could borrow a pipeful too, sometimes. But, in general, men chewed up their own smoking. Cigarettes were nonexistent. Eventually, because of the shortage, the Army decided to send in tobacco. Every fifth mule then carried a twenty-pound box of plug.

For one week nothing came through, aside from ammunition, but hardtack. And we lived on it. Then came a one-gallon can of tomatoes for each company. Quartermaster Dave Werdenschlag lined us up to pass the open can. Each man received two of our mess-spoonfuls of the tomatoes, poured down him on the spot. And it was good. One week on hardtack and water and anything is ambrosia and honey! And then we went back to hardtack.

One day General Shafter came through, riding his sagging buckboard. Another day a woman appeared, wearing a black skirt and white shirtwaist, and we heard she was Clara Barton. Sickness had begun to strike. Intestinal disorders had started; the latrines began to be flecked with blood. Above all rode the persistent hunger; it was a ravenous longing for just the taste of food, real food. All day long the truces continued. General Toral was bargaining for surrender.

The bloat of malnutrition showed itself in some. Now and again a man had to let out his cartridge belt in order to buckle it; yet his face grew leaner and his cheekbones rose higher. Even on the short trip to the latrines and back, men would lie down to rest. Men cursed more, coldly, blasphemously, obscenely, and grimly; but there was no whimpering. We soaked our hardtack in water till it swelled up to the size of a fat dog biscuit; then we fried it in what grease we had —

the rancid scraps of sowbelly, soft and a bit on the greenish side. Occasionally some Cubans might pass, and we traded hardtack for mangoes. This probably helped the germs of dysentery. But we did have coffee! Green and unroasted, just as it had come from the shaking-tables of the coffee plantations and just as it had been issued to us that night before the battle. We fried it in our mess tins and it charred to black on one side and remained its natural green on the other. Then we pounded it into broken bits in our mess cups, using the Krag-Jorgensen bayonets we had picked up that 2nd of July. Then we boiled it. The result was a vague, dishwater-colored liquid; its only resemblance to coffee was that it was hot. Our dysentery germs loved it.

Our talk was of food. We lay on our backs, our ragged hats tilted against the sun, and imagined to each other superb menus and heaping plates of what we would order when we got back to the States. Roast beef, rare; a thick steak; an English mutton chop with a kidney folded in its arm; roast goose — *gebratene Gänze,* in Joe's Rheinweinhandlung — and beer. For dessert, mince and apple pie led by many lengths — just as did roast beef for the main course — and ice cream was a poor third. We dreamed only of heavy food. It was a game, and some could not play it; they had not enough imagination, possibly, or perhaps they had too much. A group of us were playing it outside the first lieutenant's tent one morning when he told us to shut up. Thinking he was bantering, we added a few gastronomical touches. He came boiling out of his tent. "Goddam you, shut up! When I say shut up I mean it." Captain Rafferty overheard him and was as astounded as we were.

"Couldn't stand it, Captain," said the lieutenant. "Goddammit, it'd drive a man crazy. If you fellows want to talk, get the hell away from me — and I mean it." And he did. And we did.

There was a perpetual poker game. Four of the dog tents were joined together. One wall of their length was stuck up on branches like a marquee, and it made a stretch of shade. Ed Booth, Gus Pitou, John Shaw, and Ben Payne were its backbone, with occasional visitors. None had any money. Our inedible dried beans were used for chips, with the promise to settle up after the war, back in the States. The beans for poker were scrupulously kept in one pocket, and each man's stake, each day, was counted out of that pocket. The books always balanced, and there never was a bean used other than those that had been strictly dedicated to poker. And from morning roll call on — except for water detail — the game was on.

One day some mail came through; we had sent a regimental messenger back to Siboney for it. Most of our correspondents were hoping we were well; *our* mail, the after-the-battle letters, had not yet gotten through. On the morning of July 2nd, we had been told to write home — Shafter knew that the home folks would be on edge with the published dispatches of the fight — and, as we had no stamps, just to sew up the letter with thread, mark it "Soldier's Letter," and a

special staff messenger would get it out to a dispatch
boat. Many of us, like myself, had arranged for some
tobacco to be sent us once a week, or money. Nothing
of this kind ever came through. The troops in Siboney
were not much better off than we were in the trenches;
except, of course, for the transports and their supplies.
At a base, troops that suffer privations have only
themselves to blame. It was after the war that I
learned of the lavishness of supply and transport —
for those properly situated.

I shall now make a very germane digression into a
field that is uncovered for the first time. Too many
people are embarrassed by it. I knew a Lieutenant Martin; his father was in the Regular cavalry. Lieutenant
Martin was assigned on special duty to reach Cuba and
Shafter with military equipment that had been designed by General Nelson Miles and was to be used in
the Santiago campaign. This military contraption was
the testudo. It was a device known to the Romans and
had, thought General Miles and our War Department,
been neglected long enough. The testudo — as revived
by them — consisted of a solid oaken barrier about
sixteen feet long and six inches thick. At each end was
a solid wooden wheel by which it could be moved forward. It had loopholes and a thin iron plating. On its
hither side hung a ladder. At its center was a long
wagon tongue by which it could be steered. The steer-
ing and pushing was to be done by sixteen soldiers,
whom it would shelter. All that was necessary to do
was for us to push it along trails that had mired every

pack-mule train, or to shove it valiantly through the jungles while, perhaps, a troop of cavalry with machetes and brush-hooks cleared a way for it, and us. Scaling the Spanish trenches with the latter would then be simple.

"I had twenty-five tons of the damned things," said Lieutenant Martin.* "I reported to General Shafter. He — or somebody — said, 'What the hell! Hang around here and we'll feed you, or go back and throw them overboard!' So I lived right well through the Spanish War."

And at this time we didn't have rations or medicines in the trenches.

Yet I *did* get one letter. It was from the Commissioner of Jurors in New York City. It notified me that I must appear for jury duty, and when I did get back to New York there was a five-hundred dollar fine awaiting me for my nonappearance. It took a judge to get me off!

Some new, fresh sowbelly did get through and we had hardtack fried in fresh grease — and was it good!

During all this time General Shafter had been vigorously demanding surrender under threat of bombardment and assault. General Toral sent a lot of noncombatants out to the hills, and they begged our hardtack. One of our men, a stenographer and typist who had been detailed to Shafter's headquarters, was present at

* Lieutenant Martin, son of Captain Martin, of the Sixth Cavalry. Lieutenant Martin was of the First Volunteer Engineers, who served in the Puerto Rican campaign under General Nelson Miles.

various conferences between the chief generals. Shafter demanded immediate surrender. Toral's reply was interpreted — for these were verbal conferences, except for the formal written notes that followed.

"Surrender," said General Toral, "is out of the question! In two weeks," he continued, "three-quarters of your men, General Shafter, will be down with yellow fever, dysentery, or other diseases. Why should I surrender!" He was quite right, and we were already on the way.

General Shafter replied, with General Nelson Miles standing at his side: "General Toral, I will give safe-conduct to any officer you may choose to go down to Siboney and see my fleet lying off there. I have a thousand men on the way for every sick man for the next fortnight, and more thousands on the way for the fortnights to come. Fifty thousand men are on the way at this minute. *They* are on the transports this minute — on our transports that have arrived!"

It was true. There were transports crowded with soldiers lying off Siboney at that moment. But they were on their way to Puerto Rico under General Nelson Miles, and General Miles had merely stopped off to have a cup of tea with Shafter. General Toral knew of those transports loaded with troops; what he did *not* know was that they were for Puerto Rico!

From that point on, the arrangements proceeded rapidly. On July 10, Toral began preliminaries for the surrender of twenty-four thousand Spanish troops in the province and city of Santiago. Shafter had about

Our trenches on Misery Hill during the siege of Santiago.

Just one more stretcher on Misery Hill.

Captain Rafferty's special detail going to Santiago to unload rations.

Quarantined at the Hospital Detention Camp at Montauk Point, Long Island.

half that number, with the inroads that disease had already made.

There would be a little formal bombardment so that General Toral could surrender with dignity and under fire, in battle. This bombardment began with rifle fire at dawn on the morning of July 10. We were expecting it; we had been told to get into the trenches and stay there, the day before. Capron's battery had been selected to do the bombarding, or to begin it. Capron was an angry and disgusted man that morning. He was a grizzled veteran, somewhat plump, and he and his men were devoted to each other. The loss of his son Allyn at Las Guasimas hurt deep. For days he had been waiting for the time that he would see his battery in action again; and now it was here, and filled with a frustrated bitterness.

Captain Capron was a liberal drinker, though except after nightfall he never took a drink by himself. But, at night he would crawl into his dog tent and we could hear the clink of the bottle against his tin mess cup. It was within fishpole length of us. Then there would be another clink. A pause. Then a clink and, presently, you could hear the captain murmuring. There would be another clink and the murmur would become articulate. There was a sob in it. From where we sat on the trench berm we could hear it. "I'll get 'em, Allyn, I'll get 'em, goddam 'em." Another pause; and another clink and then, again: "I'll get 'em, goddam 'em, I'll get 'em, Allyn, I'll get 'em." And then he would begin to fade off into sleep. And the little row of men on the berm, gunners and doughboys, felt no touch of ribaldry; they sat there and sympathized, feeling a loyalty to the old man. We liked him.

It was dawn, and we were in the trenches.

Capron's battery was to bombard Santiago, and to hit nothing — those were his instructions!

So he began firing, slow, very slow fire. The range was easy, two to three thousand yards to the little fluttering red-cross flags of the Spanish position. The shells burst far short and high over the jungle and swamp. Captain Capron would gaze impassively into the distance. Presently he would step up to a gun, crouch, and sight it. Stepping back, he would straighten up: "Number Three — fire!" And a billow of white smoke as big as a barn bellowed forth from the parapet. A pause and we all, gunners too, peered over the trench or through an embrasure. This time there would be, just this side of the red-cross flags, a burst of tile roof and adobe brick in a cloud of dust.

Captain Capron would rave: "Who laid that gun — who fired that piece — goddammit — I'll have —" and it would fade off into roars of his inarticulate condemnation. For there might be a staff officer about. It was an act — and a good one. Once more the harmless bombardment would begin, with very slow fire. Then, after an interval and a look around, Captain Capron would lay a gun; and again — "Number One — fire!" And again there would come a burst of dust and tile from one of the buildings on Santiago's outskirts. Those buildings looked like barracks. Once again Cap-

tain Capron would fume and roar in an apparent rage
that droned off into mumbling that could mean anything.

No gunner in that battery ever hit anything, that
day or the next. But with the captain laying a gun there
were results.

Perhaps Capron's specially aimed shells irked the
Spaniards, for they turned some pointed rifle fire on us.
Capron asked for some sharpshooters to cover his
battery; our colonel sent him Sergeant George Doyle.
Doyle placed a few shots in the Spanish trenches and
the rifle fire died down. Then the Spaniards lobbed a
shell into our Third Battalion, in dog tents just in the
rear of us; and the battalion came boiling out en
masse on the run for our trenches. Amazingly, no one
was hit, for the shell burst with the fine accuracy so
much admired by artillerists, just a little above the
ground and in the very center of the tents.

By this time we could not be kept under cover in the
trenches. We wanted to see. We had placed logs across
the trenches at various points and covered them with
earth, splinter-proofs in case of artillery fire. The
trenches were hot, dirty, and muddy at the bottom. I
was near one — just in case, for I was, and am, a lover
of prudence. Along came a major of our regiment. He
was ducking — even though the bank of our trench
was higher than his head. He crouched under the splinter-proof. From its shade he looked up at the soldier
nearest him, who was perched on the berm.

"See anything, my man?" he asked.

"No, sir," the soldier said, "nothing at all."

"Very good, men," and he ducked under cover. "If you see anything — any movement — let me know." And he stayed there until it was time to inspect another splinter-proof. Forever after he was known as "Bombproof Johnny," and often from the ranks and loud enough for him to hear.

Four days later, on July 17, 1898, with the first gun fired in salute over the surrender of Santiago, we mounted the parapet of our trench and gave three cheers. Capron's battery had been named for the honor of firing the twenty-one guns of victory. Far down on either side of us stretched the trenches, on back to the blockhouse, Roosevelt's men, and beyond them. On our right they began the encirclement of the Bay of Santiago, and at our extreme right were the Cuban troops in their trenches. Miles of men in tattered and ragged blue; sick and well, waving and cheering and shaking hands.

The war was over. Now we could go home.

And what a dinner we would order!

21

The war is over! The Y.M.C.A. arrives and the chaplain takes over. Disease strikes deeper. Taps and funeral volleys are stopped. My detail goes to Santiago to unload the Vigilancia.

THE war with Spain was over. We wanted to go home.

The hot, tropic sun beat down, and in the afternoons the rain came. Our ponchos, their Army-contract rubber coating peeling in tattered shreds, gave some protection spread over the ridge of our dog tents while we crouched beneath.

Water detail was a task nowadays. The river was over a mile away. The tenseness and *élan* of the battle had faded. We were weaker and sicker than we knew. There was no bugle for sick call, for the bugler was sick too. If anyone was well enough to report sick he was well enough for duty and detail. If he dropped, then send in another. It was not brutality; there was nothing else to do. We heard rumors that yellow fever itself had broken out in Siboney.

Rations now came out from Santiago by wagon, over bad roads, but they seemed like parkways after those eleven miles of gumbo mud to Siboney and back. Mule pack trains could get through without mired and abandoned animals en route. We got beans and unroasted coffee and hardtack and sowbelly. And, once, fresh beef! The beef was dumped from the Army truck to the ground under a tree; this was the tree the regimental horses had used for their stable. There were quarters of beef, fore and hind; the quartermaster sergeants got an axe and chopped off a section for each company. Having a fashionable butcher for a quartermaster sergeant was an advantage. Once I believe there was even filet mignon for the captain. The regimental quartermaster saw to it that each company took its turn at stew meat. Anyway, I preferred stew meat; it made a gravy, or soup, when a sack of flour got through to us. Lord, how good it was! It made hardtack edible — almost.

The Young Men's Christian Association brought up a tent, almost a circus tent.

"This," said the young Christian gentlemen in charge, "is for the enlisted men, you soldiers." He jovially helped us roll the vast bundle of canvas off the wagon at the foot of our hill next to Capron's battery. Jimmy Lowe, Harry Carpenter, and I helped roll it up the hill and started to unlash its ropes. Not right. Wait. The Y.M.C.A. man disappeared. Presently he came back. Not here; over there. It was closer to the regimental headquarters. So we rolled it down one hill and up another. More volunteers appeared and we set up the poles and swayed on the guy ropes. Splendid. The tent was up, and gave shade that was not as leaky as the Arkansas roof.

"Whenever you boys want to lie down," said the Y.M.C.A. man, "just come over and lie down here — we've got writing paper and envelopes, and reading matter too — if any of you fellows want to read!"

The next day I went over. I heard that the Red Cross had sent up some cornmeal and some white flour, a barrel of it. They had, two huge sacks. It was fine flour, and I knew if you mixed it with water you got dough; and if you heated dough you got something to eat. Cooking is easy. Just dough and heat.

Behind the sacks and barrel sat our chaplain, suave and benign. Far away at the other end of the tent was the Y.M.C.A. man, perspiring, dealing out blue-lined writing paper with crossed American flags up in one corner, and also little tracts. These latter were very welcome, but not exactly for the purpose of their pious donors. Two officers lay on cots within the shade of the tent. Two of our soldiers came up and one started to lie down — for, other than the foregoing, the shade of the tent was vacant. "Anything you want?" asked the chaplain benignly.

"I was just a-going to lie down," said the man.

The chaplain's voice was still benign but with the suggestion of a military ring in it.

"This tent is for the officers, my man," the chaplain said. "Here is flour, help yourself, and over there is reading matter. Take what you want and go back to your quarters."

Two other men climbed the hill to the tent; they were sick, obviously.

Suavely the chaplain welcomed them. "This tent is for the officers," he explained. "The officers" — he waved his hands courteously — "need this. I have taken charge."

I had my tin cup full of flour. "Chaplain," I said, "I helped put up this tent. The Y.M.C.A. man said this was for the men." I looked at the two officers and the great vacant space of shade.

"That was good," responded the chaplain. "But I have taken over. Is there anything you wish?"

I went over to the Y.M.C.A. man; I needed some of his reading matter. He was perspiring and — I will give him credit — embarrassed, I think. "I helped put up this tent," I said. "I would like to lie down — there is no shade in the trenches. My bunkie, too. The chaplain says we cannot. You said this tent was for the enlisted men."

The Y.M.C.A. man appeared not to hear me. "You would like to have some reading matter — or writing paper?" he returned.

"I want to lie down in the shade — there is no shade in the trenches."

"Sorry," he replied, "but you can't. Have you the chaplain's permission? He is in charge, you know."

I took some reading matter and writing paper and went back to the trenches. The tracts that I took were

marvelous, in a sense. They had been carefully picked
by someone within the Young Men's Christian Association. I remember two of the titles to this day. One
was *Sailor Jack's Homecoming;* the other was *Little
Susie's Prayer.* And I read them both, every word, before they were used up. It was easy to feel that their
authors wept at their own pathos and were exalted by
their own desperate piety. Sailor Jack had come home
at Christmas time, and it was pleasant to know there
was such a thing as snow and ice and sleighbells while
we toasted each other in lukewarm river water. *Little
Susie's Prayer* was, as I recall, a condensed mixture
of *Ten Nights in a Bar Room* and *Elsie Dinsmore.*

The sickness was striking deeper and wider. I could
have set my watch by my chill and corrected it by the
fever each afternoon. Except that my watch had long
ceased to go at all. The shallow latrines were spat-
tered with blood, ample evidence that dysentery was
crowding upon us. We knew now, not by rumor but by
news, that Siboney had been burned to thwart the outbreak of yellow fever before it could become epidemic
or reach the trenches. One could not burn the trenches
if it ever got there.

Medicines were more than scarce. It was our regimental surgeon, Major Bell himself, when I went over
for some bismuth, who told me: "A man is as well
off in his quarters" (his dog tent) "as over here in the
tent — we haven't any bismuth; we have only three
hundred five-grain quinine pills, and no cholera mixture — and God only knows when the medicines will

come up." That same week I overheard Major Wells, brigade officer-of-the-day, say with exultation: "By God, we've only got three hundred and sixty men fit for duty and it's the smallest sick list in the brigade — and the division, too!"

Later, I passed Major Wells lying weakly by the side of the path that went to the latrine. I stooped to help him. "Go on," he said. "I'll be all right." So I knew, as we all did, what the standard was for being fit for duty, his and ours.

With the mess cup of flour from the Y.M.C.A. tent, I made dumplings. It was, as a matter of fact, the first time that the wagon came through and dumped the fresh beef on the stable ground. Jimmy and I combined our fresh beef. We added river water; then we made a dough of flour and water and dumped it in with the stew. Men stood around and looked at my boiling cup and its dumplings. In that hour I made a reputation as a veritable chef. Also, from experience back in the States, I knew how to build a fire and get it going, with the utmost economy in twigs and firewood. Going after firewood was a chore. No more did I forage for my firewood. I built and made fires for others, and saved them labor in firewood foraging. For this service I would trade a wood detail. Also I would cook a meal, or add dumplings to it, for other favors in the line of distasteful duty. I lived the life of Lucullus and of an indolent Diogenes combined.

But I frequently took water detail. Tobacco was

still desperately short and I might get some at that
Tobacco Exchange at the crossroads. Then too, once
there was an issue of hard soap; a piece one cubic
inch in size. I was lousy, like everyone else. So I
hoped to give the so-and-so's a banquet of yellow soap.
Lice are very interesting little fellows and highly epi-
curean — at least so far as yellow soap is concerned,
as I found out. There are three kinds of lice that
specialize in and on humans. There is the gray-back,
or seam-squirrel, from the days of our Civil War —
or from Caesar's legions, in all probability. There is
the louse that feasts only on the cerebral sections and
attaches himself and his progeny to the hairs of the
head. We added to the vocabulary of the louse and
named him the "Rough Rider," by which term he is,
I am informed, known even unto this day. And then
there is the crab, looking, under a glass, for all the
world like a first cousin to his well-known and larger
brother of the Eastern Shore of Maryland. This one,
the human attaché, is *Phthirius pubis,* and an ancient
writer knew him well and suggested a remedy: "A
louse," he wrote, "is a worm with many fete, & it
cometh out of the filthy and unclene skynne. . . . to
withdrayue them the best is to wasshe them oftyntymes, and to change oftyntymes clene linen." My
"clene" linen had been lived in quite steadily; so I
pinned my hope on that little cube of yellow soap.

There was a rush of water details to the San Juan
River. We were joyous in the lousy time we would

give those lousy lice. And nothing happened. The louse either loves yellow soap, or he abhors it. In either case the net result was the same. They throve.

Then it was that we turned to the ant. There were plenty of ant hills teeming with lively young ants. We had heard that ants are great fighters and ferocious against intrusion. So we would lay our clothes on an ant heap and stand there, naked, hoping for results. An almost complete area of sunburn or tan over our dermal exteriors was the sole result. But miles of naked men, studiously peering at their favorite ant hill, absorbed in the search for entomological truth, is a tribute to our American eagerness for exact knowledge.

Me? I had only the Rough Riders. It was the most genteel form of these afflictions; for others, two hands were piteously inadequate.

At darkness we crawled into the dog tents after first evicting a land crab or two. Once I found a big hairy tarantula, first mistaking it in the dimness for a land crab. It did not jump at me as I had been told it would; I speared it with my bayonet and folded it up in my soapbox as a souvenir. A few days later I learned that insects of this size are in the field of taxidermy, so I threw the soapbox away. There never was any more soap, anyway.

After dark, Captain Rafferty would sit up on the trench looking over toward Santiago. A little group slowly formed. There was Jimmy Lowe, my bunkie;

there was Gus Pitou, and Johnny Shaw; there was Ed
Booth, the gambler, and his church-going brother Jim;
two artists, a lawyer, and an engineer. Rafferty would
tell of his life in England and his membership in the
British militia. He had traveled, and had scores of
incidents and reminiscences. We had only the hum-
drum of a city to exchange. We argued mildly on re-
ligion and politics, in their broad aspects and not sec-
tarian angles; perhaps it was more morals or ethics
that we discussed under the stars. We talked about
war, and what it demanded; and this drifted mildly
into the view that war was inefficient, that its re-
sponsibilities must be met, and that killing of an enemy was not a personal matter but rather a wholly
abstract and necessary incident. We had seen but few
Spaniards. But we had killed and been killed, and been
— and were — hungry for decent food and a physi-
cally clean life. The days of the frenzied "Remember
the *Maine*" were far back, far back in the days of a
frenzied civilianism. Probably it was all very primitive and oversimplified; but we had stepped back into
an oversimplified world; we were living an oversimplified and primitive life.

There was one rather curious fact: on not one of
those nights on the parapet of the trench was a single
dirty story told; we were beyond the point where that
kind of entertainment had any appeal. We were trying
to think. It may be that men who have faced death, and
survived, feel the sense of a new day dawning somewhere within them. We were silent, and listened; or

talked with a serious groping; and the anecdotes dealt
with facets that had affected our lives. For behind us
and down the long lines of trenches men were sickening
and dying. Any one of us might have his own number
up before the next sunset. They were wonderful eve-
nings. And Rafferty was a superb captain — and man.

Major Wells came by one evening and joined us.
Then he came regularly, though dysentery had him in
its grip. An engineer in civil life, he was bossing the
building of the road that would reach around to our
right flank; mule trains would then be replaced by
wagons. The major's headquarters were with the brigade, whose officers' mess gathered around banana
leaves laid as a tablecloth on the ground. One day a
can of jelly arrived. Our chaplain had become the pre-
siding officer of the mess.

"How he got there I don't know," said Major
Wells. "There were ten of us, maybe twelve. 'A little
bit of luck today, gentlemen,' says the chaplain, and
he held up the can of jelly, 'and I think I had better
serve it, if you will pass your mess tins up.' When
he got through serving the others, half the jelly was
left. 'Ah,' says the chaplain, 'I see that there is some
left,' and with that I'm goddamned if he didn't dump
it all on his own mess tin! And the sonofabitch ate
it all."

The major had voiced the regimental epitaph for
our chaplain, who had no business being in the Army.
He belonged to the tea tables of communities where

his avid obesity would be kindly regarded as a product of affability.

Daily the sickness struck deeper. But the food was increasing. Army wagons came in regularly with meat and vegetables. The onions, turnips, and potatoes had been in the hot holds of the transports since we landed at Siboney. Half, or more, were rotten, the turnips wholly so; it took a strong man to approach their barrels. An overripe onion can even outrange its friend the turnip; joined together in aroma they defy description. The vegetables were dumped on the ground and twelve quartermaster sergeants stood just outside the area and supervised; behind them at a greater distance stood various officers, also supervising. The twelve sergeants represented our twelve companies; and each of us earnest workers was exhorted to get a good pile for his own company. Once the first whiff was absorbed we did not seem to mind. When there were twelve piles of this assorted vegetable muck a whistle blew and each man dived for the pile he had been heaping for his company. Sometimes there was a fight; it was disheartening to have selected and accumulated a choice pile of assorted vegetables and then have some claim-jumper, nearest to your fragrant assortment, hop to it. It was a highly competitive process. I was regularly on this detail and my company did not fare badly. Also I was able to do a little foraging and accumulate a little stock of private issue inside my shirt.

My dumplings, saltless and sodaless, were a regular part of the service for my clients. Only once was this a failure. Ed Booth had a pocketful of salt. He kept it in his shirt pocket, which was where he also kept some five-grain quinine pills. The sweat, the heat, and the rains had combined the two. I added some of Ed's salt to one evening's dumplings, unwittingly giving them and the stew about twenty to thirty grains of quinine. That evening I went hungry, except for the hardtack; and I had put into that stew such a lovely ration of fresh meat.

Each morning in these days we would hear bugles blowing taps very shortly after reveille. First, from off in the hills back of the trench line, a volley — the burial detail. Then the bugle. Taps, those slow, steady, and plaintive notes that mark the end of a day or the end of a soldier's life. The sickness was striking in harder. The volleys became more frequent and one bugle followed another throughout the day; they followed each other almost as if they were but echoes among the hills about us. And our regimental sick list showed only 400 men, out of our 900 remaining, fit for duty; yet we had the smallest sick list in the brigade!

Then one morning there were no more volleys. No more taps. But the little files of men with picks and shovels, a stretcher covered with a blanket or poncho, and a chaplain showed that the burials kept on. Volleys and taps had been stopped by official order from headquarters lest their frequency might demoralize us! Soldiers were buried in silence but for the chaplain.

Then reveille stopped for our regiment. Every bugler was down and out. There were no calls; guard mount was silent, and the flag came in at sundown in silence. It was as if all the watches had stopped, for we had the habit of telling time by the bugle. The bugles were Army clocks.

There was no excuse for guard; you took your trick; if you were strong enough to report sick, you were strong enough to go on guard. Anyway, each man had his supernumerary, who was named to go on if anything happened to him. One company sent in five supernumeraries during one tour of guard duty. We would watch the ragged line of guard as the new relief was being formed. A man would crumple and drop. The sergeant of the guard would yell: "Stretcher bearer!" and the man would be carted back to his dog tent. I have seen three calls for the stretcher bearer before the new guard was posted.

Then one bugler recovered. Two men braced him up the hill. He blew retreat as the flag came in from the parapet. A weak, quavering retreat, with missing notes and hissing gasps, but it was recognizable, and we gave him a hand. Each evening and morning, in the distance on either side, we could hear the reveille and retreat from other outfits, some better, some worse, but each seemed the ghastly echo of a thinning and dying army corps.

Yet, even in those difficult days there were men who knew nothing but their drill book. There were shavetail lieutenants* fresh out of West Point who apparently had succeeded to the command of companies through the death or illness of their captains, for in vacant patches on the hills about us we could see their men in drill! Fours right — fours left — right front into line, double time — fours right about, double time! All this under a tropic morning sun and when only a platoon, at the most, was able to drill! Then this was stopped. It took a headquarters order to do it. Word went around that men were dying ninety to a hundred a day.

Our surgeons had looked at these drills with amazement; and they cursed the men who ordered them. Captain Capron, next to us, cursed them too: "The goddam fools!" His men loafed; they kept their guns cleaned, and shoveled up their parapets and embrasures after a rain, and that was all. We loafed too. Men needed their strength to survive, not to waste it on double-time parade-ground exercises. The day of close-order on the battleground was past. I believe our Companies F and M, in covering Best's battery, were the last soldiers ever to go on the firing line in the old close-order.

Then came more orders from General Shafter's headquarters: we must boil all our drinking water. It

---

* The term "shavetail" originated from the custom of shaving the tails of mules newly bought for the Army. Hence "shavetail" indicated a Johnny-come-lately.

was a good order and wise. But what would we boil
it in? We had only our mess cups; we had the water
in our canteens, and two cups made one canteen. Some
men had no canteens; they had sprung a leak or just
got lost. These canteenless men hacked off a section
of bamboo and carried water in that; they left a sort
of peg at the bottom to stick in the earth and hold it
upright, and it was, as a matter of fact, quite conven-
ient.

At the San Juan River, all the water details met at
the only nearby place where the banks were not as
steep as the side of a house or matted with jungle.
Here men bathed, with or without soap, and used its
banks as a latrine. Mules came here to water. Dysentery and the intestinal germs of its brotherhood do
not wait upon sentries or prudent orders from general headquarters. The placid little creek flowed on
down to other tiny playas where other water details
gathered, and down to Hell's Pocket and Bloody Ford
where more canteens were filled daily. The sickness
steadily spread. Later we found that this order for
boiling water had been born in the office of Surgeon
General Sternberg back in his softly carpeted office
in Washington, D.C. No one of us ever disputed the
value of boiling our water, and we grinned contemptuously as we drank it, for what else was there for us to
do?

General Shafter had written to Washington: "The
death rate will be appalling. There is more or less
yellow fever in every regiment. It is really an army of

convalescents, at least seventy-five of the men have had malarial fever, and all so much weakened that they are capable of very little exertion. There are other diseases prevailing, and severe types of malarial fever which are quite as fatal as yellow jack."

This was our army, the Fifth Army Corps, one week and three days after San Juan Hill. Men were walking about, their eyes glazed with fever, doing guard duty and water detail. The hard-packed path to the latrine had its resting figures, going or coming, as others stumbled past them on a shuffling run.

Even the poker game went on in a lassitude, at one end of the three dog-tent flaps that had been put together. One of the men in that tent was out of his head. He slept and had lovely visions most of the time. He dreamed about — well, it was like this when anyone attracted his attention: One day as I was passing he called to me in a secretive whisper, "Hey, come on in — don't let anyone see you."

I stooped and crawled under. "What is it, Pete?" I asked.

"Sh-h — not so loud. It's beer, ice cold. Got a keg of it here!"

"Yeah!" I said in the Army jeer. "Yeah!"

"Sure," he said warmly, "no fooling. Don't tell. Got a keg here — cold — down under." He pointed vaguely to a corner of the dog tent. "Anytime you want some, come around."

In a minute he was mumbling to himself, and his eyes were looking vacantly out into the hot sun. He would lie there all day muttering and inviting anyone in to his keg of cold beer. Ben Payne, Gus Pitou, and Ed Booth looked after him.

In the dog tent next to Jimmy Lowe's and mine was Ed Kroupa, a quiet, steady man. He was a good soldier. He never complained and he never swore; chiefly, I imagine, because he was a very silent man. He went down with sickness, and his silence continued. We had sick call, true; and the first sergeant sent you over to the regimental surgeon where there were no medicines either; and then you came back and lay down under your dog tent. Kroupa did all of that. He was sick in quarters and did not have to answer the roll call that lined us up each morning.

Then, one morning, someone noted that Kroupa's feet seemed to be in the same position, sticking out of the little tent, that they had been in the day before. Kroupa was dead and cold. He had been dead from the day before, how long no one knew. So he was taken out, and another silent funeral was held on the nearby slopes.

Then Tom O'Brien, the chum of Chumbum, laughing, joking, always the first to volunteer for detail, took sick. Two days later he was dead, and our company had added another to the muted obsequies and flimsy headboards.

Captain Rafferty got an idea. Our transport, No. 23, the *Vigilancia,* was now lying in Santiago Bay. Why not unload her and bring up all the regimental gear, the Buzzacots, and the tentage? Army wagons were short, but we could get some stuff through. So Rafferty was told to go ahead and pick his detail. It was a choice detail — to get into Santiago, and what might not be there! Rafferty counted the fit men — fit to unload a transport and regimental stores. I thanked God that I only had a bit of fever and was counted among the fit; also I had done a full twenty-four-hour trick on guard — sitting on the worn parapet with the rifle across my knees and just loafing it through. I was lucky in being named as one of the detail of twelve men under Sergeant Jack Myers and Captain Rafferty. The captain had picked up one of the stray Army mules, had gotten a saddle, a saber in place of the regulation straight infantry sword, and a British pith helmet in place of the campaign hat. The delicate infantry sword he had always held in contempt as being in the class of weapons somewhat less than deadly. Also he had acquired spurs. At daybreak we started off.

We marched strictly at attention. For Rafferty had told us: "You boys understand we're going into a captured city. There'll be Spanish soldiers, and they'll have barracks and uniforms. They have an idea we're the better men. And, goddammit, we're going to keep up that impression!"

He looked down at his little command. My sky-blue pants were a wreck. One knee was exposed in all its nakedness by a flap of grimy cloth. My campaign hat was shapeless, drooping, and full of holes. And I was undoubtedly fragrant with sowbelly grease and rancid onions. The others looked no better; some looked worse. But one thing — we did look tough. And to this day I feel secure in the thought that no Spanish soldier, or loyal Spanish royalist, could regard us as anything but a type of soldiery to be avoided at all costs and under all conditions.

We passed in a sort of review before the colonel, who saluted, and went on. Then we marched at ease. We passed the outer sentries and on down the deserted lane that approached the city we could see in the distance. We passed the great hole in the road, and detoured around it. A Spanish land mine had been planted there. We had watched its explosion after the city had surrendered — a vast burst of black smoke that rose and billowed as great clods of earth shot through it — and we had speculated on that day at San Juan Hill: Had the Spaniards tried to entice us on past the Hill and down that road into Santiago — for it is doubtful if the Hill could have been considered as heavily defended — and then on down to the mine? It is a possibility of the Spanish strategy of that day, and only a Spanish commander could have the answer. They would have gotten some of our men, true, but not enough to have effected any stoppage. It is entirely possible that our men would have swept on and captured the city that same July 1st, and General Toral would have had to take to the hills and work his way back to the main Spanish force at Havana as best he could.

The little lane through abandoned fields, now overgrown, ended, and we struck the suburbs. We saw the

shattered wall that Captain Capron had blasted in his
personal gun-laying. Cubans stared timidly out of
their doorways and sometimes waved at us. A few
Spanish soldiers, out on a pass, stared at us curiously.
As we saw them ahead, Captain Rafferty would bring
us to attention and we would match step to step, covering and dressing as if on parade, and marching with a
guide right. We had the reputation of the United
States on our shoulders — and of the United States
Army!

I think the folks back home would have shared the
pride we felt, marching in a swinging cadence into the
city we had captured.

22

Food in plenty — Red Cross stores! We live high and so do our germs. I turn cook. Our Captain gives a dinner with unexpected results. Worcestershire sauce and brandy.

NOW there were more and more little adobe houses. Naked Cuban children stared at us and we at them. We halted in one of those public squares where there was a fountain — the neighborhood's water supply, unchanged from ancient Cuban days. Two Spanish soldiers approached.

We spoke no Spanish and they no English. They wanted souvenirs. After some very elementary sign language, we also gathered that they wanted something to eat. We had hardtack and a chunk of sowbelly. The next moment they had sowbelly and hardtack and we had the Spanish red-and-yellow insignia from their broad-brimmed, straw army hats. More Spanish soldiers came up; then we all had souvenirs, and they had food, of sorts.

We passed on. In the main part of the city there was no great amount of curiosity over us *Yanquis*. That first burst of curiosity had apparently been satisfied with the entrance of the Ninth Infantry, U.S.A., now encamped in the Santiago opera house near the center of the city. Each squad of the Ninth Infantry, we saw later, had its headquarters in a loge of the orchestra circle, or the balcony. The sergeant of the guard occupied the box office, and the lobby, or foyer, was the guardroom. From the balcony, above the orchestra pit, stretched lines on which rows and rows of blankets were drying and airing.

Outside, where a broad alley ran from street to street along each side of the opera house, was the regimental latrine. The cane-bottomed benches, which were for the less wealthy patrons of the opera, had been taken outside and lashed against the walls and the seats hacked off with a bayonet. The cellar of the opera house had been lighted by little windows that opened up from a trench just outside its foundations. Thus the cellar itself became the latrine, with a convenience and comfort that reflected great credit upon the engineering resourcefulness of some sergeant in the Ninth. True, with the alleys running from street to street — and open at both ends — there was a lack of seclusion. No one cared. Every street was a temple dedicated to sanitation. There was a public latrine, down on the water front three blocks or so away; it cannot be described. The whole city was interwoven with malnutrition, starvation, and pestilence.

Diagonally opposite the opera house was the palace of the archbishop. Beyond its open-grilled gates a bitter priest strode up and down in his lean cassock. He viewed us *Yanquis* with unconcealed scorn; we were *gringos,* accursed *Protestantes* full of the pestiferous germs of heresy. The good man would never have believed that Tom O'Brien, buried back there in the hills, would have walked barefoot over live coals to get to mass.

Down by the water front, a long deck thrust out into the bay. Along the shore were cement-floored open sheds, with corrugated steel roofs. They were piled high with Army stores, cases, and barrels. Just beyond lay the *Vigilancia,* No. 23, along with Navy cruisers and low-down little torpedo boats. It was hot — hotter than in the trenches. And the black, dim holds of the *Vigilancia* and its regimental cargo held out no allurements.

A reasonable modesty prevents my going fully into the matter of how I avoided that perspiring and laborious task. Unless one has been for days on a hot, shadeless hill, where even the leaves in the bud are baked off the spindly trees by a remorseless sun, it is not possible to realize the fascination that those vast areas of blue-and-purple shade under the cargo sheds held. It stirred my imagination; I must get under one.

I am not gifted by nature — other, perhaps, than having been given a superb sense of the value of indolence. I have often noted the close relationship between indolence and achievement. A busy person goes ahead and does the job; the indolent man thinks up a better way to do it. Thus indolence is the mother of invention.

It was, I think, when we stopped in that little plaza, where we traded hardtack for Spanish ribbons, that I spoke.

"Captain," I asked, "who is going to cook for this outfit?" I swept my hand to indicate all of us.

"Oh," he replied easily, "I've thought of that — plenty of cooks down there, I guess." He gestured to the water front. "Some Cuban, most likely."

As I turned away I murmured, but not too softly: "My Gawd — a Cuban!" I slandered a fine people; but in war no holds are barred.

The captain turned abruptly. "Can you cook?" he demanded.

"Yessir!" I said.

"What makes you think you can cook?" he demanded.

It was ridiculous. Could I cook! All one needed was a fire and something to put in it or over it. Also, if one was a good cook one simply told someone else to make a fire and what to put on and take off it. I proposed to be one of those good cooks. Since hardtack and sow-belly would buy souvenirs, why would they not buy services? So I answered the captain.

"Why not?" I asked.

"Then, dammit," returned the captain, "cook! And it better be good."

I noted that the sergeant's eye was upon me. He was a suspicious man and entirely fitted to be a sergeant. There must be no misunderstanding.

"Captain," I suggested, "do I understand that *now* I cook and unload the ship too?"

"Sergeant," said the captain, "he cooks and nothing else." I was one up on the sergeant already.

"Captain," I pressed, "I need something to cook with."

"Ah, yes," said the captain.

"Sergeant," I said, "when you go aboard break me out a Buzzacot and have it ashore with the first load!"

The Buzzacot arrived. It was the colonel's own pet Buzzacot for the headquarters mess. It was just right for our twelve men!

That night we camped under one of the big corrugated-iron sheds. We slept on the concrete on our ponchos and half-blankets — no twigs, no bumps, no chasing a land crab or wondering about a tarantula! It was luxury. We had messed at noon any old way; the night's dinner was on the Buzzacot. The dinner was hardtack, sowbelly, and coffee — same as in the trench. And all about us, under this shed and the next, were mountains of fine white flour, Pillsbury's 3-XXX's, canned beef, canned fish, jellies, sugar, roasted coffee in waterproof waxed bags — Red Cross supplies, and there were not wagons and mules enough to get them back to the hills and the trenches.

"Rations?" I asked the captain. "Nothing more in our haversacks."

"I asked this evening," explained Captain Rafferty, "and I am instructed that all these rations piled about us are Red Cross, and that we will draw three days' rations tomorrow morning."

"Yessir," I said.

"The rations," added the captain, "will be Army rations: hardtack, sowbelly, beans, and coffee. Also sugar, salt, and pepper."

"Yessir," I said. "Roasted coffee?"

"Hell, no!" said the captain. "Do you think they want us to get soft? And," he added mildly, "there aren't enough wagons to get this back into the country. It's a pity, too."

I thought the matter over carefully — carefully because a soldier should think things over carefully when great moral issues are at stake. I felt that the captain would not like to have me pillage Red Cross supplies — or, perhaps, he might not like me to get caught at it. But I was a cook and the first duty of a cook is to cook food. Few in the Army, outside of the plush-sofa offices in Washington, regarded either sowbelly or hardtack as being in the nature of food as the term is commonly used. And here I, a cook, in the land flowing with honey and protein, had nothing to cook. My duty was plain. I have, therefore, nothing to blush for when I state that we lived well.

By morning we had roasted coffee out of waterproof waxed bags. It seems that when I came back from a stroll through the shed that night, a waxed-paper bag of roasted coffee fell out of my shirt when I sat down. And it happened to the captain too!

There were two sentries to each supply shed, and

they were a nuisance — recruits, probably, and very conscientious. They were particularly odious about the pile of nice white Pillsbury 3-XXX flour. Sometimes we stabbed a sack with a bayonet and let it run out into mess tins, which we emptied into a Buzzacot bucket and hid under a blanket when the sentry was coming. But we got bolder, or more sagacious; we would haul out a whole bag of flour, intact, and lay it on a tier of canned tomatoes, or something, where it looked perfectly natural. And it was not the sentries' business to get things sorted out. Sugar? It lay stacked in tons around us! Potatoes, onions, turnips, everything. The stacks were assorted, and we found, by scouting, where there were jams and jellies, Worcestershire sauce, ketchup, canned tomatoes, lime juice for lemonade — and all for a little patience and ingenuity from time to time.

Even as I had hoped, I found those who would work for hardtack and sowbelly: two young Cubans who began to hang about that first day looking hungrily at the few remaining scraps that we ourselves had at that time. They dragged bucketfuls of water from the municipal water tap down on the bay, a block away; they broke crates into kindling and firewood and blew the embers into a blaze come mealtime. They led me to a Spanish baker up in the city; and the baker traded me sixty pounds of utterly delicious Spanish rolls for a hundred pounds of raw white flour, and threw in two pounds of sweet chocolate in addition. We traded every day, and the two little Cubans were supporting their families in luxury on what was left over. They had bread and rolls to trade each day and, between times, we could see far on the other side of this water-front esplanade a hungry woman in black with a basket to take what she, and the two boys, thought was surreptitious spoil.

We gave them all of our Army rations that we scrupulously drew every three days, hardtack, sowbelly, dried beans, salt, sugar, and pepper. "It might excite unjust suspicions as to what we were living on," said Captain Rafferty, "if we did not draw rations. So see that you draw them." I thus did my bit for Cuba and also relieved the Red Cross of some of their problems of supplying nutrition to the needy, including ourselves. Further, we found that sentries are not as forbidding as they might appear. A glass of jelly can establish a friendship of definite value, and another will give such friendship endurance, and often a bit of tobacco, of which the Regulars had a better supply than the Volunteers. For tobacco was still scarce. But by prowling a bit out on the dock underneath the mountains of supplies and the tarpaulins, I found a twenty-pound case of Piper Heidsick chewing plug. We outfitted ourselves and sent the rest back to the regiment in the trenches.

Every day Captain Rafferty rode out to our trenches. His gunny sacks, huge saddlebags, were filled with the rolls and bread of the Spanish baker, some of the chocolate, and whatever else we had been able to accumulate. It was a lovely existence — if one did not have to jack regimental freight out of a dim, hot hold of a ship, and slide it down to the lighter alongside. And I did not have to. I lolled, and the little Cubans toiled. Once we had baked beans, for a Sixth Cavalry cook alongside our shed baked them in his Buzzacot with hot embers on top of the oven pans to brown them nicely. It is true that I furnished the sowbelly for them. But, outside of that, I merely waited until he called me to come and get it, and I sent the little Cubans over.

Then Sergeant Myers had an idea. The sergeant was really a nice man when he was not thinking up something concerning the cook.

"Captain," said Sergeant Myers, "I think we should have a pie." And he gave me an unpleasant look.

"Fine! Fine, Sergeant — in fact I'll give a little dinner," responded the captain cordially. "There's a Regular officer I've met — I'll invite him — I've had dinner with him and turn about's fair play." He laughed genially. Then *I* gave the sergeant *a look!*

"Yessir, Captain," I said. "But no lard for shortening!" I had him there, I thought.

I had never made a pie.

"I brought some off the ship today," said Sergeant Myers evilly.

So we had pie. Amazing as it may seem, there were cans of superb peaches among the stores under these sheds; there was everything if you could find it. I dusted off, and washed off, a bit of the cement floor of the shed, and rolled out the crust with a whisky bottle filled with water to keep it cool.

Captain Rafferty's final words had been: *"And I'll bring a steak!"*

None of us thought we heard right.

But that afternoon there was the captain, a slice of meat half the size of one of our tattered ponchos over his arm. It *was* steak! His friend the Regular Army captain came shortly afterward and under his arms were two bottles of wine!

We started with bouillon, made from Leibig's Beef Extract in our tin mess cups. My Cuban assistants collected them and washed them up for coffee. We had steak, broiled over the coals from a fire of packing boxes and crates that had been tended all that afternoon. With the steak there were *petits pois* from a case of those little French lacquered tin cans. There were tomatoes, softly thickened with flour and a dash of salt and sugar. There were lyonnaise potatoes, boiled that morning. Then we had the peach pie, with cheese — the Red Cross thought of everything — and coffee. The Cubans washed out the tin cups again. For the Regular Army captain was uncorking the bottles of wine! He was worthy of Captain Rafferty. We had set a place for them, a little apart, on a packing box. Not for them! They moved over and joined us in our circles on the cement floor. The wine was port, maybe, or Madeira. Never was there such flavor, or such a bouquet with its gentle warmth.

Then Captain Rafferty produced cigars!

Two officers, one a West Pointer of the Regulars, and twelve dirty, ragged, fevered, and lousy men sat in the evening darkness under the iron-roofed shed in Santiago. There was no thought of rank. It was the fellowship of men in the brotherhood of a common and epic experience. Our stomachs were warm and replete with comfort. Chills, fever — hell, that was for another day.

We sang softly. They were the sentimental songs, remembrance songs, "Tenting Tonight," "My Old Kentucky Home," "The Banks of the Wabash," "Old Black Joe." That evening there was no ribaldry, nor even any of the casual, colloquial Army swearing. We were too tough to have to pretend to toughness. The Army seemed to fade, the trenches faded, the fever and sickness faded.

And we loved that West Point Regular. "Goddammit," we told each other, "you'd never know he was a Regular!"

He spoke to me while the wine was going round. "Cook," he said, "I hear you're no good at unloading a ship."

"Yessir," I answered.

"See that you stay that way," he said. I could feel him smiling in the darkness. He was that kind of a man.

The next morning Joe Howard was down with fever. It was not long before he was slightly delirious. He did not go out to the *Vigilancia,* and early that afternoon the captain sent a stretcher over and Joe was taken to the hospital. The rest of the detail were out at the ship, so I got the men with the stretcher to carry him. Hood's New Orleans regiment of "Immunes" had arrived two days before and were lined up for inspection, or parade, or something. They were all supposed to have had yellow fever and thereby become immune to it. But that stretcher fascinated them, and they craned their necks.

"What's he got, Jack?" they would call. "Yellow fever?"

"Hey, Jack, is he dead?"

You could see a pale panic run down their line. I nodded.

The Immunes were quartered under the shed next to ours, with their guardhouse within the shed. That evening we had listened to an officer giving the guard their instructions.

"Remember, men," he said, "that you are now in the country of the enemy! You will load with ball cartridge — you are in the enemy's country."

That night on the water front was the most dangerous night in Cuba that we had had since July 1st. Captain Rafferty had heard the officer too. "Be careful," he said. "Better stay at home. I'll get word around."

All that night the Immunes seethed and jittered; it was their Crabshooter Hill. At the first call of "Corporal of the guard!" the guard was a bedlam. "Turn out the guard — turn out the guard! Where the hell's that corporal — turn out the guard!" Rifles were clanking on the cement floor. Officers were yelling orders in the darkness; and somewhere the guard was lining up to repel boarders, or something. Some officer was yelling at a sleeper. There was a scream that sank into an agonized moan. "My vaccination! My vaccination!" They had been newly vaccinated, apparently, and a fresh vaccination had been kicked or grabbed. The corporal of the guard showed up with a prisoner, a ragged Cuban worker who had just come off the long dock and was heading for home when he had the misfortune to wander into the Immunes' lines. The incident was over.

All that night Immune sentries were yelling for the corporal of the guard, and the guard was being turned out with a shouting and a clatter. Our knowledge that the Immunes were in the country of the enemy, with ball cartridges, kept us hugging our cement mattress and thanking the Lord that there were piles of cases of canned goods between us and a stray bullet. By daylight the Immunes viewed us ragged blue tramps as veterans and our rags and tatters as the vestiges of battle. Also they received some directives from headquarters. It was explained to them that the city of Santiago had already been captured, and that any suspicious stroller was merely some needy Cuban seeking a latrine or a nook to sleep. The next night was peaceful.

The Yacht Club of Santiago was on the bay front beyond where the Immunes were on parade. It was here that we took Joe Howard. For the Yacht Club had been turned into an army hospital, and its spacious rooms were jammed with cots, each with a mosquito netting over it. Now and then some half-naked and delirious soldier would crawl out aimlessly, and try to walk away, stumbling feebly, until a hospital man would steer him gently back to his cot. Others lay inert, or waving their wealed hands in the delirium of fever.

At this hospital, Miss Wheeler, daughter of Major General "Fighting Joe" Wheeler, was just reporting for duty. She wore a stiff-brimmed, light straw sailor hat with a black velvet ribbon around it. Her shirt-waist, with its full sleeves, was immaculate and crisp; and her long, ankle-length skirt was of a soft gray. She was the first American woman, not counting Clara Barton, that we had seen since we left Port Tampa some two months before. Miss Wheeler was chatting with Captain Rafferty. I have never forgotten the picture she made in that brilliant tropic morning against the background of the hungry city. She was utterly lovely. Clara Barton came up and joined them. We had seen her before, but at a distance, back in our trenches, when she was on a tour of inspection.

We left Joe Howard at the hospital. He would die there.

We had left the trenches on this unloading detail as being among the healthiest in the company. And we were. But the sickness kept boring in, and with us in Santiago too. Malnutrition for weeks had left us but a slight margin of resistance. Back in the trenches Johnny

Shaw, Gus Pitou's side partner, was down; he died in his dog tent. John Dinan was down; he died in the hospital island out in Santiago Bay. Fred Engels was down, but not yet too bad; he was to die later on shipboard. Almost everybody was down, in fact, but walking around. Rafferty was back and forth each day with news.

The unloading of the ship was finished. The detail loafed and strolled up and down Santiago; there was little to see, and less to do. Each afternoon I could feel my chill begin, and then the fever. By three or four o'clock both had gone. In the meantime there was a cold clammy feeling about the stomach, nothing much but never absent, and a little worse about the time of the chill. I discovered something: Worcestershire sauce makes a good drink. We had a case of it, two dozen bottles. It warmed one. Jimmy Lowe tried it. Its salty flavor was not like liquor, but going down and inside it produced a similar cordial and gracious heat.

Not that there was no liquor to be had in Santiago, but Jimmy and I had but one twenty-five-cent piece between us. For weeks we had agreed that it was to be spent for a slug of rye or bourbon, or even rum. As our last quarter it must go out with flags flying, bands playing, and joy pervasive! The few drinks back in Capron's battery and the wine at Captain Rafferty's dinner party in Santiago had been the only breaks in our dry monotony. But, without a word of Spanish, we could not tell one shop from another. They all looked alike — a doorway and a dim interior that revealed little, with here and there a painted bottle or glass of beer on the outside wall.

I found out that the word *bodega* meant a place for drinks; hard drinks. One day coming back from the Spanish baker's, in a narrow street I had never been through before, I saw a place marked *Bodega*. It was a tiny hole-in-the-wall, with two little tables and two wire chairs. Behind a counter was a row of bottles, and on one the label read "Hennessy, Three Star, Brandy — Cognac." It was in English; and the bottle was half full.

I reported to Jimmy, and we came back and went into the café.

I pointed to the bottle of Three-Star Hennessy and laid down our twenty-five-cent piece. Two tumblers were at once on the bar, and the bottle. There was no change, naturally. A quarter for two Three-Star — it seemed incredible. The proprietor turned away. Jimmy filled his tumbler. I half filled mine — well, maybe a little more. The proprietor turned and smiled. "*Americanos*," and he smiled again. We sipped. The bottle remained on the bar.

Lest there be any mistake Jimmy sipped rapidly to reduce the liquid level in his glass, and so did I. But the bottle remained on the counter. The proprietor paid little attention to us other than to remark "*Americanos*" to his Cuban friends as he would point to us. When the tumblers were empty the bottle still remained, and we poured out another pair of drinks. For politeness' sake we left some in the bottom of the bottle — another drink, at least, though not as large as those we had had. We left, and again the cordial Cuban saluted us with *"Americanos, adios!"*

That quarter had a glorious end. No two-bits ever bought more.

23

Medicines and rations in trenches still scanty. General Shafter's ice and champagne. Home? Any day! We board the transport Grande Duchesse. *Five men to a cabin sick or well. Looting the hold. We sail for Long Island.*

SANTIAGO was pleasant and exotic and we were curious. We could have a pass whenever we asked for it; but it was not needed. A blanket over the arm, or a sack, was satisfactory to any prowling Provost Guard. "On special detail" was satisfactory. Sobriety was a pass in itself. Not that there was any prevalent drunkenness; no one had any money.

Before the chill-and-fever set in I rambled through the narrow streets and looked at the narrow balconies where the lovely ladies, in better days, would lean on their elbows and pretend to ignore the compliments and admiring glances of rapturous young bucks who passed and repassed below. I strolled into the arch-bishop's patio-garden when its iron-grille gates were hospitably open, and was ordered out by a sour cassock. Several other sour cassocks appeared so I strolled out.

I watched my Spanish baker grind his chocolate in what may have been, at one time, a paint grinder. I strolled down to the Yacht Club to see how Joe Howard was making out, but he was mostly delirious. I went out on the long wharf when we heard that the *Olivette,* a hospital ship, had come in. Others went down too. There was a load of nurses on board, but they did not, in the slightest, resemble Miss Wheeler. Shapeless and Mother-Hubbarded, they lined the *Olivette's* rail; and we hurled jocular ribaldry back and forth from deck to dock. They were the forerunners of the WAVEs and the WAACs. The military and naval minds distrusted femininity anywhere near the front lines. These had been carefully picked for the safety of all concerned. They were volunteers, we heard, and to volunteer for climes where yellow jack is endemic, and black jack epidemic, could have but little appeal for blithesome blondes. Anyway, no nurse was allowed ashore.

Maybe they *were* nurses. But we had the feeling that New York must have been left a mopless and scrubless city and an undefended prey to dust and mice. Then they, and the *Olivette,* disappeared. We heard that they had been returned by order of the commanding officer in Cuba, and it could be so.

The streets of Santiago were swarming with beggars, no dirtier or more ragged than we, although they lacked our general uniformity. All day long they sat across from our landing sheds; sentries kept them back from the mountainous stacks of food that, beside the cases in our sheds, stretched under acres of tarpaulins far out on the long wharf. It seemed incredible that so many people could be so eager for hardtack and sowbelly, and our details gave them plenty.

Nearby our shed the mule pack trains were loaded. Fifty mules to a pack train and but three packers and a boss packer! Long before the last mule was packed there would be mules at the head of the train lying down, tired of waiting. To get a mule up, a packer twisted his tail — though this was strictly against orders — and more than one mule had a broken and lacerated tail at its base. Hunger was against orders too, but it happened. I watched the packers, as I had in Siboney, and learned more about the diamond hitch, which goes back to the dawn of history in ancient Persia; every mule-packing people knows it. It is simple, but a marvel of ingenuity in which every section of the pack rope strains at every other section to make a tense lashing. Every mule knows every phase of its preparation, and is nonchalant — up to a certain point. That point is where the packer throws his weight into the final heave; before that the pack rope weaves loosely back and forth. At the correct instant the mule takes a deep breath and holds it; he is swollen to a girth that, when the pack rope is tightened, will allow him to deflate himself for ease and comfort like a lady removing her corset at eventide. The answer, by Army regulation, is patience; let the mule deflate himself when he can hold his breath no longer! This takes time, and when you have fifty mules and five packers, time becomes of the very essence. Thus when the mule begins to swell the wily packer does not tighten the pack rope; he waits. At the apex of the mule's long breath the packer brings his knee up into the mule's belly; the mule deflates with a thunderous snort and in the same instant the pack rope hauls taut, is made fast, and the mule is packed. A loose pack makes for saddle galls — and being turned out to pasture to cure them. The mule knows this too. He would rather have galls and pasture than listen to applause and praise.

Every other day there was a special pack train of three mules specially commissioned for the headquarters of Major General Shafter. There were two muleloads of ice and one of champagne; it was current rumor that this came from Colonel Astor's yacht, which was reported to be somewhere in Santiago Bay, and Colonel Astor was a member of General Shafter's staff. It was an unfortunate coincidence that the trenches surrounding General Shafter's headquarters were short of medicines and hospital supplies during this champagne-and-ice period of headquarters hardship. A mule carries 150 pounds; three mules can pack 450 pounds — which is quite a lot of medicine and supplies. But General Shafter was ill, so champagne may have come under medical supplies. In fact there was quite a bit of special correspondence between President McKinley and Secretary of War Alger in regard to the illness. Sympathetically they offered to bring him home and replace him with General Wheeler, who was next in command, and who had also been ill. General Shafter's illness proved not too precarious. It was gout.*

Yet, gout and all, he had made sound military judgments, and his choice of strategy was good. He had not succumbed to General Kent's desire to retreat after we had captured San Juan Hill, he had played superb military poker with the Spanish General Toral, and he had captured more Spanish soldiers than he had men in his whole Fifth Army Corps, more machine guns, and more artillery as well! Any criticism of General Shafter rests, with better grace, upon the complaisant contract-brokers in the War Department in the Washington of those days. However, the headquarters *might* have been moved into Santiago, closer to the ice and champagne, where one Cuban with a wheelbarrow could have delivered it.

It was August 7, at dusk. I had just returned from the Yacht Club; I didn't see Joe Howard, he was reported as well as could be expected. Captain Rafferty rode up on his mule. He had been on his daily trip back to the regiment in the trenches.

"There's news," he said. "The regiment will be here in the morning. We're going home tomorrow!"

Home.

In his gunny sacks the captain had twelve new uni-

---

* *The Fight for Santiago,* by Stephen Bonsal, Appendix, Note *S,* p. 526.

forms, khaki. "Save 'em till we get aboard," he suggested. "Maybe we'll get a bath there."

We packed our haversacks and foraged for empty flour bags. Into them we stuffed Spanish rolls, chocolate, Worcestershire sauce, fancy *petits pois,* canned peaches and pears — anything we could carry. We measured life in terms of food, or its lack; and we didn't trust Army commissary. We admired the captain's new khaki and stroked our own; it felt like silk! Till then we had not realized how filthy we were. I could scrape the grime and grease off my ragged pants.

Breakfast the next morning was a jittery affair. We sipped our coffee and kept our eyes over the rim of the tin mess cup, looking up the Santiago streets for the first glimpse of the regiment that was on its way. Then, from the left and unexpected direction and along the esplanade of the water front, we saw a column of men, in khaki, not blue, and carrying our colors. It was the regiment. They swung "fours-right" into line — line of battalions — just beyond our shed. These were the men we had known back in the States, on the transport, and in the trenches. Lean, tanned, with gaunt, hard cheekbones, with bright glistening eyes and ragged beards through which the bared teeth of emaciation showed. There was F, our company; there was Gus Pitou, a corporal now; there was Ben Payne, a new sergeant; between them they were bracing up Arthur Pendleton — a skin-tight, shrunken wreck — to help him make the transport and *home!*

We hated the general hospital, and feared it; to be

left in the trenches or Santiago was death; men struggled to keep themselves in the ranks, and were braced by the men on either side of them. There were others as badly off as Pendleton. Tom Wynn, dying, dead before we reached New York. Fred Engels was helped and half carried aboard by his bunkie, Amos Barnett, and died a week later and was buried at sea. There were not ten men in the company fit for duty or even fit to be out of a hospital — a hospital at home. That line of battalions halted and sat down, half the men not sitting, but lying on their horse-collar packs. Yet they, and we, yelled back and forth. There was the false tingle of health that followed each chills-and-fever spell; and we had the inspiration of moving, of marching again, and of going home. We would have sworn we were well men!

Next morning we went aboard. It was the transport *Grande Duchesse,* of the Ward Line in her former civil life. A Spanish tug brought us alongside the towering deck of the ship; we clambered through a cargo port and were guided through dim holds and up companion ladders to the main cabin deck. All the cabins faced outward with their doors opening to the sea; their locks and hinges were brass and their white paint immaculate as if we were paying passengers — but not quite. There were no mattresses or pillows or sheets. The bunks were bare boards and the floor too, but what of it; we had slept with land crabs and tarantulas, and nestled on cement floors in comfort. The transport was luxury — it smelled clean too! Five men to a cabin, two for the lower bunk and one for the upper, and two on the floor — or any other arrangement our ingenuity might devise. We could exercise all the ingenuity of a sardine in a can. Four of us generally slept on deck, with the sickest inside, in the lower bunk. But when it rained — those driving tropic downpours — we all went inside and gasped through the night.

The crew had watched us come aboard and climb through the cargo port. We were accustomed to each other — fever, emaciation, and gauntness had become our normal appearance. But the crew stared at us. "You fellers ain't et much!" one said. Farther on, a boatswain — I think it was — said, as my squad was climbing a companionway: "This goddam boat ain't been half unloaded — come back and I'll show you." He gave the word to other companies and squads too. So, after stowing our packs and haversacks and rifles, we went back. He pointed to a hatch down lower. I went down. A half-dozen soldiers were passing up boxes prying them open — canned goods, like those we had under our Santiago shed. I joined in — I filled a box with cans and bottles of lime juice and tins of choice bacon. I climbed out and started up for our cabin on the upper deck. At the head of the last companionway stood an adjutant. He smiled evilly as he looked down at me.

"Plundering stores is against orders," he said sternly "Bring that box up here." I knew he was going to confiscate it. I had stumbled on the very companionway he had moved to. I was at the foot of the ladder; I

knew he could not see me well on the dim lower deck.
I threw the box down. I didn't care if I was shot at
sunrise.

"Bring it up yourself, goddam you." And then I disappeared in the dusky hold. I still maintain that my remark, and the intensity of its emotion, made it more of
a prayer than a swear. The officers had the cabin mess
and with regular cooking to look forward to. He had
stolen from me and my company; he did not need it.
We did, and events proved it. I wondered if the Cal-
vinistic hell of my forebears could be entirely adequate
for such an adjutant.

Then I went below and gathered another box, but
the choice stores of that first trip were gone; I got only
second-rate stuff with no peas and mostly tomatoes,
and one bottle of lime juice. Also, however, a large
package of candles! And these, later, were most valuable. We cooked over them!

I went back again but by then there was nothing but
the trash of broken cases. Fortunately there were
other holds, and a sailor led the way to one. "I don't
know what's there, Jack," he said, "but you can find
out." The hatch cover was partly off so that one had
to crawl as through a tunnel. Ed Booth was with me,
and I had a candle. The hold was filled with boxes, tier
upon tier, and none had been broken. It was a treasure
house of canned goods and proteins. We battered open
a case. It was toilet paper. We broke open another.
Toilet paper. Another soldier crawled in and we broke
open more cases. Toilet paper. Hope kept us going and,

as we worked, we piled the broken cases behind us; there must be something somewhere. Then from one side we heard a wail that held a note of terror.

"I've dropped it, I've dropped it! The candle — and it didn't go out!"

Ed and I crawled over to him, and fast. We piled boxes behind us. Far down in the narrow space between the skin of the ship and the stacked boxes we could see a tiny glow, the shine from the candle. Ed emptied his canteen down the space. The glow continued but we could hear the little sputter of hot grease as some drops of water splashed into it. My canteen was emptied. The glow flickered but still continued. There was no alternative but to get down there, and fast. We began throwing cases behind us, and each case added to the barricade between us and the single opening under the tilted hatch cover, that would block our retreat unless that vicious little glow was killed.

We got there; but there was not much margin. The candle was burning and sputtering in its own pool of grease; one box corner was charred. We stamped out the candle and then, in almost pitch darkness, began unpiling the cases of toilet paper to work our way back to the slit of light under the hatch cover.

We went back to screening the other hold, though there was not much salvage there; yet a dozen soldiers who had only just heard of it were there finding an occasional case of tomatoes. Once they paused. There was a scream from somewhere aft of us in the dimness, a crash and a thud. A soldier had fallen into an open hatchway. A moaning came from deep down somewhere. No one paid any attention; it was a member of the crew who finally reported it. I know, because at Montauk Point I was in the same hospital tent with that soldier. He had broken his right arm and left thigh.

Back in our cabin we hooked open the door to get the breezes of the Bay of Santiago. Jimmy Lowe and Gus Pitou rigged up a blanket as a hammock and lifted Pendleton out and lashed the hammock to the rail. All day Pendleton lay there, semiconscious, until he was lifted back into the cabin at night, his eyes glassy and drooling pus. There was no hospital on board.

Distilled water was issued twice a day, hot. A cask on our deck was filled with ice, and the hot distilled water turned on it. If one fought one's way there in time, it would be cool, sometimes cold. This was for the stronger, tougher men who could jam their way in first. There was no water in which to wash our tin cups or our shallow mess tins, and both were rancid with old grease or coffee. The canned corned beef and hardtack of the travel ration had begun again. There was, we heard, a mess for those strong enough to get to it, but it was hardly worth while even for those who could. For they served canned corned beef, hardtack hash, and coffee. Once, we heard, there was dried-apple pie.

In our cabins we fared better, perhaps. But no one had much appetite. We missed coffee, and men would go to the mess for that alone, and bring it back for their cabin squad. Supplies from that looted hold went quickly. The superb canned bacon went into our mess tins and was cooked over four or five candles inside the cabins out of the drafts. The candle smoke mingled with the aroma of bacon, and no one cared. The canned peaches went fast; so did the canned pears and the cans of little peas. I still had some of the sweet chocolate from the Spanish baker, but appetites faded quickly, and hunger became a minor emotion. I have heard that this is a condition that is common for those who have undergone periods of malnutrition.

We swung in the idle waters of Santiago's landlocked bay that first day, and the next, and the next. At night we watched the surface of the bay where the sharks were cutting figure eights or patterns of graceful curves that left brilliant phosphorescent arcs on the dark waters as though some vast hand was striking matches or doing the Dutch roll on phosphorescent skates. Now and again tarpon would break the surface in an explosion of luminous spray, like the shells we had watched before San Juan and from the trenches. It was one of the most brilliant displays of phosphorescence I have ever seen. Night after night it never lost its radiance nor the sharks their curving grace. The night was full of pale blue-green arrows and sudden fountains of soft luminescence. We slept in fitful naps and woke to the bugle's reveille. From there on we waited for the clank of anchor chain that would mean the first leg of the trip home.

From dawn to dark a line of irritable men stretched

through the thwartship alley that led to starboard where the regimental and battalion surgeons had their quarters. It was the same as back in the trenches. There wasn't a grain of bismuth, and the whole ship was septic with dysentery. There was a little quinine and some compound cathartic, just as back in the trenches. And our deck, the sick-deck, was carpeted with sick men. They shuffled weakly from port to starboard and back as the tide or the tropic sun moved the shade on the decks.

There was but one latrine for the enlisted men. It had been for the second-cabin passengers, or steerage, in the former civilian days, and with it was combined a washroom with four taps and bowls along one side. It was wholly inadequate for the thousand men now on board the *Grande Duchesse*. There were two battalions of my regiment, and one battalion of Regulars, with the Regular's regimental band. The rest of our regiment was on the *St. Paul*. The inadequacy was recognized and was met by thrusting two six-by-six-inch timbers out over the fantail of the stern and lashing thereon a crude platform that was almost as wide as the ship itself. It helped; and its customers were continuous, night and day. One man weakly climbed the ship's rail to this platform and then doubled up like a jackknife in sheer exhaustion and was caught just before he would have slipped into the churning wake thirty feet below. This was after we were at sea. He lay on a coil of rope to get back his nerve, and then crawled back to his cabin.

Down below, forward, in the former steerage-class latrine, was always a line of sickly men. One morning the door was half open, blocked by the body of a dead man whose yellow hand extended across the opening. He had died that morning in there, most likely from heart failure and dysentery. At half past three that afternoon, when I went back, the body was still there, grotesquely huddled, but it had been pushed under the washstands and no longer interfered with the door.

All night sick men stumbled over sick men going to one or the other latrine. They cursed and crawled, steadying themselves against the ship's rail. There was no rank in the darkness, and an officer would be cursed for disturbing the deck, whether he was sick or not. The monotony of the bay, and its shores, closed in upon us. That first thrill of swinging into column and aboard the Spanish lighter was gone.

Then, early one morning, there was the whir of a winch up forward and we could hear the anchor chain clanking in. It was hove short. Then up and down. The whistle of the *Grande Duchesse* burst out in a shattering roar above us. The ship trembled as we felt the first throb of her engines and saw the red-roofed buildings along the shore start slowly sliding past the stanchions. On the deck above, the regimental band struck up "Home, Sweet Home" and then drifted into "Hail Columbia." Men crawled up the ship's rail and cheered — sickly men and a sickly cheer. There were men who choked as they cheered, and many lips trembled to hold back their emotion. Some men cried with silent tears; it is certain that there was not a dry eye on board.

Steadily we gathered way and headed for the narrow channel that led to the sea. We passed that little hospital island in the bay where, we had been told, Lieutenant Tiffany of the Rough Riders had been taken.* To be taken there was to die. We waved at the little figures of nurses and doctors gathered at the dock, and they waved back. We were lucky! We cheered the transports at anchor that were not yet ready to sail, and they cheered us. We passed the wreck of the *Merrimac* that had not succeeded in blocking the channel, and we cheered it. We did not know then that the President's brother Abner got a fat profit while it was still junk afloat. We steamed silently past the *Reina Mercedes,* sunk in the channel for the same purpose of blocking it, which also failed to do so. Clear of the channel, past the *morro* forts at the entrance, now we were well out in the Caribbean, bow swung eastward. Home lay just ahead!

---

* It was this little death island and Lieutenant Tiffany's being sent there that inspired Paul Dresser's ballad "Take Me Back to New York Town If I'm Going to Die."

24

A bath! The silhouette of Long Island at dawn. Quaran-
tined. Prisoners or patients? The fight for survival. We
forage for food. Fever and dysentery. How we measured
time.

THE mountains of Cuba slowly sank into one long,
undulating bank of thin blues and purples. Cape
Maisi lay ahead. Cape Maisi gave us two superb
thrills: first, as we passed it and swung west for the invasion of Cuba and eager adventure, and now as we
passed it again when every pulsing throb of the engines
meant home and the simple decencies of human dignity.

I had not yet changed into my nice new khaki uniform. I wanted a bath. To slide into those crisp pants
and immaculate jacket needed a better and more sanitary foundation than I could yet offer. What bath facilities there were for us enlisted men on the *Grande
Duchesse,* I do not know to this day. I know we were
not allowed to use the firemen's room that was large
and splendid and filled with ample, spraying jets. I had
reconnoitered the officers' quarters aft, which, strange

to say, faced the latrine that had been built out over the stern. Mostly they used the boat deck above us. Just forward of the built-out latrine was a door and a flight of steps down into the officers' dining saloon. At the bottom of these stairs, off a small landing on the right, were three bathrooms for exalted luxury. However, at the door of the dining saloon was a sentry whose duty was to ward off any stray who in fevered delirium might fall down the stairs on his way to or from the latrine. Further, his job was to prevent any such unlicensed scum as I from access to those immaculate bathrooms. I cased the joint carefully. I noted that the sentry mostly faced the dining room and watched the laying of the tables for the next meal with concentrated interest. This helped.

I hung my nice new khaki pants over my arm, and the blouse as well, together with the new blue shirt that came with them. I hung about the fantail as one who did not dare to leave the neighborhood much, and waited until the deck sentry had turned a corner, and then I sidled rapidly to the door that led below. I did *not* sneak down those stairs; I walked boldly down trying to make a footfall like an officer, not too loud but like an irritated officer. The sentry's back was still toward me as he faced the dining saloon. I gave the door at the foot of the stairs a mighty slam shut — an angry officer might do that — and darted to the right and into the first mahogany-and-silver bathroom. Outside I heard the sentry inquire, "Who's there?" I never heard him because the water, hot and cold, was rushing into the tub with such a torrent of splashing that any officer, naturally, could not have heard any inquiry. Besides, no sneaking prowler would have come banging down those stairs and begun slamming doors. He was a tactful sentry.

Luxury? Hot and cold water, for there were both salt and fresh water taps! Soap — hot water and fresh soap! Face towels, little and big, and a vast turkish bath towel about as large as both sections of one of our dog tents. I luxuriated. Never, never was there such a bath. I stuffed my old outfit through the porthole, including the last romantic bellyband from New York, by now a mere strip of red flannel. The tub was full. I splashed in it as might an officer, heavily, like some old walrus. I used up most of the soap. I looked at the tub and its contents in repulsion. I drew another tubful, nice and tepid. I rinsed. I took my time. If I was destined for the brig or the guardhouse I wanted to feel that I had had my money's worth. Presently I climbed out, immaculate, and enfolded myself in the turkish towel. I arrayed myself in my new khaki; I had my new Army shoes too; only the socks were the same as in the trenches. Then the moment came.

I stepped out briskly to the landing. The sentry's back was turned, and I slammed the door shut. He turned and saw me on my way up the stairs. I did not stop to bandy words with him, but I could hear him. He was using the good old Army vernacular, prefaced frequently by the word "lousy." Well, I had been lousy, very; in that he was accurate. Once on deck I had luck, there was no sentry in sight. I made for the latrine and was lost in its indistinguishable shifting of customers. But, with that bath, I was a well man — almost.

Perhaps there was inspection of the *Grande Duchesse*. I do not know. Sometimes an officer strolled along our sick-deck. Every morning a hospital steward and a surgeon would come down with a pouch of something slung over his shoulder. Perhaps most of the pills were of bicarbonate of soda. Surgeon General Sternberg was capable of most anything; for it was he who said of us, in the trenches, that we should be moved back some twenty or so miles into the higher hills and mountains where it was healthier! They couldn't get sufficient food into the trenches when the trenches were only two or three miles out of Santiago — and how would they get it out twenty miles or more, without roads, and with the rainy season on! A mind like that would be capable of prescribing shiploads of bicarbonate of soda for malnutrition, since the special focus of both is in the stomach.

Irritation now became easier and more frequent. Sick men cursed each other and, too sick to fight, swore to beat each other to death when they were well enough. Pendleton's blanket hammock was tied to the rail each day; and he lay there, eyes half-closed and glazed with fever, drooling, indifferent to food other than some condensed milk diluted with water. He got the same medical attention as the rest, maybe less, for no one expected him to last the trip. But he survived the Montauk camp, too, and recovered.

Fred Engels did not. One day he was discovered in his cabin, dead. How long he had been dead no one knew. How long his side-partner had been sprawled beside him, unconscious or delirious, no one knew either. The stateroom was filthy with dysentery and neglect. Later there was a burial at sea, from our deck.

The sea was calm for the entire trip. Once we passed a night of rain squalls with our cabin doors closed against the driving water — for we were on the windward side — and our five men, one in delirium, cursed each other in the tangible stench. With morning, the sun, and the broad stretch of open sparkling sea, when we could get out onto the open deck, we felt again that alternating surge of health and strength. We laughed and the fights were forgotten. Then we started the same routine all over again — the feeble scramble for cool water at the cask, and the warm liquid that was the share for most of us; the hope for coffee from the able-bodied mess; the aimless, dreary hours in which even the trips to the latrine became a welcome break in the monotony of sun and sea during the endless hours.

Then, in one slow, sweet cool of dawn, we saw against the horizon the low, purple silhouette of the hill of Montauk Point, Long Island. The throb of the screws slowed down and stopped; we heard the hoarse rattle of anchor chain through the hawsepipes. We

were home. The early morning air was bracing; it was
cool after the hot Cuban sun, yet it was August. Sick
men slapped each other on the back; men clawed up
the ship's rail and looked hungrily at the distant shore.
Stronger men helped weaker to the rail. There was
wine in the very air.

One of the old Coney Island iron steamboats, its
paddlewheels churning a lovely wake on either side,
was coming out from a tiny dock. Fenders were put
over and she made fast to us. On our deck names were
being called, the names of the sick men, who were the
first to go ashore. A gangplank went over to the upper
deck of the little side-wheel steamer. Men, with their
packs, rifles, cartridge belts, haversacks, and canteens
lined up to the call. An officer passed along: "Leave
your rifles, men," he said, "and belts — you'll not need
them." The little line shuffled along to the gangplank.
Four sailors helped the men climb the rail and steadied
them on the gangplank. Others lined it to pass the men
along so they would not slump through its guard rail
to the water below. Men from the Coney Island boat
grasped each soldier to steady him as he came aboard.
Men were protesting that they needed no help — no
one had helped them before. "Hell, I'm all right. I feel
all right now!" Men fought against sickness as if sickness were yielding to something effeminate. Captain
Rafferty was at the rail checking the sick men over. "Go
on, go on," he'd say, "you're going to be all right —
steady." A deckhand on the Coney Island boat said in
surprise: "Hey, you fellows don't look so bad. We

heard you was all sick." His standards were high; I doubt if anything less than *rigor mortis* would have met his views. Yet, in its way, I think it was a compliment.

On the deck of the little steamboat men tried to walk, and then sat down. Very quickly men were lying down all over. Litter cases like Pendleton were being passed over the rail, but there were very few. So many men wanted to show they were not sick. They waved and called up to the decks of the *Grande Duchesse*. Someone started to sing "A Hot Time in the Old Town Tonight," and a few joined in, but the singing died down quickly.

As we neared the narrow beach and the little dock, we could see a few ambulances in the background and some trim figures in blue and some in khaki — hospital orderlies and ambulance drivers. Again, for a few moments, there was a thrill in the air and the inspiration of health in our bodies.

A medical officer came on board as we tied up to the dock.

"All who can walk," he directed, "walk to the ambulance over there; they'll take you."

The feel of American boards under our feet, of American sand to press upon, and the sandy sedge grass beyond was wonderful. Men walked, helping each other. A medical officer saw it: "Here, you," he shouted. "Let him alone. Bring a stretcher," he called to a hospital corpsman, and the stretcher came. And men protested against being put on a stretcher!

Back in the trenches when the sickness struck and
men stumbled as they walked or went on guard, there
would come the flippant shout: "Walk! Walk, goddam you, walk!" There was no jeer about it; it is the
way, I think, that men keep up each other's nerve when
the going gets rough. "Walk, goddam you, walk!"
was a pungent gesture in contempt of fate, a gesture of
rugged sympathy for worn men. And the worn men
smiled back, too.

Ambulances went off with the stretcher cases. Presently they came back and the walking sick were loaded
in. We crowded into the ambulance and more were
crowded in after. My ambulance carried thirteen men
and two more on the seat with the driver. Most of our
gear, except for haversack and canteen, had been left
on one boat or the other. There were not enough ambulances and not enough stretchers. From the little
wharf we could see, only a short distance away, a large
hospital tent with the yellow flag of pestilence flying at
its staff. Yellow fever! Who cared; we were home.
Maybe we had it ourselves — for we were being taken
to the quarantined Hospital Detention Camp under suspicion of yellow fever, with a guard from the Tenth
Cavalry thrown around it so that no one could come in
or out without rigid inspection and an official pass.
The rigidity of this quarantine may be imagined from
the fact that when the New York City postal authorities went out to establish postal facilities for this hospital — there were five streets of tents and eighteen
tents to each street, with five to eight men to a tent —

the Army medical authorities refused them permission to enter. We were all under suspicion of having some form of dangerous and communicable tropical diseases.

This quarantine hospital camp was on a little plateau that rested on top of a high hill overlooking Montauk Bay. We climbed out of the ambulance and joined a scattered group of a hundred or so that were lying on the grass, and we too lay down where we were. More ambulances arrived and more men lay down. We saw the tents beyond and knew that we would be assigned to them. But there was no one in charge of us.

Presently a medical officer came and looked us over. Few had a blanket; and the breeze seemed cool, for we had just left the tropics.

"All those," he called out, "who can walk had best get to their regiment — it's about a mile off. You'll get more there than we have here. It's for your own good, so if you can make it, *walk!*"

He disappeared.

Some few men tried it; but soldiers get wise, and we thought he was merely trying out for malingerers. Malingerers, hell! The few that got up were damned by the rest. "Lie down, you damned fool — they've got to do something."

Not a man was fit to walk a mile to his regiment — and some regiments were farther off, and no one knew where.

We were landed at about nine that morning. Once —

it seemed to be afternoon — a hospital sergeant came around with some milk; it was enough for only half the men lying there. He disappeared and did not come back. A little later another hospital sergeant came among us with some beef extract, about a wineglassful to a man. This came to about one man in four. Then there was no more. I missed out on both. The afternoon sea breeze was cooler — it was cold to us. Then a few stretcher bearers came and began moving us to the tents. It was dusk when my turn came. The tent was shelter from the wind, and there were blankets in it. The grass of the plateau was its floor. Four men were already there. One was the soldier who had fallen down the hold of the *Grande Duchesse;* two were men of the Rough Riders who had never been in Cuba but were kept on some special detail in this country. The fourth man had dysentery and fever, and spent most of his time in delirium or begging for a bandage around his head.

It was after midnight that night when an elderly, kindly civilian, a volunteer nurse, of which there was one for each tent-street, brought in some food in an iron pail. It was a pailful of greasy water, lukewarm, and filled with ragged morsels of mutton and gristle and sinew, with potatoes here and there. It had the flavor of tallow, slightly moldy or rancid. We ladled it out by the light of his lantern, and I drank what I could in the dark.

In the morning the two Rough Riders dressed, combed their hair, adjusted their blue polka-dot neckerchiefs, and went out into the tented street to the mess shack at its farther end. It was quite a walk; they were the only ones in our tent — it was in the last row of the camp — who could make it. When they came back they talked of the oatmeal and milk, the fried eggs and the bacon, and reviled it, all but proud of the fact that they were taking the hardships of war on the chin. How they got into that quarantine camp I do not know. In recollections over many years, I find their memory precious. They spoke educated English and talked of dances and parties and summer beaches and of the vast minutiae of the *haut monde*. But they never brought back an egg or a cup of coffee to us; our only food supply was the volunteer civilian nurse. We got, in our turn, about noon, some milk from one pail and some oatmeal from the other; sometime long after dark he would be back with a pailful of stew, luke-warm, and another pail of bread. There were almost twenty tents in our street, and he had about a hundred men to feed. He did all he could, faithfully and stead-ily. If he had not, we would have had nothing; no man, from the beginning of the war to its end, has my greater respect.

It was on the third day, possibly the second, that a medical student came into the tent and examined us. He was what was known as a "contract surgeon" and he must have had two years in a medical school to qualify for such a job; a medical course is four years. He gave the delirious soldier a bandage around his head; to me, five two-grain quinine pills and one fuzzy

blue-mass pill of about veterinary size. The soldier
with broken bones was told to lie quiet and later he
would get a change of bandages! Lie quiet! How much
sprightliness could you achieve with your right arm
and left leg broken, and maybe a rib or so! Also, the
"surgeon" insisted that I must get into hospital pajamas, which the civilian nurse would deliver.

The next day the pajamas were delivered, along
with a hospital man to get me into them. The delirious man got into his on the promise of a new bandage
around his head. The broken-winged man could not be
maneuvered into his without a derrick. The Rough
Riders were out somewhere. The broken-winged soldier and I had agreed that I must not get into my pajamas. "You can't get out of this camp if you're in pajamas — you can't run the guard. You've got to get
out. There's plenty help outside. Get yourself out!"

So the orderly and I struggled. He would have had
to cut me out of my uniform. And, anyway, I do not
think he really gave a damn one way or the other; no
one in that hospital camp did. If you died, so what; if
you lived, that's your luck. I never did get into pajamas. But the delirious man did, with many others.
He got a fresh bandage around his head; it was what
he wanted to cure the pain, or ache, in his stomach!

I swallowed the quinine pills, but I threw out the
blue mass, a sort of compound cathartic made from
mercury, I believe, and a very popular remedy nearly
a century ago. It was the last medical examination I

received in that quarantined hospital, and the last medicine.

The broken-winged soldier and I talked things over. I knew that if I could get out I could get word to newspapermen somewhere. Whatever the hospital camp had been intended to be, it was not; it was in utter breakdown. Days came and went. About noon we got breakfast, oatmeal ladled into our mess cup and a dash of diluted condensed milk added. After dark came dinner — mutton stew — and then a wait until the following noon. We tore up a handful of grass from the floor of our tent and swabbed out the mess cup after the oatmeal-and-milk. The next morning we swabbed out the grease of the mutton stew and waited for the oatmeal. The two Rough Riders were out most of the time. They came in at intervals with various supplies — where they got them is still a mystery. They had a can of peaches, a can of condensed milk, some fancy crackers, and a jar of Chinese ginger in candied fruit, which they hid under their blankets or ate as they sat on their cots while we watched them with amazed eyes. They finally left — they were utter fakes as men — and they left to me their jar of gingered fruit. We threw it out, in our pride, as not fit to be eaten by decent men.

One day another civilian came into the tent. He was a thin, pale little man with silky, curling first-growth whiskers and a conspicuous Bible under his arm. He had heard us.

"You men — oh, you men!" he was ejaculating in tones of horror. "Such blasphemy, such taking the Name. You soldiers, who have been so near to death — to use such language! Oh you, you, who have been in the presence of death, who have faced your God! I am praying for you. I am praying for you!"

We suggested, and in unrestrained secular language, that less prayer and more food might help. He turned the thought aside. Presently he went to another tent, in utter earnestness and in complacent uselessness. The Bible never left its place under his arm, and he never lifted a finger to help that civilian nurse who was our only attendant, and for some hundred other men too. At any hour of the day or night, or at dawn, he would thrust himself between the tent flaps and, with rapturous eyes, launch at us his excited prayers. For this world, this hospital, he had no time; we were merely a peg upon which to hang his pallid egotism. The Assistant Postmaster of New York City (my uncle) was not permitted to establish any postal service in that camp, though he made a special and official trip for that purpose. Yet this pious, worthless nincompoop was set at large to pray upon us.

I thought I was getting better, and I tried for the mess shack. The shack was for the cooks and officers; the open was for us. A couple of planks on horses were the tables; you gathered an empty crate or box where you found one. A cook's assistant came out of the shack with a Buzzacot pan filled with fried eggs.

He placed it at the end of a table and there was a stampede of men. The pan was hardly down before it was empty. Those who had not succeeded in getting an egg went back on the grass and waited. Another batch of fried eggs and another rush, and back on the grass while the winners ate. I got an egg, once. It was a stale egg, fried till its edges were crisp celluloid, and cooked in a grease that must have been brought up from the Cuban trenches we had left, in a spirit of Army thrift. Then came coffee. The cook's assistant appeared with a huge pot of it. There was an instant rush for the table. If you had a seat at the table he would fill your mess cup; if you had no crate to sit on, you got no coffee. Whether he or the medical headquarters staff had devised this strict table etiquette I never knew. I do not think the cook had sufficient imagination to have thought of it. There was no officer in control; the cook was a civilian contract cook who could do as he damned well pleased, and he did. There was white bread on the tables, but the struggle was over butter. No sooner was butter on the table than eager hands grabbed it. Sick men are not mannerly, and often bare hands grabbed it, for table utensils were scarce.

I got some white bread and went back to the tent. I passed a man who had just left the table. "Hey, Jack," he said, "want an egg?" He pointed to his on his mess tin. "It's yours if you can eat it." I couldn't. Yet some were wolfing them.

I was strong enough to get down to that shack

once a day, and pouch a little bread for the tent. *Thou shalt not steal* was the cook's motto and upheld with an angry iron spoon wielded by an assistant. The food was fairly snatched from the pans the moment it touched the table, and an instant later there was none left. Theoretically, there were three successive tables; actually it was one long melee that the assistant cooks stopped with an iron spoon as the formal hour for feeding was passed. We hated the cooks as cordially as they hated us.

In these days the grass between the tented streets was flecked with blood and dysentery. Few could make the latrine at the far end of the camp. Tents were latrines. One could not merely stumble and drop; one must keep his eye searching for an oasis. At night it was not so simple. Then packing cases, sawed in half lengthwise, were brought in — one for about every five tents. They were neither emptied nor treated with chemicals, but they were a luxury measured by the effort that had gone before. One poor devil, weak and emaciated, toppled over and lay until he gathered strength enough to crawl off. Through all this the civilian volunteer nurse kept plugging away. I have often wished I had known his name.

It is difficult to realize the utter emptiness of time in those days. We measured time in food; in the time between chills; and when the fever left us, and we were partly brisk and living again, we measured it in dysentery, and in latrines. How the broken-winged man measured it I do not know; he lay all day in his cot,

with the tent for his latrine — even the boxes in the
street were beyond his reach. Yet, somewhere, Army
contracts were glowing in the gentle warmth of political protection.

Then came the storm.

The storm was an act of Providence — for nothing
less could have ended this ingrained orgy of incapacity that stigmatizes, for all history, the vain regime
of Sternberg, Surgeon General of the United States.

25

Saved by the storm. Tents go down in the night. Preparing for the Secretary of War's inspection. I am appointed spokesman for my tent. I get a pass.

THAT evening I had scrubbed out my mess cup with grass — ready for breakfast. It was dark, though early, for storm clouds were gathering. I had turned over to sleep in the not too unpleasant exhaustion that follows chills and fever.

I had been in one of those dozes of the unwell. I was dreaming. I was back on San Juan; but there was no danger; I was half eyewitness and half soldier. The little bullets were z-zinging through the air, and none of them could hit me — I was immune to them, and knew it. I was in the battle, but not of it. Now and again there was the blast of a field gun. It was all highly dramatic, and I had an orchestra seat. Men were shouting commands and so were officers. The shouting rose, but it was not I; it bore into my dreamy consciousness. It was the broken-winged man over in the corner. Slowly I returned to the tent. The spatter of bullets dissolved into raindrops — machine guns of them — beating on the tent fly above us; the flash of the field gun was the blast of thunder. The broken-winged man was yelling: "Get out — get out!" In the flashes I could see that the tent poles were slanting and its ridgepole lowering under the blasts of wind.

The delirious man with his bandage and his belly-ache was at the forward tent pole and heaving against it. I jumped up and joined him. His delirium was gone. The canvas front of the tent was as hard as a board against the gale. We heaved against the tent pole; it meant nothing. Steadily it pressed back, and stronger. We could feel it going. From his cot the broken-winged man was shouting to "get out — get out, you can't hold it! Go and get help!" The pole pressed in and, in a final burst, came down on us in a massive bundle of wet canvas and pole. Somewhere in that mess was the man with the head bandage. I was swathed in the stiff, soaking canvas, in total darkness that not even a lightning flash could penetrate. And the pole was across me somewhere, pinning me across the middle. I felt the leg of my cot, and it gave me the direction in which to crawl. I wriggled out of that canvas and from under the pole, but it took time. I learned something about panic too. Outside, the rain was pouring and driving in blasts before the gale. In a lightning flash I saw a tent fly sail through the air like a witch on a broom. The tent next to us was sagging like ours, and down toward the foot of the tent street not a tent was left. I pushed around to where the front of the tent had been. The man with the bandage around his head was already there. He was running in a little circle and making hoarse, inarticulate animal noises; he was wholly out of his mind, his eyes saw nothing, but he still had the blanket around his shoulders that was flapping like a signal flag.

But there was the little colporteur with the curly black beard. In the lightning flashes I saw that he had his Bible under his arm as he clasped and unclasped his hands in a jerky hysteria. He was sobbing dry sobs and over and over again saying, "Oh my God — oh my God — so many men in the presence of their Maker tonight — oh my God — oh my God!" He could not hear me when I spoke to him. "Oh my God — oh my God," he kept on. I put my hand on his shoulder, and he did not feel it — he did not know I was there.

"Get help!" I shouted. He never heard me. By the lightning flashes I could see his eyes staring vacantly as he chanted.

The sentry of the Tenth Cavalry came up; this was on his post and he joined us. "This is awful!" he said.

"Call the guard," I said. I had no fever, no chill, I was soaked through, and I never felt better in my life.

"I called the guard — they don't hear." He called the guard again. "Co'pral o' the Guard Number Seven!" He had a good resonant voice, but the words were whipped from his lips and went howling out into the black gale. "I've called 'em aplenty. No one hears — not even the next post — I been down there a-callin' too — they can't hear me an' I don't hear no calls a-going back."

"Fire your piece," I told him.

"Can't do that — lessen there's a fire or insurrection — or fightin'."

"Fire your piece," I demanded, "this is an emergency."

"No," he responded, "I can't fire no piece."

Even that might not have been heard. Then I remembered the broken-winged man down under all that wet canvas. I went back and crawled under the tent where his cot was. There was no one in the cot or under it. I went back to the front. There he was, he had just arrived. It must have been agony to get out, but he had made it by himself. The sentry was still shouting, "Co'pral of the Guard, Number Seven," and it whirled out into the gale and was lost in the wind. I told broken-wing that he wouldn't fire his piece.

"Fire your piece, goddam you," said broken-wing.

"Can't do it." He raised his voice in another call. It was no use.

"You go for help — up at headquarters," said broken-wing.

I knew where headquarters was — farther away than the cook shack. I slopped through puddles ankle deep. I stumbled over guy ropes, tripped over tent pegs. I went through a pile of tent wreckage and saw tents askew with now and again a tent fly ripped off or billowing in the streets. The flashes of lightning helped. I reached the headquarters of the surgeon in charge of the camp. It was on a platform reached by a flight of steps. It was around midnight and a hospital sergeant was sitting inside at a desk with a lantern for a light. On the porch a sentry stopped me. I was drenched, I was dirty, and he suspected I might be one of the delirious inmates and on a rampage, or crazy.

"I want help," I said. "My street is all down — we need help!"

"G'wan," said the sentry not unkindly, "back to your tent, Jack — everything's all right." Medical sentries had evidently been instructed to be kind to nuts. But I raised my voice in anger. If a row started I knew someone would come to stop it. I hoped an officer would come. But it was the hospital sergeant from inside. He was nice and dry and comfortable.

"Get the hell back to your tent!" he ordered.

"He says the tents are going down," explained the sentry.

"We need help," I shouted. "The tents are going." There were other words, mine and the sergeant's. A row would bring an officer. It did. He sounded irritated; it was around midnight. I felt better.

"Man says tents are going down, sir," said the sergeant.

"What is it, my man?" asked the officer.

I explained, excitedly, and quite likely deliriously and with incoherence. The officer listened.

"Well," he said soothingly, "we'll have a look. Sergeant, get this man back to his tent." The sergeant picked up the lantern; I felt what he was thinking, nice dry officer sending a nice dry sergeant out to get wet. He was not cordial. "Come on, Jack," he said, and I followed. "Where's your goddam tent?" I pointed in the general direction.

By some freak the gale had not damaged the first rows of tents, those on the bay side. Mine was in the last row, the worst hit. The hospital headquarters had only a touch of the storm — just "some rain." The sergeant suggested I get into a nearby tent and he'd look me up in the morning. He too was slopping through puddles of water ankle deep and often street wide. It made no difference to me, I was soaked. We came to the street just before mine; some tents were down and many warped and bent; it was bad. Then we came to mine. There were, as dawn showed, but five of the eighteen left standing. Some were crumpled masses of shapeless wet canvas and some, like mine, had vanished completely. The sergeant took one look.

"Good God!" he said. "Here, you, get into any of those tents back there — I'll take care of this."

The sentry had gone; so had the man with the bandage around his head; so had the colporteur and his Bible; only the broken-winged man was left where our tent had been. "I'll take care of him," said the sergeant.

Daylight came. Report circulated that five men had

been found dead in their rain-soaked blankets and cots. And of all this the official records set forth only that "there was some rain."

That night I found a tent with a board floor, on which I slept. In the morning I rescued my two sketch-books. Then I was assigned another tent at the head of the second street and one of the nearest to the la-trine. Also, before noon of that day, something had been stirred up. There were civilian laborers in the streets with brooms and pails of water: they were *washing the grass* and removing the packing-case la-trines, to be burned outside the camp. They were not replaced, but orders were sent out that not to use the one official latrine was a guardhouse offense! We heard one man had already been arrested for not being able to get there! Rumors were flying. There was to be a new medical commandant. Rumors were that one had thrown up his hands in despair and stayed drunk. There was a rumor that we were all to be discharged. There was another that we were all to be shipped to the hospitals in New York City! It was a good rumor. And it was rumored that Secretary of War Alger would visit the camp tomorrow! This proved to be true, and it made us angry.

That the grassy streets should be washed with brooms and the street latrines moved and sick men threatened with arrest if they could not make the head of the street and back, all so that Secretary of War Alger might not know of the scandals of stupidity and incapacity, gave us a hot resentment. Yet, it was possible that Washington *had* heard of us and that something would happen. Our street crowded into other tents.

We heard there was plenty of milk for the asking up at the cook shack. I went up to find out. And it was true. Eight big quilted-and-canvas-covered dairy cans of milk were lined up outside the cook shack. We could have all we wanted. Men were converging on the cook shack — milk, fresh milk!

"Milk?" someone called to the cook's assistant in the doorway of his shack.

"Sure," he said. "Help yourself." He pointed to the row of hooded cans.

There was a rush for the cans. The quilted covers were tossed off and men plunged their cups in. Some of those nearest poured it into the cups of those behind. The news was shouted down the streets. More men came, some running. I was not in that first front rank, but a man edged his way out and poured his cup into mine. Men were jostling to get at the cans; men struggled out to where they had elbow room to take their drink. Milk spilled and splashed. It was a small riot — but there was no anger in it. In the doorway of the shack appeared the red face and burly form of the head cook. Perhaps the noise had irritated him.

"Get oudt!" he shouted angrily as he waved a heavy, long-handled milk dipper. There was a protest from those nearest. They had been told they could have the milk. In that same instant the cook charged, his big milk dipper flailing on the head and shoulders of those nearest. He was savage in a raging ferocity. A couple of men were knocked down, for there was little room to back away in the press where they stood. Then the crowd turned; it pressed forward in sheer mass. It was a riot of sick men, but of sick men whose anger made them well for the moment. He could not swing his dipper. He backed away and men pressed forward. His assistants rushed up; a table was overturned and its parts could be nasty weapons. He was calling for the guard now, and his face was less ruddy. We would have killed him had we been able — and I say *we* thoughtfully, for I would not have shirked the decent instincts and impulses of that moment. These were no tame tabby-cat men. That camp was from every regiment of the Fifth Army Corps of the Cuban invasion. They were men who only counted the odds when the fight was over. In fact, that is why and how Bloody Ford and Hell's Pocket stopped nothing and that San Juan fell.

An officer and a hospital sergeant roughed their way through. The cooks retreated inside.

"No milk," ordered the officer brusquely. "Get back to your quarters. Sergeant, put a guard over the cans."

We drifted back to our tents and lay down.

The milk? I had forgotten it, almost. I could not drink mine; it was cold, but soured. Few could do more than sip a bit of it.

The next day Secretary of War Alger came to the camp; everything had been slicked. Surgeon General Sternberg had ordered that everything must be a model for the Secretary. And it was, except for the men in camp. The Secretary walked through each street in a frock coat and a silk hat; slightly behind him came his staff, golden and immaculate. He was a small man, and slight, with a gray mustache and a goatee. He stopped at a tent and asked pleasantly how everything was. He was told bluntly that everything was rotten. A few said everything was all right, thank you, and were given hell by their squad. He talked to more tents, and kept his staff at a respectful distance. In the street of tents next beyond that he was then inspecting, men went ahead and passed the word: "Have someone speak — give 'em hell — he wants to know. He's asking." The street I was in was next. Back of my tent a voice was whispering: "Get up, get up and tell — Alger's asking questions — have a man speak — Christ, we'll die if we stay here!"

I was hastily picked to speak for us.

The Secretary stopped and looked through the open tent flap.

"Attention!" someone called. Men rose from their cots.

"At ease," said the Secretary. "How are you, men? Can we do anything for you?" His voice was pleasant. It may have been only the ordinary routine question. From the rear of the tent I could hear a tense whisper: "Go on — get going!" I saluted. I have never forgotten that moment.

"Mr. Secretary," I said, "I am speaking for this tent and many other tents. We are dying here without attention, without rations or medicines. Five men were picked up yesterday morning, dead. For two days men have been washing the grass with brooms so that you would not see the blood and the dysentery or know the facts. Latrine boxes were in the streets; they have been removed. Every effort has been made to make this place nice for your inspection. And it's a lie. We're dying of neglect."

I was conscious of an audience behind me; men were pressing against the rear wall of the tent. There was another hoarse whisper: "Go on — give it to him straight."

I could see the official staff, two paces beyond, stiffen; one of them, I knew, must be the surgeon-commander of this camp. Maybe they could shoot a sick man at sunrise, but not in front of the Secretary of War. I did not care.

"You have been lied to in this inspection, Mr. Secretary," I went on, "this hospital is a lie. Anyone who tells you different is a liar. We have friends at our homes and we can't get to them. I have had five quinine and one blue mass since the transport landed. We will die if we are kept here."

The Secretary listened. "There, there, my man," he said mildly. "We'll fix everything." This was just soothing talk to a sick man.

"Give us a furlough," I answered, "so we can get to our own people and friends. Those men back there are lying to you. Everything is to make a nice camp for you to see. Give us a furlough."

"Tut, tut," said the Secretary, "you must not talk like that. We'll do better than a furlough — we're going to give you your discharge."

"I'm telling you the truth," I answered. "We're dying here without care."

I dropped back to my cot. From other tents he got the same, I heard. Now and then someone would say that everything was fine, but there were many who told him the truth, and even cursed as they did it.

The night came on. Secretary Alger's visit was feverishly discussed. Was there hope — a furlough — or a discharge? No one could tell, and the numb waiting returned.

Then, in the morning came a rumor. Passes to New York City were to be issued — were being issued! A man showed me one. It was true! Slowly the details spread; an adjutant's tent had been set up at one end of the camp; one applied there. Promptly I applied. No passes to New York. Yes, there had been some, but they were gone, a cut-and-dried sergeant major explained; go back to your tent. Then came another rumor. Passes *were* being given out, but you first had to prove that you could walk to the railroad station, and that was almost a mile away. Hell, the men who most needed the passes couldn't get them! Walk to the railroad station? What were those Army wagons doing, and the ambulances? A railroad baggage car could be used as a hospital; men had slept on floors before!

I tried again. A little line of men waited outside

the adjutant's tent. The word passed down the line:
"Don't sit down — you've got to walk to the station
or no pass." So we stood up. I had long ago forgotten
my bunkie, Jimmy. Somehow he too was in this camp
and on this line. We lost a place on the line in order to
be together; we leaned against each other for support. He had his haversack with his sketchbooks and
I had mine; nothing else mattered. Jimmy had a boil
on his forehead that was, in truth, as big as half an
egg. Together we stepped into the adjutant's tent.

"What's this man doing here?" demanded the adjutant.

"He's my bunkie," explained Jimmy. I was behind
Jimmy and had him by the back of his shirt to steady
him. A pass was made out.

"Go to the bath tent," explained the adjutant, "take
a bath, get into this uniform. Then come back here for
the pass. Can you walk to the station?"

"Yessir," said Jimmy.

I went through the same routine, and told the same
lie. We knew any Army teamster would give us a lift.
Outside, a hospital sergeant beckoned us over to a
rather large hospital tent that was the bath house.
There was a new pump some fifty feet away. Inside
the tent were three round wooden washtubs, each full
of foul water with a greasy, soapy scum floating over
it. Thick, dirty cloths were scattered over the wooden
floor; they were towels, and mixed with them were
fetid heaps of abandoned uniforms. The sergeant
handed out new uniforms, new socks, new underwear

— a complete outfit — donated. "From Helen Gould," he said.

All that morning men had been taking a bath in these tubs of unchanged water and leaving behind them the fevered accumulation of weeks. "You can get new water at the pump," said the sergeant. "You take a bath, or no pass. Suit yourself."

It was ingenious. If you were strong enough to walk to the station you were strong enough to lug water. And those tubs held some two hundred pounds. Two sick men were out pumping even now; they were still pumping when Jimmy and I finished. Jimmy and I undressed slowly as we eyed those tubs. This irritated the sergeant, or maybe he had a kindly heart — it is nice to think so. The lack of speed seemed to provoke him. "For God's sake, get a move on!" he said. "I'll be back in ten minutes. And no faking — you take a bath!" He went out. Sixty seconds later, sergeantlike, he poked his head between the tent flaps. "Say," he said, "hurry up with that bath!" He saw two naked men surveying the scummy tubs. This time he went off to the adjutant's tent; the time before he had not, for we had been peeking. He returned — and it had not been ten minutes. Two naked men were whirling towels about their heads, the floor was pools of water, for we had dumped some over to stand in. Our hair was wet — we didn't care what happened to our insect friends — and the sergeant seemed satisfied. Jimmy, more conscientious than I, had actually stepped into a tub.

The adjutant issued each of us a ticket from Montauk Point to New York City and five dollars in cash. Now we could eat!

Under my new uniform blouse were buttoned my two sketchbooks; they were dirty, greasy, and wholly unhygienic, I suppose, like everything we had. We had been ordered to leave everything behind when we put on the new uniform and underwear. In those sketchbooks were men who had died and men who had lived; there were the trenches — one sketch under fire — and Jimmy had made a sketch of me and I of him on that Misery Hill.

A Tenth Cavalry sentry inspected our passes and we went through his line. Beyond him the hill sloped sharply. We slid down that slope and waited at the bottom for an Army wagon. The first one that came along stopped as it reached us.

"You boys from up there?" the driver asked, as he pointed to the hospital plateau above. "Want a lift?" A civilian beside him reached down and we climbed up. "Get down there." He pointed to the wagon box behind him. "I ain't supposed to do this." He indicated the civilian beside him, "Except for him, he's Red Cross."

We got down out of sight and he started up his four-horse team. The Red Cross civilian began asking questions. He wanted to know about that hospital camp. He was the secretary to some New Yorker in the upper brackets of wealth and philanthropy.

"I've wondered," he said, "why they won't let the Red Cross inside that hospital. I've tried, but they say they need nothing. I have money."

We told him of the food, of the storm, of the dead picked out of it, of no medicines — everything. He offered us money, but we did not need it.

The wagon pulled up at the freight shed and Jimmy and I climbed out. We hunted up the passenger station; it was crowded with soldiers, some from our camp and many from the regiments brigaded around it. There was a lunch counter, and it was jammed. In the confusion I lost Jimmy, but I got to the counter and a stool. The excitement of freedom was freshening. Again I felt that wine of health. And I was hungry. I was swollen with the bloat of malnutrition; my belt would barely meet. I was buoyant. There was pie, milk, coffee, sandwiches, and bananas. I craved all of them; it was not hunger, it was craving; and I had five dollars. I drank two glasses of milk, tall ones. I bought a whole can of peaches and ate half of it; the rest I saved for the train trip. I bought a bunch of bananas to go with the peaches on the train. I knew the value of food on a train. I had two cups of coffee with milk and sugar, plenty of sugar, and a piece of peach pie. The girl behind the counter gave me a paper bag for my can of peaches, the bananas, and an extra ham sandwich, and I went out to look for the train. It had not yet come in, but when it did it would turn around and start right back.

The station platform was crowded with soldiers

shuffling about and also waiting. I could not find Jimmy. We had agreed that we were going in on the Pullman, and we knew there would be a rush for seats. The Pullman would have a soft carpet on the floor, and we could lie down on it. Presently we could see the headlights in the distance, then the passengers alighting. There was a Pullman, but the porter would not let me in. You had to buy a ticket from him, and he would not sell one until the train had been turned around and pulled back into the station. I sat on the steps and rode around the yard during the switching. Then, as we pulled into the station, he opened the door and sold me a ticket. It was the last one he had, the others had been reserved. Jimmy was nowhere to be seen.

From New York City to Montauk Point, this one-track Long Island Rail Road was the only transportation. For one hundred and twenty-five miles this railroad had a monopoly, and there were thirty thousand troops at the Montauk end of it. Its railroad yard had been laid down overnight. The nearest town to Montauk camp was Amagansett, eighteen miles away — over a day's march for infantry, and for wagons it was sandy roads, fetlock deep, among the sedge grass of the dunes or scrubby pine barrens! It was the town of Amagansett that supplied the labor and dug the few wells for this camp, and the water for those workers had to be, at first, hauled from that town. The Long Island Rail Road certainly knew the right hands to shake in Washington in order to get that camp established at the end of their one-track line. Every dollar of their profits was flecked with the blood of dead and dying men. But, in those days of Mark Hanna and the complaisant McKinley, they were neither better nor worse than the meat packers with their "embalmed beef" and the canned meat made for Japanese coolies and salvaged for American soldiers.

For the first few minutes the Pullman seat was comfort; for the first minute it had even been luxury. But it was too much. I lay down on the carpet. The car filled up with officers and their wives; there were only two or three privates like myself. When we pulled out I tried to make my way ahead through the day coaches; I wanted to find Jimmy.

26

Into New York via the famous Long Island Rail Road. I reach Roosevelt Hospital. Food, rest, and delousing. I survive.

THE Pullman was the last car on the train. The day coach ahead was jammed to the doors. Men were lying in the aisle. Slowly I worked my way through to the next coach; it, too, had men carpeting its aisle, and someone had to move even to let the door be opened. I gave up and went back and lay down.

Back in the Pullman officers were also lying in the aisle or half under the seats; it was as carpeted with men as were the day coaches. The night came on, and the lights, the click of the rails, and the sickly soft-coal smell of the old car blended into confused, dreamy sensations. I lost all sense of time. A gracious lady appeared and I came to. I knew it was the colonel's wife, because the colonel was with her. He knew me, I was one of his men. I tried to rise and salute. "Lie down," said the colonel. She spoke, and it was very nice. I dreamed some more. Yet, I suppose, it was not

all dreaming. Would I live to reach New York? I
hoped I would, but I did not care. There was no more
of that wine-of-health feeling; I was past it. A curious
kind of contentment floated through me — home,
New York, and then my thinking stopped.

Then, through this dim, feverish wandering there
came a sudden shout: "Long Island City!"

From the coaches ahead there came the noise of
yells and cheers. It rose above the clicking of the
switches and sidings of the railroad yard. We could
see lights from the saloons in the scandalous bailiwick
of Mayor Pat Gleason — a tribal chieftain surviving
from the Stone Age. We were slowing down. Then
we halted. I was up. I felt my sketchbooks under my
shirt to make sure they were still there. I gathered up
my paper bag of bananas and peaches and uneaten
sandwich and tipped the porter. I found myself being
helped down the steps by the porter and an officer.
All down the train shed there was a frenzied mass of
men, yelling and slapping each other, and shuffling
down to the gates that led to the ferry. Everybody
was helping everybody. Someone took my arm, and
braced my shoulder.

"I can make it!" I said, and swayed as I said it.

I felt fine, a little weak, maybe, but that was all; I
was full of strength!

"I can walk!" I said pridefully.

"All right. I'll just steady you a bit," said my companion; it was the civilian Red Cross man of the Army
wagon. Well, my knees *were* a bit weak.

He steadied me down the slip and onto the ferry. Jimmy was there waiting for me when I came aboard. There was New York across the dark East River, the faint glow from the city's light rising like phosphorescence above the buildings. Again there was that wine in the air, and again the flush of health. The slip at East Thirty-fourth Street began to show in detail. There was an ambulance; there was a driver, and my good friend Dr. Wright beside him. Dr. Wright lived next door to my old West Tenth Street studio building. An ambulance — a hospital — good old New York! I straightened up, I felt the strength of ten! I tried to shake off the helpful arm of my Red Cross friend. I started across the gangplank. I tried to call to the doctor and wave my hand. My voice was mute, and my hand would not wave. I slipped down like a piece of wet string through the arms of the Red Cross man. I was not crying, but the tears were little rivulets on my cheeks. There was the ambulance driver with a stretcher, and they were putting me on it. And then came the last flicker of strength. *I would walk to that ambulance.* And I did. It was my last flash of strength, the last dram of that wine of health; the flask was empty. I still clutched my paper bag of peaches and bananas and sandwich, which I would not surrender, and I could feel them pressing against my sketch-books. It was a comfortable feeling.

Then there was that lovely roll through the still streets of after midnight. The ambulance springs made velvet of the cobbles and car tracks. The clop-

clop of the horse's hooves was cadenced music. We
went over the asphalt of Fifth Avenue, down which we
had paraded so ruggedly only a few months before.
Uptown — crosstown — then we swung into the narrow yard of Roosevelt Hospital. Ladies greeted us,
all beautiful in their spotless white and crisp nurses'
crowns, and there were orderlies to wheel the
stretcher.

Everybody stared at me. I was the first man back
from San Juan Hill and the trenches.

I was taken to a little room just off the ward which
was to be my home for three months to come. It was
a receiving ward for one, for no one knew what sort of
tropical germs I might have.

In the morning the hospital began having in guest-
medicos who were experts on tropical diseases. Various learned persons looked me over learnedly; I was
punctured for blood samples, given thermometers
every hour, and then dumped into a tub wherein a
twenty-pound lump of ice was floating. A fashionable
doctor, in a white piqué vest and gold-rimmed eye-
glasses, chuckled and said, "Cold, ain't it!" I was still
alive when taken out. Then they gave me an ounce of
spirits and poured slush-and-ice over me until they
grew tired. I was still alive by morning.

Later, they told me I was delirious most of the
time. Or maybe it was the opium. Officially, I was one
of the four per cent who was given opium. I remember there was a sociable white cockatoo perched on

the foot of my bed who said the wittiest things, which, in my lucid moments, I could never recall to tell the nurses. Time was obliterated except as an interval between the ice-water bath and the glass of egg-and-milk that was, for weeks, my only food; the *white* of egg, at that!

Then, one day, came a custard. Presently, I learned to walk all over again. And then, one day, I was well.

My ailment? Well, it was a fever; and there was much dispute about it. Some medicos said one thing; some another. They were all eminent men and not easily disputed. A compromise was arrived at, and in the archives of Roosevelt Hospital an official label reads: "Compound-Enteric-Typhoid-Malaria."

I was lucky. I had survived.